George B. Schaller
STONES OF SILENCE
Journeys in the Himalaya

Illustrated with
sketches by Jean Pruchnik

BANTAM BOOKS
TORONTO · NEW YORK · LONDON · SYDNEY

STONES OF SILENCE
*A Bantam Book / published by arrangement with
The Viking Press*

PRINTING HISTORY
Viking press edition published March 1980
A Selection of Book-of-the-Month Club, February 1980;
Macmillan Book Club, February 1980;
Reader's Subscription, July 1980 and
Times-Mirror Book Club, October 1980
Bantam edition / August 1982

*Bantam Books are published by Bantam Books, Inc. Its trademark,
consisting of the words "Bantam Books" and the portrayal of a
rooster, is Registered in U.S. Patent and Trademark Office and in
other countries. Marca Registrada. Bantam Books, Inc., 666 Fifth
Avenue, New York, New York 10103.*

PRINTED IN THE UNITED STATES OF AMERICA

0 9 8 7 6 5 4 3 2 1

Acknowledgments

My project in the Himalaya received generous support from several organizations. It was financed by the New York Zoological Society and the National Geographic Society, and it was conducted under the auspices of the New York Zoological Society whose general director, William G. Conway, provided constant encouragement and help. My institutional host in Pakistan was World Wildlife Fund Pakistan, and in Nepal I am indebted to His Majesty's Government for assistance.

The individuals who accompanied me on long journeys or helped in gathering data are mentioned in the text, and here I want to express my gratitude collectively to Pervez A. Khan, Zahid Beg Mirza, Melvin Sunquist, Andrew Laurie, and Peter Matthiessen. Amanullah Khan holds a special place in my esteem, and a few words cannot acknowledge my debt to him. Intermittently over a period of four years we traveled together, from the heights of the Hindu Kush to the deserts of Sind. His interest and assistance were a major contribution to the project. The people of Pakistan are known for their hospitality and, indeed, so many helped me, each in some important way, that I can do little more than list a few: Syed Babar Ali, Shahzadas Asad-ur-Rehman and Burhan-ud-Din, Malik Muzaffar Khan, W. A. Kermani, S. M. H. Rizvi, T. J. Roberts, Syed Asad Ali, and Ghulam M. Beg. E. R. C. Davidar, John Gouldsbury, and Rashid Wani were of special assistance to me in India, and John Blower and Phu-Tsering Sherpa in Nepal.

Richard Keane drew the two plates of sheep and goats and their relatives, and Jean Pruchnik made the other sketches. I am grateful to both artists for enhancing this book with their talents.

I am indebted to the University of Chicago Press for permission to reproduce material from *Mountain Monarchs*. Parts of chapter 4 appeared in *Animal Kingdom*, the magazine of the New York Zoological Society.

The National Geographic Society generously provided photographic assistance during the project.

Peter Matthiessen, my companion on a Nepal trek, read several chapters and made many helpful comments. In 1978 Peter published a book based on our journey, a beautiful work of observation and reflection entitled *The Snow Leopard*, from which I quote on several occasions.

The life of a field biologist is often lonely, away from family and home. But he, at least, follows his own vision. Even lonelier is the wife who awaits his return. On previous projects I was able to move my family into the study area where Kay made a home for us. This was not possible in the Himalaya. I traveled widely in remote areas and often under difficult conditions, and Eric and Mark had to attend school. For two years they all lived in Lahore, Pakistan, and at other times they remained in the United States. Either way, separations were long, periods of togetherness all too brief. The burdens of raising a family and maintaining a home devolved on Kay. It is customary in publications to acknowledge a wife, but Kay's contribution went far beyond mere assistance. The fact that she not only waited but also encouraged me in my work in spite of the pain my absences caused, that she raised our children through critical years of development, creating persons of whom I am immensely proud, and that, in the end, she edited and typed this book, a book about journeys she wanted to take with me but could not, can only elicit my admiration, devotion, and love.

Contents

Acknowledgments   v

List of Illustrations   ix

Path to the Mountains   1

The Snow Leopard   8

Beyond the Ranges   51

Karakoram   74

Mountains in the Desert   115

Cloud Goats   150

Kang Chu   174

Journey to Crystal Mountain   203

Appendix   279

Index   283

Maps

The main study areas in the mountains of South Asia   2

Route traveled through the Hindu Kush   54

Routes traveled through the Karakoram   77

Route traveled in western Nepal   206

Distribution of markhor goat   281

Distribution of sheep in northern Pakistan and India   282

Path to the Mountains

"The high altitudes are a special world. Born of the Pleistocene, at home among pulsating glaciers and wind-flayed rocks, the animals have survived and thrived, the harshness of the environment breeding a strength and resilience which the lowland animals often lack. At these heights, in this remote universe of stone and sky, the fauna and flora of the Pleistocene have endured while many species of lower realms have vanished in the uproar of the elements. Just as we become aware of this hidden splendor of the past, we are in danger of denying it to the future. As we reach for the stars we neglect the flowers at our feet. But the great age of mammals in the Himalaya need not be over unless we permit it to be. For epochs to come the peaks will still pierce the lonely vistas, but when the last snow

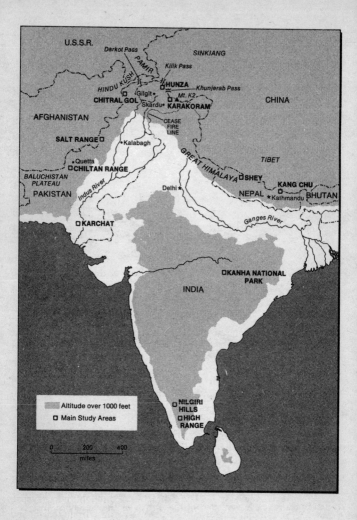

leopard has stalked among the crags and the last markhor has stood on a promontory, his ruff waving in the breeze, a spark of life will have gone, turning the mountains into stones of silence."

With these words of hope and despair I concluded my book *Mountain Monarchs*, a scientific treatise on the wild sheep and goats of the Himalaya. This book begins where that one ends. A research report can present only the facts of a study. During my three years in the Great Himalaya, Hindu Kush, Karakoram, and other nearby ranges I did indeed gather many facts about wildlife; however, as William Beebe stated, there is also a need of "softening facts with quiet meditation, leavening science with thoughts of the sheer joy of existence."

At first it is daunting to contemplate a project in the Himalaya, because the mountains are so immense. From Afghanistan in the west to China in the southeast, the main Himalayan system curves in one gigantic arc for nearly 2,000 miles to create a frozen barrier between the Indian subcontinent and the Tibetan Plateau. For convenience, geographers have divided this expanse of peaks into various ranges, and I visited many of them in northern Pakistan, India, and Nepal. Each range has a character of its own. The Pamirs, the Bam-i-dunya or Roof of the World, as the Persians called it, consist of broad valleys flanked by smooth glacier-worn mountains extending southward from Russia to Pakistan's border. The Hindu Kush in northeastern Pakistan is arid and almost treeless, a stark range belonging not to the Indian subcontinent but to the steppes of Central Asia. Farther east is the Karakoram, a mass of bristling peaks and twisting glaciers, the rawest, wildest range of them all. South of the Karakoram and lying within the big bend of the Indus River begins the Great Himalaya, which extends on eastward through India, Nepal, Bhutan, and India once more. Unlike the arid Hindu Kush and Karakoram, moisture-laden clouds reach the Great Himalaya during the annual monsoon that sweeps northward across India, with the result that the southern flanks are verdant with forest. The same period of geologic upheaval that created these great mountains also shaped a series of lesser ones in the deserts of western Pakistan, where from a barren plateau protrude several low and haggard hill systems, the Kirthar, Salt, and others, which seldom exceed a height of 10,000 feet. I visited parts of all these ranges to search for wildlife and to study it, the maps on pages 2, 54, 77, and 206 showing my routes and research sites.

So little was known about Himalayan wildlife that I first needed to collect basic information on the distribution and status of species. At the same time I looked not only for suitable study areas where animals were still sufficiently abundant to make research worthwhile, but also for areas that would make good national parks or reserves. The first three chapters in this book describe such surveys in northern Pakistan where I met many animals, marmots and wolves and high-altitude birds. But none possessed me as did the snow leopard, a rare and elusive creature which lured me on, only seldom permitting a glimpse.

However, I was in the Himalaya on a scientific quest, not just to make wildlife surveys: I was there to study the world's greatest variety of sheep and goats, known by such obscure names as markhor, tahr, urial, argali, and bharal. These are little-known animals outside the fraternities of big-game hunters, and at first their names may be as confusing as the names of the many Himalayan peaks, glaciers, and rivers. Taxonomists have established the subfamily *Caprinae* and placed in it twenty-four species, among them the various sheep and goats. A table listing all species appears as an appendix, and the sketches on the endpapers illustrate the various members of the subfamily, but only a few concern us. Just as there are thinhorn and bighorn sheep in North America, so there are two species of sheep in the Himalaya, the small urial and large argali. Each is classified into several races, based on minor differences in horn shape and coat color; only the Marco Polo sheep, a type of argali, is well known. Unlike the stocky, cliff-dwelling North American sheep, those of South Asia are lithely built, almost antelopelike, and devoted to rolling terrain rather than to precipices. North America lacks true goats, the Rocky Mountain goat being actually a goat-antelope, a primitive member of the subfamily *Caprinae*. By contrast, the Himalaya has three species of true goats, all of which I studied. The ibex inhabits the highest peaks, ranging upward to the limit of vegetation, its most distinctive feature being a series of knobs along the front of long scimitar-shaped horns. The other two species live at lower altitudes, usually below 12,000 feet. The wild goat also has scimitar horns, but with a sharp keel rather than knobs in front, and the markhor has uniquely spiraling horns. South Asia is the home of yet another type of goat, the tahr, with one species living in the Great Himalaya and another in South India. The Himalayan and Nilgiri tahr differ from true goats in that they have short, curved horns instead of long, sweeping ones. Finally there is the bharal or blue sheep of Tibet, an animal so intermediate between sheep and goat in its physical characteristics that taxonomists have had trouble classifying it.

Any scientific endeavor needs focal points beyond the desire to gather knowledge, and the Asian sheep and goats present fascinating biological problems. The wild goat is the progenitor of domestic goat and the urial of domestic sheep, yet no one had tried to find out whether the wild and domestic forms differ in behavior, whether 12,-000 years of domestication modified what evolution created in several million years. Is the bharal a sheep or goat? A study of its ecology and behavior might provide an answer.

With such questions in mind I made several trips to the Himalaya between 1969 and 1975. The project began in the autumn of 1969 with a study of Nilgiri tahr in the highlands of southern India. I was in Pakistan for several months late in 1970, and in Nepal during the spring of 1972. In mid-1972 I moved with my family to Pakistan and remained there until mid-1974 except when I visited Nepal from October to December, 1973. Afterward I made two more trips to Pakistan, in late 1974 and early 1975. My search for wildlife in Pakistan often led me into terrrain where few or no foreigners had been since the British withdrew from the subcontinent over thirty years before. Nepal, which remained essentially closed to the outside world until 1950, still contains little-known valleys where one senses a nostalgia for that heroic past when explorers penetrated the wilderness. A large part of this book describes my journeys—the mountains, the people, the daily routine of travel. Each journey presented problems: some were political, for the Himalaya borders such sensitive areas as Tibet, Sinkiang, and Russia; others were logistic, for recalcitrant porters, reluctant baggage animals, and washed-out trails are an integral part of any mountain journey; and still others were climatic, whether fierce heat in the desert mountains or piercing winter winds on the Tibetan Plateau. It is somehow anachronistic in this age of high-speed travel to plod behind a string of porters or lead bulky yaks over a glacier trail—it seems like a late expression of the romantic era, of Henry Stanley, Richard Burton, and Sven Hedin. I did not always enjoy these modes of travel, yet, in writing about my trips, these are the parts I dwell on with quiet longing, for one tends to complain of discomfort and relish hardship: the more difficult a journey, the greater the satisfaction in having completed it.

I wrote part of this book while on a new project in the dense forests and vast swamps of the Mato Grosso in Brazil. Life pervades that area, it intrudes, it smothers one like a crowd on a city street. There are thousands of species of plants and animals, each trying to survive, each defending itself and its niche against competitors with thorns, spines, claws, toxins, and poisonous stings. The human intruder, too, is forced to enter this struggle, constantly combating encroaching vegetation and insects just to maintain his tenuous foothold. Such an existence promotes little reflection. By contrast, mountains and deserts, with their spare life at the limit of existence, make one restless and disconsolate; one becomes an explorer in an intellectual realm as well as in a physical one, and the following pages include some of my lonely thoughts born of windswept mountain passes.

One October day, I ambled up the Dachigam Valley in Kashmir. The mulberry, walnut, and willow trees had already turned yellow with the first frost, and Himalayan black bear searched among fallen leaves for the last acorns; early winter snows covered the alpine meadows and would soon claim the valley as well. From the slope above, near a stand of pine and fir, I heard a mournful yet insistent sound, at first soft, then growing louder, until it filled the whole valley, *eeoouuuu*, before dying away. And from upvalley came one answer, *eeeoouuuu*. The Kashmir stag, a subspecies of red deer, were in rut. However, where once the mountains echoed to their wild bugling, only a few lonesome sounds now broke the stillness, only a few stags had descended from the high summer pastures in search of hinds. The rest were dead, shot by the many hunters in these hills. At most a few hundred deer survive in the Vale of Kashmir, their only home, yet as recently as 1947 there were over 4,000, the animals having been brought to the verge of extinction because no one cared. There are many species similarly threatened, all in need of someone concerned enough to fight for their needs. The fact that a living being can vanish from this earth solely because of man's improvidence and neglect is appalling, and the utter finality of it touches the consciousness of far too few. I have met many species without a future, and each time had the forlorn hope that somehow I might be able to extend their existence for at least a few years. Pen and camera are weapons against oblivion, they can create an awareness for that which may soon be lost forever, and if this book has a main purpose, it is to induce others to care for the dying mountain world of the Himalaya.

The Snow Leopard

When the snow clouds retreated, the gray slopes and jagged cliffs were gone, as were the livestock trails and raw stumps of felled oak. Several inches of fresh snow softened all contours. Hunched against December's cold, I scanned the slope, looking for the snow leopard which was somewhere a thousand feet above near a goat it had killed the previous day. But only cold prowled the slopes. Slowly I climbed upward, kicking steps into the snow and angling toward a spur of rock from which to survey the valley. Soon scree gave way to a chaos of boulders and rocky outcrops, the slopes motionless and silent as if devoid of life.

Then I saw the snow leopard, a hundred and fifty feet away, peering at me from the spur, her body so well molded into the contours of the boulders that she seemed a part of them. Her smoky-gray coat sprinkled with black rosettes perfectly complemented the rocks and snowy wastes, and her pale eyes conveyed an image of immense solitude. As we watched each other the clouds descended once more, entombing us and bringing more snow. Perhaps sensing that I meant her no harm, she sat up. Though snow soon capped her head and shoulders, she remained, silent and still, seemingly impervious to the elements. Wisps of clouds swirled around, transforming her into a ghost creature, part myth and part reality. Balanced precariously on a ledge and bitterly cold, I too stayed, unwilling to disrupt the moment. One often has empathy with animals, but rarely and unexpectedly one attains a state beyond the subjective and fleetingly almost seems to become what one beholds; here, in this snowbound valley of the Hindu Kush, I briefly achieved such intimacy. Then the snow fell more thickly, and, dreamlike, the cat slipped away as if she had never been.

Having visited many of the earth's wild places, I am well aware that a wilderness that has lost its large predators, whether wolf, snow leopard, or other, lacks an essential ingredient. I can feel the difference; there is less vitality, less natural tension. But my meeting with the snow leopard went beyond this. It occurred in 1970 during my first visit to the Chitral region of northern Pakistan, and over the next four years when I spent a total of about six months there, the snow leopard represented not just a rare and beautiful cat whose habits I wanted to study, but also the symbol of a search for something intangible that seemed forever elusive.

Some 4,500 square miles in size, Chitral encompasses the drainage of the Kunar River in the northwestern corner of Pakistan bordering Afghanistan. Until 1969 the area was a semiautonomous state presided over by a royal family whose ruler was called the mehtar. After Pakistan's independence in 1947, the royal family progressively lost power until, just before my visit, the government incorporated Chitral into the Northwest Frontier Province. With this decline, many members of the royal family abandoned their mountains for such cities as Peshawar and Rawalpindi, and correspondingly neglected their properties, including the private hunting preserves. With restraints removed, villagers killed wildlife, and by the time I arrived only tiny remnants persisted where once animals had roamed by the hundreds. However, a few preserves had been at least casually maintained. One of these was the Chitral Gol, a valley belonging to the mehtar, just west of Chitral town. The finest remaining herd of markhor goat in northern Pakistan was said to inhabit this valley, and snow leopard were known to frequent it too. It seemed like an ideal place to begin my research in the northern mountains, and, after obtaining permission from the royal family, I spent the first of several months there.

The Chitral Gol is about thirty square miles in size, all of it consisting of rugged mountains up to 17,600 feet. One stream drains the area, and perched on a bank above its turbulent waters is a partially collapsed hut of earth and rough timbers that once provided royal hunters with shelter; it became my home during this first visit. There was nothing suggestive of charm and comfort in the hut, nor, for that matter, in the valley as a whole. Nothing had prepared me for such winter bleakness as in the Hindu Kush. Usually an area looks desolate only until one sees the details, but here even they seemed forsaken. The area lies beyond the monsoon's influence, and its vegetation belongs to the steppes of Central Asia rather than to the Indian subcontinent. Southern Chitral, including the Chitral Gol, does have forest, stands of spruce and fir and evergreen oak, but somehow the trees have the stark look usually associated with desert or arctic wastes. One's main impression is of barren slopes, subdued in hue, surmounted by peaks flinging themselves up into the realm of perpetual snow. The ground is almost bare, consisting of crumbly shale which gleams gunmetal-gray in the wintry sun. Except for an occasional tuft of grass or a timid forb, there is only sagebrush, but the pale-leafed plants are stunted and submerged into the landscape.

A path led from the hut through patches of conifers upward until trees gave way to alpine meadows. My eyes passed over these bare slopes to the crest of the ridge where cloud shadows wandered; on our left was a colossal limestone cliff, its upper ramparts sprinkled with snow. Pukhan, our guide, was in the lead. An angular, gap-toothed fellow with a perpetually seeping nose which he wiped on the sleeve of a faded tweed overcoat, he was one of several game guards in the preserve. Following him was Zahid Beg Mirza, the curator of Lahore's Punjab University Museum, whose interest in wildlife had brought us together. I plodded along in the rear, stopping occasionally to watch birds, using the halt as much to rest as to identify the species. Here at 8,000 feet, few birds remain during winter. Crested black tits flitted among fir trees, nutcrackers hurried by, and once a black-throated jay investigated me from a low bough.

Pukhan had loped ahead and now waved to us, excitedly pointing to the limestone cliff. At first I saw nothing, but finally spotted several markhor, faint brownish dots lost in the immensity of rock. Hastily fastening my spotting scope to its tripod, I watched the goats I had traveled so far to see; the long, slow process of gathering data had begun. There were sixteen markhor, including two males, five females, and nine young. Twinning was obviously common and the survival rate of young seemed good. Scattered over the cliff, the animals foraged on plants that had somehow found a foothold in cracks and bits of level ground. Though stocky in build, the goats were incredibly agile, traversing ledges so precarious that footholds seemed more imaginary than real. The single adult male caught my attention. A magnificent animal, at 150 to 200 pounds about twice as heavy as the nondescript females, he was beautifully adorned with long spiraling horns and a white, flowing neck ruff. Poets may praise the deer and nightingale; I celebrate the wild goat. A markhor male standing on a promontory, ruff shining in the sun, is a far different goat from the small, disheveled, smelly beast that domestication has produced. The male's black tail was folded up over his rump, a characteristic of rutting goats. I looked forward to the rut, for at no time of the year are hoofed animals more active and is social organization more distinctive than during the mating season. We watched the goats for an hour, until they filed out of sight behind a spur, and then we continued our trek up the slope.

Near the base of the cliff, just above where sheer rock gives way to scree, I could see a cave. When Pukhan saw me examine it through binoculars, he told Zahid something in Urdu, and Zahid, as my interpreter, relayed the information that black bear used the place as a winter den. The Asiatic black bear has a wide distribution from Iran eastward to Indochina and Russia, including the forests of the Himalaya. Distinguished by its long black hair and a white blaze on its chest, and weighing between 150 and 300 pounds, it is a powerful beast whose short temper the villagers justly fear. Bears were unfortunately rare in the Chitral Gol—no more than one or two visited the valley judging by spoor—and I never saw them there. Although the cave tempted me, it was not until a subsequent summer trip that I had an opportunity to explore it without fear of arousing a dozing bear. Carrying a lantern and rope and followed by a reluctant Pukhan, I clambered into the cave. There were two chambers, the largest nearly 40 feet long and 30 feet high. Old bear droppings littered the floor, peculiar droppings resembling dried coal tar laced with grass. A few also contained walnut shells and markhor hair, the latter probably scavenged from a dead animal. This small sample of droppings gave no idea of the actual range of foods eaten by these bears. I have examined autumn droppings in the Dachigam Sanctuary of Kashmir and found acorn, walnut, hackberry, grape, maize, rosehip, apricot, apple, wasps, and feathers, to list a few items. At one end of the cavern was a tunnel just large enough for me to squirm through. Leaving Pukhan at the entrance, I entered, my lantern piercing a darkness that had never seen light before. The tunnel slanted down, then up, and after about 30 feet opened into a chamber some 15 feet wide. The place was disappointingly empty: no bones, no nest material, nothing but smoothly worn bedding sites where generations of bears had slept.

We labored up toward the head of the valley. Oak had ceased to grow at 8,500 feet and now at 10,500 the conifers almost gave out.

Mountains should be climbed at one's own speed, step by step, only the present occupying the mind. As he trudges along leaning into the slope, a climber's view tends to be limited to the ground at his feet, and I did not like what I saw, for the terrain was riddled with livestock trails and droppings of domestic sheep and goats were everywhere. The vegetation had been devastated by domestic herds which forage here in summer; all grass was gone and so were most forbs. Only those plants that could somehow deter the voracious mouths managed to survive, among these being small pincushions of *Astragulus* and *Acantholimon* whose long spines, like those of porcupines, protect the splendid but unpluckable leaves and flowers. Almost no wildlife existed in this wasteland: once a black-naped hare skittered off, and later a rattling *kak-kak* revealed a small covey of chukor partridges.

Reaching the crest, we looked down a ravine toward the main Chitral Valley and the rampart of peaks beyond. Scattered far below were tiny fields wherever chance had made the ground fairly level. So much terrain, yet so little of it can sustain life! On a patch of snow were tracks of a large cat. I measured them: about 4 inches long and 3 wide. Only snow leopard or perhaps lynx could have made these prints, and full of anticipation, I hurried along, looking for other spoor. Soon I came upon a scrape in the soil, two parallel grooves made by a cat raking its hindfeet on the ground. This, I knew, was a means by which large cats such as leopard, lion, and tiger mark their range, leaving a sign of their presence. A snow leopard had patrolled the ridge, and during the long descent toward our hut my mind was occupied with devising a means of arranging an encounter with the cat.

Snow leopard are creatures of high altitudes in the mountains of Central Asia. Their range extends from the Hindu Kush in Afghanistan eastward along the Himalaya and across Tibet, and northeastward over the Pamirs, Tien Shan, and Altai to the Sayan Mountains near Lake Baikal. A rare, shy inhabitant of remote habitats up to an altitude of 18,000 feet, the snow leopard had never been studied in the wild. Although the naturalist Peter Pallas carefully distinguished snow leopard from common leopard in 1779, accounts nearly two hundred years later still said little more about the cat's habits than that it moves seasonally up and down the mountains following such favored prey as ibex and bharal. Not even zoos provided much information. In 1970 a total of ninety-six snow leopard were in zoos but of these only twenty had been bred in captivity, a dismal record. It was known that the gestation period is 96 to 105 days, that there are usually two to three cubs in a litter, that the eyes of young open after about a week, and that the first teeth erupt at about three weeks. But the snow leopard's life remained unwritten.

At dusk we reached our hut, weary but exhilarated with so many new sights and impressions. Sher Panah lit a fire and soon brought us strong sweet tea. Sher, like many Chitrali men, was short, angular, long-faced, and slightly bowlegged. His usual job was cooking for the staff of the royal household, but as I discovered later, his culinary talents were held in such regard that there was general rejoicing whenever he accompanied me on a trip, as he later did on all my journeys through Chitral. He took care of camp, and knowing my needs and idiosyncrasies, made certain that our travel went more or less smoothly. In remote areas, among villages which may not have seen a foreigner for many years, it is essential to be accompanied by a local person not only to allay suspicions, but also to act as interpreter. Most people in the mountains speak only their local language, whether it be Khowari and Bashgali in Chitral, Burushaski in Hunza, or Kohistani in parts of Dir and Swat, to name only a few, and to ask even a simple question could be tedious. If, for instance, I wanted to know how many markhor were in a particular valley, I might ask Zahid in English, while he, in turn, inquired of Sher in Urdu, who then queried the guide in Khowari. A lively discussion lasting several minutes would ensue until a monosyllabic reply filtered back to me.

No dictionaries are readily available for local languages, but Eric Newby in his amusing travelogue, *A Short Walk in the Hindu Kush*, mentions a Bashgali-English phrase book:

Notes on the Bashgali (Kafir) Language, by Colonel J. Davidson of the Indian Staff Corps, Calcutta, 1901, had been assembled by the author after a two-year sojourn in Chitral with the assistance of two Kafirs of the Bashgali tribe and consisted of a grammar of the language and a collection of sentences.

Conversations around the turn of the century must have been heroic in this area if the phrase book is an indication.

"I saw a corpse in the field this morning."
"How long have you had a goitre?"
"Thy father fell into the river."
"I have nine fingers; you have ten."
"I have an intention to kill you."
"A gust of wind came and took away all my clothes."
"A lammergeier came down from the sky and took off my cock."

Not all these phrases were of use to me.

Crowding the fire for warmth and light, Zahid and I wrote our notes while Sher prepared dinner in a nearby lean-to. Eventually he brought pieces of boiled goat and *juwari,* a flat, thick, unleavened bread the size and weight of a discus. In these mountains it is best to eat the local cuisine as much as possible, rather than a poor imitation of the Western one. Dinner signified the end of our day, for as night cold gripped the valleys, a sleeping bag provided the only cozy haven. By eight o'clock we were in bed.

Zahid and I soon settled into a daily research routine. He took Pukhan to look for markhor near the hut, while I wandered down-valley each dawn. At first the route passed through a gorge so narrow that the stream filled its floor, and the trail had to trace ledges, surmount ice-glazed boulders, and cross the torrent on single trembling logs. Sun seldom penetrated this gloomy defile and even the birds had a somber plumage. Occasionally a whistling thrush, blue-black and with a yellow bill, skulked among the willows. A few wall creepers, so inconspicuously gray that I seldom saw them, haunted the shadows; when flushed they bobbed off like butterflies, revealing crimson wings. Where the slopes retreated, the trail climbed high above the stream. Often only a foot or so wide, it presented a marvelously sporting proposition, especially when slippery with snow and ice. With so little vegetation to hold the soil, constant avalanches of scree eliminated sections of the path and an occasional lone pebble or boulder hurtled down with remarkable velocity. But from this trail I could observe markhor easily on the opposite side of the narrow valley. Even the falling rocks conferred a benefit: markhor may dislodge stones as they walk and it was this clatter that sometimes made me aware that the goats were nearby.

Most hoofed animals must forage some eight to twelve hours daily, and consequently markhor are usually on the move all day with only a lessening of activity between 10:30 A.M. and 1:30 P.M. while they rest and chew cud. The markhor's range seemed to have little food, and I was curious about how the animals might obtain an adequate diet, one enabling them to survive the stresses of winter. A grazer and browser like a markhor would seem to have ample food available, even in a place like the Chitral Gol where livestock has devastated the slopes. But not only must food be available, it must also be nutritious enough to sustain life. Animals prefer the young, growing parts of plants to dormant or dead ones because the former contain more protein and have fewer indigestible fibers. Furthermore, availability does not necessarily mean palatability. Some plants are too prickly to chew, and others, such as sagebrush, juniper, and mint, contain aromatic chemicals that are toxic, capable of causing death if an animal eats more than its system can degrade in a given time. Although markhor ate a variety of plants, including a sourdock and the foliage of *Pistacia* trees, their main food was the leathery leaves of evergreen oak. With a fat content of 4 percent and a protein content of 9 percent, these leaves were relatively nutritious. Markhor nibbled leaves off low-hanging branches, often standing bolt upright, but not satisfied with that, they also leaped up into the trees, bounding like monkeys from branch to branch in search of tender leaves. It was startling and incongruous to look 15 to 20 feet up into the crown of an oak and see several of the goats there, calmly munching. However, oak leaves were not a preferred food. When two years later there was a huge acorn crop, markhor almost disdained leaves to eat mast. In a severe winter, when snow covers their forage and the nutritional value of leaves is low, markhor may find it difficult to survive. Those animals that have stored fat while on the high summer pastures can draw on reserves until spring brings a new flush of green. But young of the year use much of their extra energy to grow, entering the winter quite lean, and many apparently succumb to the stresses of that season, judging by the population statistics I collected during my daily rounds. An average of 1.3 young accompanied each adult female in November, when about six months old. A year later only about 0.5 per adult female remained, a drop of nearly 60 percent.

I usually wandered downstream as far as Merin, not far from where the river joins the main Chitral valley. The royal family had a large bungalow at Merin, but one by one the heavy log and earth roofs had collapsed until only two rooms remained usable. I often stayed here after heavy snows in late December made the trail into the upper valley too dangerous to use. Several stony fields were at Merin and large herds of domestic goats; wood collectors from town made daily visits, and herdsmen lopped branches off the oaks to feed their livestock. Although their habitat was being destroyed, the markhor themselves were not molested while I worked in the valley. Years ago so many markhor lived here that herds with 100 or more animals were common. Now average herd size is 9, and the largest I saw numbered 35. After meeting certain markhor repeatedly in the same area, I soon learned that the Chitral Gol population was divided into six loosely organized herds each of which favored a specific part of the valley. Some adult males were exceptions in that they roamed widely both alone and in small groups.

MARKHOR

Straight-horned

Astor

Kashmir

Based on a detailed knowledge of the population, I estimated only 100 to 125 markhor in the valley. And this is the best reserve for the species in existence.*

The markhor as a species is restricted mainly to Pakistan, but small populations also exist in eastern Afghanistan, in adjoining parts of Russia, and along the western rim of the Vale of Kashmir. It is essentially a goat of low altitudes, requiring only cliffs in areas with little precipitation, deep snow being especially avoided. Although they may ascend to 13,000 feet and above in summer, they prefer altitudes of 7,500 or below for the winter. Markhor differ somewhat in appearance from area to area. West of the Indus, between the town of Quetta in Baluchistan and the northern edge of of the Indus Plain, are the straight-horned markhor, also known as Sulaiman or Kabul markhor, depending on the area. Its straight horns are twisted like corkscrews. By contrast the Astor markhor

* The Chitral Gol was opened to trophy hunting in 1977, a sad action by a country which has otherwise made progress in wildlife conservation.

along the upper Indus and its tributaries has widely flaring horns with at most one-and-a-half twists, and the so-called Kashmir markhor of Swat, Dir, Chitral, and neighboring Afghanistan has only moderately flaring horns, but with as many as three complete twists.

Having recently completed a study on lions in the Serengeti National Park of Tanzania, where one is nearly always within sight of wildlife, I found these mountains depressingly continent. After hours of hiking I would encounter a small markhor herd or two, and with luck something else, perhaps a yellow-throated marten. On the trails were the tidy, spindle-shaped droppings of red fox, but one rarely met one of these nocturnal predators. At least the droppings revealed what the foxes ate—yellow-necked field mice, Turkestan rats, rose-hips, *Pistacia* and other seeds, and around human habitations, scraps of goat skin and maize. The reserve is much too small and prey too sparse to support resident large predators, and only at intervals did wolves or snow leopard pass through.

In fact I met wolves there just once. Although it was only 2:40 P.M. the sun had already vanished behind a ridge. The whole valley had the pallor of ice, and the huge limestone cliff was imprisoned by clouds. Shivering, I pressed into a rocky niche so as not to disturb a herd of nine markhor feeding nearby. Suddenly two wolves raced into view, side by side, along the contours of the slope. Startled, all markhor bolted for a cliff about two hundred feet away, all, that is, except one young which mindlessly veered alone up the slope. But the wolves did not see it. The smaller of the two wolves came to within thirty feet of a markhor before halting at a precipice; the other wolf, a handsome buff and gray male, pursued another markhor onto a cliff and was almost close enough to grab it when his foot slipped on an icy ledge and he wisely gave up the quest. The two wolves joined, angled up the slope, and vanished. While all other markhor remained irresolutely on the cliff, a young male headed alone up the mountainside, crossing the wolves' trail. Had the wolves tarried nearby they might well have caught him. Having first seen the panicked youngster and now the needlessly bold male, it did not surprise me to learn later that predators kill a disproportionately large number of males and young.

Although these various encounters with animals fascinated me, it was the snow leopard that became my private quest. Sometimes in the mornings I found the fresh tracks of one which I then followed with the hope of at least seeing a shadow vanishing among the rocks. But the views were so wide that even a distant cat could easily detect my approach and retreat. Following an old set of tracks at leisure was often more enjoyable than tensely tracing a fresh one. Once I traveled for five hours along a fir-covered ridge while deducing a snow leopard's doings from its spoor. It was piercingly cold at 10,000 feet, not a breath of wind, nor a cloud. To the north snow peaks speared the sky. I first found the pugmarks among tracks of black-naped hares, meandering as if the snow leopard was searching for one of these animals. Then the tracks of the cat headed straight to a huge fir, and in the needles beneath it made a scrape—a calling card. After plodding steadily through the snow for a while, the snow leopard halted at a fox dropping, probably sniffing it. A few minutes later it left the crest to detour to another fir, which it circled, perhaps looking for the scent marks of other cats. Farther on, beneath two sentinel firs, it deposited its own mark, another scrape. Although usually solitary, snow leopard nevertheless are members of a community. By leaving signs of its presence—scrapes, feces, and urine mixed with scent—each snow leopard in an area learns not only that someone else has been at a particular spot, but also probably who it was, about how long ago it was there, and in the case of a female, whether she was in heat. It is no coincidence that snow leopard leave their calling cards on prominent locations such as at solitary trees, on hilltops, and on mountain spurs. The tracks I was following veered off the crest, then down the slope, and soon after that, where the snow gave out, I lost them. With wildlife depleted and livestock carefully guarded near the villages in winter, snow leopard must travel far for a meal. I followed tracks for a total of twenty-six miles in Pakistan and Nepal and in that distance saw sign of only one hunting attempt, a successful stalk of a bharal or blue sheep. As with most large cats, hunts end in failure more often than not. C. H. Stockley, in his book *Stalking in the Himalayas and Northern India,* relates how he once watched as "a snow leopard suddenly raced across the hollow in which they [ibex] were feeding and made an attempt on a buck, which started away just in time. The leopard's outstretched claws raked a great lump of hair from the ibex's coat as it wheeled away. . . ." The extent of a snow leopard's travel remains unknown, but it must be considerable in areas where prey is scarce. Once we waited a month for snow leopard in the Golen Gol, another Chitrali valley, and only once did a cat travel through.

Hunting accounts written in the late nineteenth and early twentieth centuries rarely mention snow leopard because the authors seldom met one of the cats, even after months and years in the mountains, which is not too surprising, for only those animals that remained elusive survived. In Kashmir they were legally treated as vermin until 1968. For example, in the course of many Himalayan trips, the naturalist A. Ward sighted five solitary snow leopard and a group of three —and he shot five of the eight. I could not depend on luck alone to meet a snow leopard. Having observed and photographed tigers in central India by tying out domestic buffalo as bait, I decided to try the same technique here. I sent Sher to purchase three goats and these I tethered where I had seen snow leopard spoor, feeding the animals oak leaves and water as needed. Each morning I checked them, full of anticipation, and each morning three lively goats greeted me with cheerful bleats. Snow leopard are known to hunt by day as well as by night. For instance, the Indian mountaineer Hari Dang saw them stalk bharal three times, tahr once, and snowcock once, all in daytime. This being so, I built a small blind of juniper boughs near one of my baits and spent many hours there quietly waiting. My presence did not disrupt the rhythm of life in the valley. Flocks of yellow-billed choughs floated on updrafts along the cliffs just above me, their effortless motion producing a kind of transitory art as they traced wind patterns in the sky. Sometimes a markhor herd moved into view. The rut had begun, and the dominant male in each herd remained close to any female in heat, holding himself erect, trying to impress her with his beauty and other males with his power. Sometimes he enhanced his presence by spraying urine over himself, dousing his chest and face; his beard possibly acts as a sachet. A female may respond to a male's persistent attention by running away, but the male follows and the two race over slopes and among trees.

Mountains usually give me a sense of space, but in the Chitral Gol the views were always blocked by slopes and peaks, hemming me in except at night. Tucked into my sleeping bag, with the mountains dissolved into formless darkness, I gazed at the clouds drifting by until I was almost dizzy from hurtling through space and only the scent of juniper and the whispering stream far below reminded me of my mountain perch. No snow leopard passed my blind while I was there. But two days after I discontinued the vigil, one detoured to my blind and even entered it before continuing up the slope without touching the nearby bait. Two weeks of effort had produced no result.

Then one morning, as I approached Merin, Pukhan hurried toward me, waving his arms and pointing with his stick. *"Burdum!"* he called, using the Chitrali word for snow leopard as he held up two fingers to indicate that there were two of the cats. A goat was dead. Peering through the scope I saw my first snow leopard. She reclined on a promontory with a small cub beside her, a tiny black and white puff of fur. She watched as several jungle crows descended to the kill, the tip of her long tail flicking, and then stalked to the goat to protect it from these scavengers as well as from the Himalayan griffon vultures that circled overhead. The cub soon retreated into a rocky cleft, but its mother remained in the open. After a few hours I decided to find out how close an approach she would permit. Casually I meandered up the slope, alternately sitting and drawing closer in a seemingly purposeless manner until at 250 feet I halted. Crouched on a boulder, she stared at me with frosty eyes. I left her then, but returned several hours later with another goat. As I approached she slid backward off her rock. Molding herself to the contours of boulders and shrubs, she became almost invisible as she glided uphill to an enormous rock behind which she halted to watch me, only the top of her head visible. I left the goat tied to a sapling. And exhilarated by her casual acceptance of me, I ran down the mountain and up the valley to Kasawere to pick up my sleeping bag, then back to Merin to spend the night, needing only one-and-a-half hours for a trip that normally required over four.

At dawn I took my scope and began watching the snow leopard from the valley floor. The cub was clambering among rocks about 15 feet from its mother when suddenly, as if needing reassurance, it bounded over to her to touch its forehead against her cheek. It ate from the goat carcass for forty minutes, then returned to its mother and rubbed cheeks with her in greeting, licked the top of her head, and vanished from sight into its rocky cleft. I guessed that the cub was about four months old, probably born in August and conceived in May, though according to the local people, snow leopard usually court in March or April. Two weeks pass before a newborn cub can walk and not until four weeks of age does it venture from its den, judging by zoo observations. With cubs being relatively immobile for the first two months of life, a female needs secluded haunts and easily available food to raise a litter successfully. Pukhan told me that this female had been seen with two cubs a few weeks earlier. Somehow she had lost one. Nevertheless, it was remarkable that even one survived. With wildlife so scarce, snow leopard must depend increasingly on domestic sheep and goats. Droppings revealed just how important livestock was to the cats in this area: 45 percent contained livestock remains. Slow to kill and eat, the cat with its prey is soon discovered by a herdsman who either chases it away or shoots it. In winter, desperate for food, snow leopard may skulk around village huts to snatch unwary dogs or claw their way into livestock sheds. Cornered by irate villagers, the timid snow leopard may then be beaten to death with staves and axes. Although a snow leopard is as large as a regular leopard—a female at the Bronx Zoo weighed seventy pounds, a male eighty-seven pounds—and potentially dangerous, no record exists of one having become a man-eater.

I decided to spend the night near the leopardess and her cub, and in the fading light unrolled my sleeping bag on a level ledge 150 feet from her. As soon as I was settled she returned to her kill. Here in this unpeopled night world, the mountains were hers, the eternal desolation of rock and snow investing her with an archaic permanence. Soon darkness engulfed us, and then there was only the sound of wind sweeping along icy mountain flanks and occasionally the grating of tooth on bone.

The moon surmounted the ridge, turning the slopes to muted silver, but the kill remained deep in shadow. Still later it began to snow, moist flakes that soaked through my bedding. When the rocks finally emerged from darkness, I rolled up my sodden belongings. In the fog and swirling snow I could just see the snow leopard, dry and protected in the shelter of an overhang. I had learned nothing new that night, but the hours of silence, the celestial beauty of the mountains in the moonlight, and, above all, the knowledge of having been a part of the snow leopard's world filled me with quiet ecstasy.

Within three days the snow leopard became remarkably tolerant of my presence, permitting me to approach to within 120 feet before retreating. However, the cub seldom showed itself. The female spent much of each day near her kill to protect it from scavenging birds. In addition to crows, griffon vultures, and an occasional golden eagle, the kill had attracted five lammergeier (bearded vultures)—two adults and three juveniles—which banked past the cliffs on eight-foot wing spans as they surveyed the kill site with ruby eyes. Lammergeier are known to carry bones high up into the air, then drop them onto rocks so as to obtain marrow from the shattered fragments. Almost daily I presented the snow leopard with a fresh goat, enticing her to remain in the area. Usually she killed it after dark, but late one afternoon I witnessed the event.

After watching the goat intently for forty-five minutes, she slowly moved down the slope, body pressed to the ground, carefully placing each paw until she reached a boulder just above her prey. There she hesitated, then suddenly leaped to the ground behind the goat. The startled animal whirled around with lowered horns, and equally surprised, the snow leopard reared back, swiping the air once with her paw. But when the goat turned to flee, she lunged and with one smooth motion clamped her teeth into its throat while grabbing its shoulders with her massive forepaws. Slowly the goat sank to its knees. A light tap from her toppled it on its side. Crouching or sitting, she continued to grip its throat until after eight minutes all movement ceased.

Abruptly, one night the snow leopard and her cub departed. I traced their tracks uphill through a stand of conifers to some precipices and then paused. Should I follow or leave them in peace? Deciding on the latter, I reluctantly turned back down the slope. For one week they had provided me with a unique experience, and I longed for the day when I might renew our acquaintance.

It was now December 21. My survey of wildlife in the Chitral Gol was finished. Zahid had returned to Lahore some days ago, and it was time for me to go too. Loaded with heavy packs, Pukhan, Sher, and I left for Chitral town the following morning. The trail angled up the slope to the crest of a ridge where we stopped to rest. Under our feet, far below, was the town, another world with buildings and terraced fields. Across the valley rose peaks, jagged and hard, and to the north, filling the head of the valley, was Tirich Mir, at 25,290 feet the highest peak in the Hindu Kush. It alone had distinction in these anonymous mountains; it alone possessed the mind and lingered in memory. "Clouds hang heavy upon Tirich Mir like sorrow upon a man," goes a Chitrali saying. But even when it wore such a shroud of clouds, one's eyes still searched for the mountain as if only it provided permanence in an ever-changing world.

As we rested, the mehtar, H. H. Saif-ul-Maluke, came hiking up the trail with an entourage of nine. Home on a school holiday, he was en route to his preserve. A pleasant young man of about nineteen, he was growing his first moustache and stroked it surreptitiously as we chatted about wildlife. His round face held genetic memories of Mongol hordes, of the horsemen of Genghis Khan, but there was a softness in his eyes and a laxness in his temper, as if his blood had forgotten its past. He had never ruled this small mountain state. Early in the 1950s, his father had died in a plane crash and his uncle, Prince Asad-ur-Rehman, took over as regent. Prince Asad was weak, lacking commitment and a firm hand, and little effort was made to improve the conditions of his desperately poor subjects. As family properties began to crumble, Asad withdrew from the turbulence and problems of this world to prepare for the next. Finally the government deposed the family and took over full administration of the state. After wishing the mehtar a pleasant journey, we descended the barren slope toward town, a slope which within living memory had been forested.

Chitral town is essentially a bazaar, a row of shops lining nearly a mile of unpaved road which is muddy in winter and dusty in summer. Each shop consists of an open-fronted shack with wares lining the walls while the proprietor hunkers in the center. Most shops specialize in such items as bolts of cloth, aluminum pots, dried apricots and walnuts, or cigarettes. Some feature a few tinned foods, very ancient and rusty, and others sell rough chunks of salt resembling cloudy quartz. Goats, stripped of their hides, hang head-down in butcher shops, and draped over poles like grotesque pieces of cloth are their fat-lined mesentaries. Shoemakers fashion sandals out of old tires. In winter the proprietors hunch over reticent wood fires burning in kerosene tins. With brown mantles called *chogas* drawn tightly around their shoulders against the chill, they spit dejectedly into the road. Chitral is a town of idle males, Muslim dogma having banished women to the seclusion of their homes. Men stand around in huddles or sip milk tea in restaurants, loitering the hours away. Once Chitrali men dressed in handsome clothes made of brown felt cloth, but most now wore seedy, ill-fitting jackets and overcoats donated by foreign charitable organizations. Only the fact that every-

one wore a *bakhol*, the flat, curled-up felt cap that is the badge of every mountain man, prevented an aura of complete dereliction.

Like many peoples whose lives follow a fixed and dreary pattern, Chitrali men are inveterate gossips. I was a new zoological phenomenon and rumors about me were rife. The vacuous gaze of idlers followed me as I walked through town and my doings were invariably reported to the local political agent. It was said that I could hypnotize snow leopard and pick them up in my arms. And, more vexing, it was said that I was here to establish a missile base. In a part of the world which has a phobia about spies, the latter rumor could affect my work. In India someone had whispered to a government official that I might be a CIA agent with the result that I was denied further research permits. Although this is a well-known technique of Indians to eliminate foreigners for ignoble personal reasons, I was afraid that these baseless rumors about me in Chitral might have a similar effect. Fortunately, they did not.

Downslope from the bazaar, past some government barracks and past fields that served as the town latrine, was the so-called royal palace. Perched on a bank above the Kunar River, the palace was but a small fortress built of timber and earth, with squat, rather sinister towers and high walls. From outside it had an abandoned look; inside, past a high iron-plated gate, was a courtyard with rusting cannons and crumbling battlements. Staircases in the buildings were treacherous, broken and dark, and the hallways and rooms were hollow with plaster flaking off the walls, little more than repositories for dusty trophy heads of Marco Polo sheep and markhor. Ancient retainers, as decayed as the fortress, scuttled down its passages. Only the banquet hall had a semblance of former glory. Of moderate size, with gold-painted woodwork, the room displayed various photographs: of previous mehtars, all bearded and corpulent; of family portraits, showing only the males; of troops arranged in neat formations; of confident British political agents who had held the real power in this area since the 1890s. The neglect of the palace was depressing; I felt a sadness, a sense of irretrievable loss over an era that had already vanished into history, yet persisted into the present, unwanted, unmourned, hundreds of years of history ending in a pathetic ruin.

I once asked Prince Asad how long his family had ruled Chitral. "I am not certain," he replied vaguely and softly with a dreamy smile. "We have no written history. The family probably started here with one of the sons of Babur's brothers in the 1500s." Descended on his father's side from the great Turkish conqueror Timur and on his mother's side from Genghis Khan's second son Chaghatai, Babur rose to power in Samarkand and Kabul and in 1526 became the first Moghul emperor after defeating the ruler of Delhi. However, Prince Asad's family did not attain power in Chitral until late in the seventeenth century and then it was shared with the Khushwaqt family of northeastern Chitral.

The recent history of Chitral is one of intrigue, murder, and treachery. In 1892 the death of Aman-ul-Mulk plunged Chitral into anarchy. In his fascinating book, *Twenty Years in the Himalaya,* Charles Bruce notes: "On his death there were only two serious claimants for his throne, his eldest legitimate son, Nizam-ul-Mulk, a hand-

some and weak man and considered immoral even by Chitrali standards, and his younger brother, Afzal-ul-Mulk, by no means a bad
person at all, although his instincts were ferocious, almost tigerish."
He demonstrated the latter on his father's death by killing several of
his brothers and forcing Nizam to flee. His uncle Sher Afzal thereupon invaded from Badakshan, which adjoins Chitral in Afganistan,
and surprised Afzal in the Chitral fort. Afzal was killed. The
British, who had by that time established themselves in the neighboring Gilgit Agency, backed Nizam, and they sent a small military
mission to place him on the throne. But knowing British prejudices,
this military presence bothered the local nobles, for each felt that he
would, in Bruce's words, "no longer be able to sell his subjects as
slaves in the open market with impunity." While this was happening,
Drosh, a town about twenty miles downstream from the palace, was
taken over by Umra Khan of Jandol and his Pathans from the southwest. Then in 1894 Nizam was murdered by his brother Amir-ul-
Mulk and the nobles revolted against the British. About a third of
the British force of 150 was destroyed and the rest retreated into
Chitral fort. For forty-six days during March and April of 1895, the
soldiers remained under siege. A column of troops from Gilgit and
another from Peshawar, which fought its way northward through
truculent tribal territories that had never before been penetrated by
the British, relieved the fort and installed a new ruler, Shuja-ul-Mulk.

The British now had the power, the rulers the privileges, and the
life of the villagers went on much as before. Ten percent of the annual harvest still had to be paid as tax to the ruler. But now there was
peace. With remarkable prescience, Sir Aurel Stein, the greatest of
the scientist-explorers in this part of the world, predicted problems
after a visit to Chitral in 1906:

> The very *pax* britannica must earlier or late raise grave economi-
> cal problems; for the population, no longer checked by slave-selling
> and feudal fighting, is bound to increase rapidly, while the reserve

of arable land still unoccupied is likely to be exhausted within a measurable period.

Chitral had 55,000 people in 1895 and has three times as many today. All arable land is under cultivation, yet there is a desperate food shortage. Many men leave the mountains each winter for temporary jobs in the cities; flour, rice, and sugar must be flown in by military transport planes to augment the meager local supplies. And the government aggravates shortages by its mere presence. Government offices alone need 10,000 manloads or 800,000 pounds of firewood per year. Each office is allowed one manload per day, yet one seldom sees a fire. Wrapped in overcoats, shawls, and caps, officials shiver through their duties. Where is the allocated firewood, I wondered? Office workers divide it up to take home, for on their meager salaries they cannot afford the five rupees or about fifty cents which a load costs. Goats damage the hills, yet their milk is needed, and from the sale of meat and hides a villager can earn a little cash. "Chitral was once a land of just enough," Wazir Ali Shah, the extra assistant commissioner and a man from an old Chitrali family, said to me one evening. "But now there is not enough." We sat cross-legged in front of his fireplace, absorbing the warmth, and eating bits of roasted lamb. The fire and food were in my honor and I felt guilty that I, an outsider, was also depleting the resources.

Most Chitrali nobles have now withdrawn from the area or into themselves, but not Prince Burhan-ud-Din. He looks like the reincarnation of a mehtar from the past century but acts like a boisterous bear, hugging friends in the bazaar, passing candy to children, and inviting stray foreigners such as myself to his home for a meal. Something of an evangelist, he may boom to a departing visitor, "Let me give you a message for your country. Let there be peace among men." Burhan has perfected the Pakistani art of being friendly and hospitable, but remaining remote. I sometimes stayed at his home for days, yet learned little of the man himself, and according to Muslim custom, never even glimpsed the female members of his household.

Our animated discussions frequently revolved around wildlife. Burhan, now as in the past, liked to stock his winter larder with markhor, and even though it was illegal, he still invited guests to shoot in his private reserve.

"Only a few hundred markhor are left in Chitral," I would argue. "Just as you strive for peace among men, so you ought to fight for peace between man and beast. The Muslim religion teaches not to kill except in times of need. And you don't have need and besides you set a bad example to the villagers."

"Yes, yes, yes," he would reply. "You are right. There is too much shooting. I am worried about the ibex in my reserve in Agaram. You must go there to see how many there are. Take my gun and shoot as many as you need. Have you eaten ibex? No? They are very good."

For all his effort to comprehend a new order of things, he remained a prisoner of a pattern of being, and at no time was this more evident than with the incident of the snow leopard. Burhan has a markhor reserve at Tushi, about eight miles north of town. The reserve consists of a piece of mountain slope adjacent to the road and at that time contained about 125 markhor. I seldom watched these animals because most adult males had been shot, leaving the population with an atypical composition. Attracted by the prey, an occasional snow leopard came to Tushi in winter. I had asked Burhan to notify me if one did so, and on January 15, 1973, a runner arrived at the Chitral Gol with a note announcing the presence of a cat. On January 17, I arrived at Burhan's house.

"Where have you been?" he greeted me. "You are too late. My keeper shot the snow leopard yesterday. It was killing my markhor."

I was stunned. The deputy commissioner, the divisional forest officer, and several other officials were at the house for a luncheon. Not one deplored the killing, even though snow leopard were legally protected. We all went out to look at the fresh skin grotesquely stuffed with straw and hanging in a shed. I joined in the lunch, a sumptuous meal of rice, spiced hamburgers, chicken curry, and stewed apricots followed by green tea, but I had no appetite. Seeing my dejection, Burhan suggested that I stay for a few days in his hut at Tushi in the event that another snow leopard might come. I agreed without conviction.

Crowded between road and mountain on a fragment of ancient riverbank, the Tushi hut was a gloomy place surrounded by winter-bare apple and apricot trees. Clouds rolled gray against the mountains and I felt imprisoned by this waste of stone. I need to establish empathy with an area before I can devote myself to it; here I felt like an alien. The character of a region has much to do with the character of the person describing it, for we see our own heart in a landscape. I knew that in part my melancholy was based on the pervading presence of man in these mountains; I seek the unpeopled world. My spiritual home lies in the Alaskan wilderness where I did my first wildlife studies, and once adopted, a wilderness becomes not just an entity but a state of imagination. Nothing had prepared me for these wounded hills of the Hindu Kush.

I tied out two goats hoping to bait in snow leopard. While scouring the slopes for fresh tracks, I had found four recent kills, three male markhor and a young, but these probably represented the last meals of the cat whose empty skin I had just seen. My search for fresh spoor was unsuccessful. But at least I had followed fox trails, observed markhor young in play, seen two golden eagles swoop at a hare. . . . And suddenly one morning a goat lay dead on the scree. I focused my scope on the site, but noted only a disheveled carcass. Perhaps, I thought, a wolf had killed the goat, eaten its fill, and moved on. Yet some magpies sat expectantly nearby as if afraid to approach. I looked again, and the rocks moved; stone turned to life, as like a gray haze a snow leopard departed with a motion so smooth it barely conveyed a sense of movement. It was a female. She hid that day somewhere among the precipices while scavenging birds stripped her kill. I tied out another goat and waited. At 4:45 P.M. a lammergeier flushed from its rocky perch. Creeping down the slope was the snow leopard, but instead of attacking the goat she calmly waited for an hour behind some sagebrush until dusk blurred her outline. Soon after, a brief dark struggle.

This female roamed through the same area as had the dead male. Do snow leopard travel in pairs as some naturalists assert? During my wanderings I came across twenty-nine sets of tracks of which twenty-five were of solitary individuals and the rest of pairs, and the Indian mountaineer Hari Dang met twelve lone snow leopard and four pairs. Obviously the cats tend to be solitary. When two or three are together they may comprise a male and female, a female with fully grown cubs, or litter-mates. However, the sexes of slain or sighted animals are seldom reported. In 1972 a villager in the Kesu Gol, between Chitral and Drosh, shot a group of three snow leopard which consisted of a female with two large cubs, male and female. An animal may be solitary yet not necessarily asocial. Residents in an area know each other and possibly meet on occasion and share a kill, as is the case among tigers. Unfortunately I could not unravel the details of the snow leopard's social life.

Lying behind some boulders at dawn, I watched the snow leopard and filmed it. Several magpies were there already, teasingly hopping within six feet of the cat and nimbly leaping aside when she lunged; vultures glided in and settled on the surrounding rocks. It was now fully light and the snow leopard became uneasy about being in the open. Three times she walked away, but returned with a rush to chase magpies from the carcass. Finally she departed, moving across the scree and along the base of a cliff until she vanished around a spur of the hill. It was the last time I saw her. My first encounter with a snow leopard in the Chitral Gol had left me exhilarated, but this one left me regretful and melancholy, as if seeing something beautiful fade away forever. It reminded me of these words by the Roman poet Virgil: "There are tears in things, and all things doomed to die touch the heart."

Generally my trips to Chitral were made in winter. At that season, when snow lies deep on the ridges and cold grips the crags, most wildlife descends into the valleys. This is especially true of markhor, which remain at low altitudes from November to May. Snow leopard naturally follow their prey. With wildlife concentrated, it is then relatively easy to make a census and study it. However, to enter or leave Chitral in winter presents various challenges.

Any map will show the bold red line of a road heading north from Nowshera near Peshawar. It enters the hills just before Malakand, crosses southern Swat, and continues through Dir over the 10,230-foot Lowari Pass into Chitral. Indeed, a road is there. But snow closes it around the Lowari Pass for at least six months of the year, and in many places the road is so poorly aligned along geologically unstable slopes that any rainstorm causes landslides, and in the absence of culverts, erodes the surface into canyons. There are three flights a week from Peshawar to Chitral, but many are canceled, especially from December to May, for the Lowari Pass is a notorious breeder of bad weather. Mornings are often clear but by noon clouds settle into the pass. Naturally, flights are scheduled to leave Peshawar around noon. Consequently only three of my nine attempted flights into or out of Chitral left on the appointed day. To obtain a seat on the heavily booked flight is so difficult that one is not easily tempted to give it up and go by road. So on flight day one goes to the airport again to be confronted by a pushing, shouting mob clustered around the check-in counter, everyone burdened with bedrolls, tin trunks, and formless objects tied into cloth, like evacuees from some catastrophe. A hundred years of British rule never taught Pakistanis to form an orderly queue. As often as not I had to brave the mob again to retrieve my luggage after the flight was canceled. After several such futile treks to the airport, especially in winter when bad weather sometimes halts air service for several weeks, I not surprisingly preferred the rigors of the road.

A fast approach by plane robs the journey of anticipation; a slow approach by road always begins with the hope of a pleasant trip and continues with the hope of simply reaching the destination. Either mode of travel has its drawbacks, and one of my road trips, in January,

1973, illustrates a few. Brad House, a former curator of mammals at the Bronx Zoo, had joined me for this trip to Chitral. At the Peshawar bazaar I had to find a taxi willing to take us the 120 miles to Dir, and after considerable haggling over the price, a driver agreed to make the trip for the equivalent of twenty-five dollars. The car had a gasoline leak which filled the inside with fumes, and the tires were so worn that we soon had a flat. Then a wheel cracked. Although we had it welded at a village shop, we soon heard metal grinding on metal again. We continued. North of Mardan the barren hills rise abruptly from the Indus Plain and here the narrow road winds through the mountains. The afternoon passed; it grew dark and a cold rain fell. The occasional roadside shops were boarded up for the night, but finally we saw a tea shop, a poky shack whose kerosene lantern cast a faint light across the deserted village street. We had an omelet, chappaties, and tea, then drove on. A policeman waved us down and told us that bandits had blocked the road ahead. Traveling through the area in 1904, Charles Bruce noted that "it is still unsafe to travel the road without an escort." Now, seventy years later, conditions were just as good. We returned to the tea shop, expecting to spend the night. However, soon two trucks with about a dozen armed policemen arrived, and we joined the convoy which after a few miles halted at a sharp bend in the road. The police leaped from their trucks, rifles ready; flares were shot off, lighting the hills, but there was no one. We continued alone. Rain still poured, and farther on, it turned to sleet; the ruts in the road had become torrents. Approaching the town of Dir, the road climbed steep hills and up these we had to push the car through snow and mud. Finally, at 10:30 P.M. we reached town. After hammering at the door of the Saheed Tourist Hotel we were finally admitted. There was neither heat nor light and our room smelled of urine. Scanning the bed with my flashlight, I noted that the time for the annual change of sheets must be close at hand and I knew that bedbugs and fleas would be my companions. At least it was a place to sleep.

At dawn I went to the bazaar to ask about porters, but the loiterers there responded with indifferent grunts. Finally one old fellow said he could get the two required porters. Last night's storm had blown over and the day was crisp and clear. It was nineteen miles from Dir to the Lowari Pass, an easy trail with most of it following the snow-covered road. Three miles from the pass is Gujar, a hotel of sorts, an open-fronted shed resembling a malevolent outhouse. The snow drifts around it were decorated with excrement, and inside porters slurped tea, then belched raucously. Brad had dropped far behind, not used to high-altitude hiking, and by the time he arrived it was too late to cross the pass. At dusk the proprietor set up charpoys, beds made of ropes stretched taut over a wooden frame. The following morning Brad wisely decided that mountains were not his métier, especially as he had only recently recovered from a bout of pneumonia. He turned back toward Peshawar while I mounted the pass and descended into Chitral, covering the remaining fourteen miles in five hours. The road was soon clear of snow, passable to jeeps.

Narrow and steep and with sharp curves, most mountain roads can only accommodate jeeps. A traveler has two alternatives: take a jeep or walk. The former provides a unique experience, but the latter is safer. Discarded by the United Nations as derelicts, jeeps next become mountain taxis. First the vehicle is loaded with several hundred pounds of flour, rice, or other supplies for delivery to various shops. When the springs are flat, the personal baggage of the passengers is piled on top. And finally some eight passengers crowd onto the load while another three squeeze into the front seat. Each jeep is manned by two persons, a driver and a helper whose task it is to fill leaking radiators and to put rocks behind the wheels whenever the vehicle stalls. Since there are always passengers to push, functional self-starters are considered superfluous. Tires are usually worn smooth and rags may be stuffed into holes to protect the inner tubes. Overloaded, overcrowded, the jeeps careen through the mountains, under only limited control, for the engine is switched off to save gasoline when going downhill. I was usually tensed, ready to leap in case of mishap. Once I kept a morbid tally of accidents in the

Gilgit area: in one month five jeeps fell off the mountains, killing twenty-three persons. In this instance I reached Chitral town at dusk, the trip from Peshawar taking three days instead of one hour by plane.

Solitary, rare, and elusive, snow leopard generally foiled my attempts to study them. The old naturalistic techniques of following tracks, examining feces, and glimpsing an occasional animal were obviously not the best means of studying the habits of this cat. If I could place a radio transmitter mounted on a collar around the necks of several individuals I would be able to locate them by picking up the signals on a receiving set. This technique had been used successfully on grizzly bears, tigers, and other species, and I wanted to try it on snow leopard. In January, 1974, Melvin Sunquist, a biologist and expert in the use of radio telemetry, brought equipment and two box traps in which to catch snow leopard. Mel is tall, lean, and easygoing; he had previously studied sloths. We moved into the Chitral Gol, and as Mel was not particularly fond of climbing, I searched the valley alone for snow leopard spoor but found nothing. Pukhan told us that no cats had been there for several months, and according to Prince Burhan, none had visited Tushi either.

I was concerned. A year earlier I had seen the cats or their tracks in both areas. But I also knew that during the winter of 1971-72, Prince Muta-ul-Mulk, a brother of Prince Burhan, had wantonly shot two female snow leopard at Shogore, near Tushi. That same season at least four other snow leopard were killed in the Chitral Valley. The following winter a male was shot at Tushi. These seven deaths had seriously decimated the valley's population. Now I wondered if there were any left for me to study.

As we waited one day for snow leopard in the Chitral Gol, the game warden, Mirza Hassan, arrived on a visit. Wiry, small, and with eyes that dance like wild mice in his beaked face, he is an exceptional individual. Whereas most officials remain in their offices doing nothing and are proud of what they do, Mirza Hassan toured the district and conscientiously tried to enforce regulations. Earlier

I had asked him to check on the status of snow leopard in various valleys and he had now come to report. His English, while not good, was better than my Urdu, so our conversations proceeded in a style somewhat less than elegant.

"How many markhor you find?"

Consulting a scrap of paper he read: "Drosh Gol—ten, Chinal Gol —fifteen, Garhit Gol—ten, Bombret—twenty-five . . . Markhor too few now," he concluded. To his total of 120 I added my own censuses of the Chitral Gol and Tushi reserves and estimates for a few other valleys. An optimistic figure for Chitral as a whole was 500–600 markhor. Thirty years ago that many animals lived in each valley, according to old-time residents. Unfortunately the time-honored slogan, "If it moves, shoot it; if it doesn't, chop it down," was still vigorously practiced in Chitral even though the deputy commissioner had prohibited all killing of markhor, ibex, and snow leopard the previous year.

Checking his watch, Hassan suddenly interrupted our conversation to kneel, facing Mecca. Five times a day he recited his creed: "There is no God but God and Muhammad is his prophet."

Then, in his somewhat breathless manner of speaking, he returned to the subject of markhor: "Burhan is causing trouble more than sufficient. He shoot markhor this month. But proof is not present. Forest Department now make court case against Muta-ul-Mulk. Between 15 and 19 January he shoot four markhor."

I congratulated him on his initiative. Villagers cannot be expected to abide by laws if princes hunt with impunity.

"You know Mikelroy?" he asked. I looked puzzled. "American," he prompted. "Kill markhor last year and quickly leave."

Hassan had mispronounced the man's name, but now I remembered. A representative of the Los Angeles Safari Club had shot markhor illegally.

"We have court case now. We *chalan* him if he come to Chitral again," concluded Hassan.

The hunter wisely avoided arrest by staying out of Chitral. I met him the following year, this time shooting Punjab urial, another legally protected species. He was pleasant but limited in outlook, interrested mainly in gaining status by adding trophies to his private mortuary. An aim of his life was to kill specimens of each species and subspecies of sheep in the world, and preferably of goats too. He was annoyed that he could not obtain a permit to shoot the rare Walia ibex in Ethiopia. When I pointed out that the animal was on the verge of extinction, with fewer than three hundred left, he emphasized that he too was concerned about conservation. Showing me his Ducks Unlimited tie, he noted: "This cost me three hundred bucks."

My conversation with Mirza Hassan turned to snow leopard, but he had little to report. He had just spent three days in the valleys of Rumbur, Bumburet, and Birir, to the south of the Chitral Gol, but the Kafir people there had seen no recent sign of snow leopard. Sometimes blond and blue-eyed, the Kafir are of unknown origin. Kafir means "unbeliever" and to Muslims their culture is anathema, for they believe in not just one god but many, their women are not secluded, and during the *pore* festival in September a strong man is selected to service childless women. In 1893 the Amir of Afghanistan forcefully converted the Kafirs in his country and only those who fled to Chitral retained their way of life. However, even there cultural change is accelerating. Once, for example, they made life-sized wooden statues of men and of figures on horseback, impressive grave monuments in memory of prominent persons, but this art form has now been discarded.

I hired Subidar Afzal to help in our search for snow leopard. As a retired member of the Chitral Scouts, a paramilitary unit in charge of border patrols, he knew the area well. When he reported that the Golen Gol, about twelve miles from Chitral town, might be a good place for snow leopard, we decided to move there. A few miles upstream from town the Kunar River divides, one branch becoming the Arkari and the other the Yarkhun, which has its headwaters in the northeastern corner of Chitral some hundred and fifty miles away. We followed the Yarkhun by jeep to near the mouth of the Golen Gol, and from there porters carried our belongings up a gloomy gorge until the valley widened and the villages of Golen and Bobaka could be seen against the slope. There was a foot of snow and the cliffs had an icy sheen; even the stone huts radiated an iron coldness. Unable to rent a room, we slept in a partially built shop. Fortunately Sher Panah found two rooms for us the next day. That night a snow leopard passed the village, overlooking the one goat bait we had tied out. The cat came downvalley, following the base of a cliff, and at a boulder field deep under snow it leaped from stone to stone down to a stream, where it walked along the edge to several ice-glazed rocks. There it jumped six feet onto one rock, seven feet to another, its claws raking the slippery surface, and with a final leap, reached the opposite bank. Skirting the village, it traced a stone wall, angled up a scree slope, and zigzagged up over a precipice. We were elated: surely another cat would soon pass by.

Our life settled into a daily routine. Mel studied the brown dippers which were abundant along the stream. Though it was only mid-February these hardy birds were already courting. Each pair claimed some 1,400 feet of river and defended its territory vigorously against other pairs. Occasionally one stood before its mate and with raised bill and quivering wings burst into strident song. Alone or with Subidar Afzal I explored Golen Gol, which wound about twenty-five miles into the mountains. The valley was once famous for its wildlife, but markhor were now gone and ibex rare. Upvalley from our base were three more villages, tiny clusters of huts in a narrow defile tied together by a snow trail.

One day we went beyond the last village, beyond Ustor where the valley narrows then rises abruptly at an ancient landslide. A stand of junipers grows here, a stand which will soon die by the ax, judging by the many raw stumps protruding from the snow. I particularly like these mountain junipers; their bark is ragged, their trunks gnarled, their branches tattered. Unlike the majestic firs, these trees are approachable, comfortable. They have a pungent, wild odor and white-winged grosbeaks like to feed on their berries. We walked slowly, scanning the slopes for ibex trails. After two hours the peaks retreated to form a mile-wide flat; we were at 10,600 feet, at a place called Rogenali. Three huts cowered in this expanse, so much a part of the landscape that from a distance only a thin column of smoke rising through the hole in a roof revealed them to be more than snow mounds. As we drew closer, I could see firewood stacked beside the walls, and by a haystack several sheep hunched against the cold. A few cottonwood and birches grew nearby, mutilated, their branches lopped for livestock fodder. Two dogs barked. Like most of these mountain dogs, their ears had been cut off. Villagers like to lop things. Two men came to the door, both dressed in coarse brown cloth and wearing goatskins tied with thongs to protect their feet. They invited us into the guest room where, taking off our boots, we settled ourselves cross-legged on a layer of straw in front of the fireplace. Soon the kettle boiled for tea, and later, for dinner, we were given boiled potatoes with salt. I like Pakistani hospitality. Even the poorest villager offers what he has with lack of servility, with individual dignity. It grew dark as we sat in the dim light of the fire— —the poor cannot afford candles or kerosene lanterns—and the three men gossiped in muted tones. They gave off a primitive odor, half-human, half-animal, a mixture of sweat, smoke, and farmyard. There was no trace of Western culture to distort the evening. Here it was easy to see the excesses of civilization in perspective, to realize the value of simplicity. I would not want to return to such an existence, but made aware of the waste in one's own life one makes a silent promise to conserve. My ancestors lived like this. And perhaps some day my descendants.

The following morning one of the men took me southeast, up a valley toward some glaciers. It was piercingly cold, around 0° F. judging by the way the snow squeaked beneath my boots, and the sun remained only a pale disk behind a veil of cloud. Deprived of the sun's radiance, the peaks were dead, desolate piles of rock and ice. First we walked on the overflow ice of a stream, and then plodded through knee-deep snow. High above we saw ibex tracks, but no sign of the animals themselves. We ate our lunch, a lean meal of dry bread, while stamping our feet to keep warm, and then it was time to return home. The guide checked the slopes once again, more from habit than hope, but this time he handed the binoculars to me with a grin and pointed. Far away and very high were ibex, dark spots near the crest of a ridge. I counted six females, three young, and three subadult males with scimitar-shaped horns no longer than eighteen inches. Several of the animals were feeding. With snow lying belly-deep they had to use a special technique to find their forage. An animal faces uphill and paws vigorously with a foreleg, sweeping the snow backward and sideways; then it nuzzles around in the crater for something edible, expending much energy for a mouthful—or perhaps for nothing at all. In winter ibex often descend from the high crags to seek food on the lower slopes, although these have mostly been denuded by livestock, and watching the animals as they dug so laboriously for each morsel, I wondered how they could survive severe winters. The amount of energy needed to keep warm, plow through snow, partake in the rut, and in the case of females, nourish a fetus, must be so great that the balance between survival and death from malnutrition is tenuous indeed. In northwestern Chitral, near the Dorah Pass that leads into Afghanistan, I once made a vegetation survey in prime ibex habitat where livestock had ravaged the slopes. At first glance, there seemed to be abundant forage, but the surviving plants consisted mainly of unpalatable species. Only 2 percent of the groundcover was made up of well-liked grasses and forbs.

Fortunately the ibex as a species is adaptable, existing over a vast range in a variety of habitats. Of the four subspecies, only the Walia ibex lives in a moderate environment. All others are exposed either to searing heat or cold, where life is barely endurable. The Nubian ibex inhabits the deserts of Egypt and the Arabian Peninsula, the Alpine ibex the high altitudes of Europe, and the Kuban ibex the western Caucasus; the Asiatic ibex, which I was now observing, ranges from the Hindu Kush across the Pamirs and the Tien Shan to the Sayan Mountains in Russia, as well as along the great Himalayan chain eastward to the Sutlej River. All day the valley had seemed bitter, the peaks pitiless, the antithesis of life. With the ibex herd above us, I felt somehow less alone and the mountains became more companionable.

Subidar Afzal and I returned to our hut at Golen the following morning. Two days later one of our goats lay dead, its demise advertised by cawing jungle crows. I hoped our wait for the snow leopard was now over, but when I checked the carcass and saw the deeply slashed throat I knew that a wolf had killed my bait. Cats are tidy killers. Although uncommon, wolves are obtrusive and herdsmen cordially dislike them for their habit of sweeping into a herd, killing an animal or two, bolting some meat, and vanishing as suddenly as they arrive. C. H. Stockley witnessed such an attack:

> He then spurted suddenly in the most amazing manner into the middle of the flock and pulled down sheep after sheep with such wonderful speed and dexterity that there were five lying on the ground within a distance of thirty yards. . . . He came up on the right side of each sheep . . . and, seizing the galloping sheep behind the right ear, jerked its head downward and inward so that it pitched on its nose.

Having waited in the Golen Gol for twelve days, I decided that Mel could continue the vigil with Sher while I checked for snow leopard in other valleys. Subidar Afzal and I left on foot for Chitral town where I again visited Mirza Hassan, the game warden, who invited me to his room. It was bleak and impersonal, so typical of those belonging to itinerant officials who have with them only a bedroll, a change of uniform, and some toilet articles. Like most civil servants, he could not afford to bring his family to Chitral during his tour of duty. No wonder everyone applies for transfer as soon as they are assigned to the mountains. We sat on his bed and drank tea and nibbled crackers I had bought in the bazaar. The temperature in the room was near the freezing point. My one recurrent wish was to be really warm, warm all over, not just hands or front or back or whichever part of my body happened to be near some puny fire. I inquired about snow leopard. Yes, Hassan said, one had been seen near town. But he was obviously preoccupied with another matter and finally asked:

"The dying man? What happened?"

It took me a few seconds to realize that he referred to an incident in the Golen Gol. One morning, near our hut, I saw blood spattered all over the snow. A messy way to butcher a goat, I thought. Later that day I discovered that during the night a villager had shotgunned another in a dispute over a woman. And now I learned that, according to bazaar rumor, the wounded man had crawled to my bed to die in my arms.

Hassan knew a man who had trophy horns in his home and he offered to show these to me. We walked through a maze of narrow and muddy lanes flanked by high stone walls behind which hid flat-roofed bungalows and small gardens with apricot and mulberry trees. Hassan entered one courtyard and I waited at the gate while he announced our arrival, warning all women that a stranger was near. Several trophies hung on the veranda. I measured each one, a 45-inch markhor, a 40-inch ibex and others, dusty mementos of once-vital beasts. As I worked, another villager came to watch. He told Hassan that he had some urial trophies and would show them to me if he would not be arrested for possessing them. He was assured that there was no law against owning horns. One subspecies of urial sheep, the Ladak urial, occurs in the mountains along the major river valleys. During the 1930s the mehtar used to send his men into the hills to drive sheep down the forested slopes to where they could be shot easily in the open near what is now the Chitral airport. These slopes are now bare of trees and the urial is so rare that I never saw any in Chitral.

I was particularly interested in ascertaining the age of each trophy. Horns continue to grow throughout the life of an animal, most so when there is nutritious food available and least so during winter. This fluctuation in growth rate produces an easily visible winter "ring" each year, enabling one to age trophies precisely. The oldest markhor in my notes died at the age of thirteen years, the oldest ibex at fifteen, the oldest urial at ten and a half. All these trophies were large enough to rate entries in the obituary columns of record books. Remembering that the world-record markhor measures 64 inches and ibex 56 inches, some hunters bemoan the fact that they have never seen, much less shot, a beast of such size. However, for horns to reach record length, good nutrition and a long life are needed, a combination that few animals now enjoy.

Subidar Afzal and I then walked the eight miles to Tushi, but no snow leopard had visited the area. We continued north to Shogore, inquiring of travelers and villagers about the cats. One, we were told, had passed through recently. From Shogore we continued up the Arkari, along a foot trail which first wound up over a cliff and then traced a turbulent stream whose course alternately passed between gorges and by clusters of huts perched on alluvial fans and raised banks. We stopped at one hut to talk to Gulbas Khan, a game watcher employed by Prince Burhan. Tall and strong, Gulbas approaches life with great zest; I was pleased when he agreed to accompany us. It began to snow. At dusk we reached the village of Mizhigram where I hoped to speak with the owner of a private shooting reserve called Besti, probably the finest ibex area left in Chitral. I had visited Besti to study ibex the summer of 1972 and now wanted to check the area again, this time to look for snow leopard. The owner was gone for the winter, but the caretaker invited us in to spend the night. It was still snowing when we left the next morning. After two hours the Besti Valley joined from the left and we ascended it over a narrow trail obliterated by snow and avalanches. Crossing unstable scree slopes high above the river, I found it disconcerting to have the trail slump away underfoot, and I was quite willing to have Gulbas in the lead. Finally the valley widened and ahead we saw the village of Besti squeezed so tightly against the mountain slope that one man's veranda is another's roof. Hill people must conserve space; land suitable for agriculture is too valuable to waste on houses. A tiny room with a bed of straw and a fireplace became our home. The Subidar made tea and baked juwari bread on the hot coals. Meals become the main diversion in a life of waiting. In these mountains one must always be resigned to waiting for something, for the snow to stop falling, for porters to arrive; only a small fraction of the total time is spent in actual research. Here in the village the people waited too, for spring. They almost hibernated. Only one snow trail left the village. Occasionally someone hurried between huts, cloak pulled over head for warmth. It was silent, a medieval silence without motors and few sounds beyond the muted voices of men and livestock.

Still the snow fell. Determined to do some fieldwork, I walked up the valley a short distance, but soon stopped, realizing the futility of my venture; with the snow and clouds roiling low on the slopes, I could see little. Suddenly the ground quivered, the tremor lasting several seconds, and like giant beasts shaking themselves, the peaks discarded their mantles of fresh snow. Avalanches rumbled, the valley hummed and vibrated, and sharp ice crystals borne by gusts of wind pierced my face. Only I seemed stable in a white, moving void.

Next morning the snow stopped and the clouds began to disperse, revealing the dim lines of peaks and an occasional fragment of ice against a brilliant sky. Breaking trail with my snowshoes, I plodded in the lead while Gulbas struggled behind. Although snow may isolate villages for weeks, the local people never developed snowshoes to ease their travel. Avalanches constantly funneled down ravines before fanning out in the valley, and I viewed these shimmering cascades with trepidation. Certainly they made my choice of route of more than casual interest. Halfway up a slope, in a gully swept clear of snow, we spotted an ibex herd with seven animals; later we met another, this one with nine animals, again feeding on an avalanche path. Obviously the ibex sought such snow-free sites where food could more readily be found. The second herd contained two magnificent males, their knobby horns sweeping up and back for almost 40 inches. Unlike the drab-brown ibex males of Europe, the Asiatic ibex is strikingly adorned with a grizzled white face, a silver saddle, and white rump which contrast with the rest of his dark pelage. As I watched the animals the last wisps of cloud withdrew. Soon heat waves quivered over the snow, dancing among the ice monuments, and once again the landscape was full of motion, brilliant with an unrelieved radiance that had an almost hallucinogenic quality. On this day and the next I found 8 ibex herds, totaling 40 animals. Gulbas told me that perhaps 200 survived in the 55 square miles of the Besti drainage. His estimate seemed accurate. The Besti Valley divides near the village and previously, in August, 1972, I had surveyed one of these branches, the Gulumbukt Valley, and found 72 ibex.

I enjoyed those summer days in the Gulumbukt. From my tent camp at 11,300 feet, on a level place among stone corrals, I had roamed the hills, climbing high up on the sagebrush slopes until only the silver bulk of Tirich Mir and I had the sky to ourselves. I had meandered up the valley through the flowers, white daisies, yellow louseworts, purplish mints, and, hidden in the grass, edelweiss. I liked to find a rocky niche protected from the wind, where, sitting quietly, I ceased to be an intruder. Sometimes a skink basked in the sun with me. I was surprised to find these lizards as high as 14,500 feet. Longtailed marmots had dug their burrows where soil was sandy and vegetation lush. At this season they urgently stuffed themselves to grow fat enough to survive their long winter sleep. Sometimes I watched ibex, and one afternoon I spotted a herd of 31 males moving far up the valley. After collecting my sleeping bag from camp, I followed the herd. The valley ascended in a series of huge steps, level green turf dotted with yellow cinquefoil alternating with precipices and boulder fields down which a stream cascaded. Dusk overtook me at 14,000 feet. Marmots scolded, a harsh *bri-bri-bri*, as I unrolled my bed on a bar of glacial silt. At dawn I continued, up toward the sun that crept down the peaks and glaciers. At 15,000 feet there was a pond at the base of a moraine, and along its shore were tracks of hare and marmot, but not ibex. I climbed on, over the moraine, its surface gray and tossed, and then along a scree slope toward a col. Here at 16,000 feet, among the great ice-carved peaks, where only the hardiest plants can survive, I again found spoor of the ibex herd. Moving upward, the animals had foraged on isolated plants, nibbling on purple vetch and yellow-flowered *Draba*. Scattered, procumbent, and hidden in the protection of boulders, plants grew too sparsely to support a herd; each tuft of grass was its own oasis. The ibex had moved over the col into the valley beyond, but I did not mind. Wandering these heights, the hard rock underfoot, seeing an eagle against the sky, was reward enough.

In my mind I had passed to another world and returned. I had to leave the enchantment of the high summer pastures for the icy bleakness of Besti in winter. I wanted to flee; I wanted flowers and grass. There were no snow leopard here, and the following morning, in a snowstorm, we left. At the entrance to the village is a boulder into whose surface someone long ago chipped crude figures of ibex and wolves. When the huts of Besti have turned to dust and the last ibex has vanished into the belly of a hunter, these petroglyphs will remain, speaking of the past in a silent voice to silent hills.

By the end of February I had checked for snow leopard in many valleys. I had evidence of four or possibly five animals in about 1,200 square miles of mountains. Four years earlier, after having observed my first snow leopard, I left Chitral with the expectation of returning to study the cat. I had waited too long, and now it was too late; I could not justify a lengthy project on so few animals. I also had to leave Chitral to observe the birth season of Persian wild goat. Mel remained for another week, still hoping to trap a snow leopard, but after a month and a half of effort he too gave up and left the mountains. In only four years the status of the snow leopard in Chitral had changed from tenuously secure to seriously threatened. The animals had been shot neither for their hides nor in defense of livestock, just wantonly because they were there. No snow leopard visited the Chitral Gol during the winter of 1973–74, and none did so in 1974–75 either, according to a letter from Sher Panah. After that I did not seek further news. Markhor may still scamper over the precipices of the Chitral Gol and chukor may cackle among the sagebrush, but one of my dreams vanished with the last snow leopard. I do not want to return to the valley.

The snow leopard as a species is not threatened with imminent extinction, but in Pakistan, where possibly fewer than 250 survive, its future is not assured. Will Pakistan's mountains soon be deprived of snow leopard as the plains have already lost lion, tiger, and cheetah? Legally all hunting is prohibited, as is the sale of pelts, but it is difficult to enforce laws in remote mountain tracts. Besides, snow leopard do prey on livestock, something a villager cannot be expected to tolerate unless he receives compensation for his losses from the government. In conservation both idealism and realism must be served. Because of these problems it is all too easy to leave the snow leopard to its fate. It survived the icy rigors of the Pleistocene, when many other species vanished from our earth, and it has so far survived the onslaught of man on its mountain realm. But I know that the Chitral Gol does not feel its soft tread anymore and that many other valleys too are deprived of its presence. Imagine the peaks without snow leopard.

Though the cats can perhaps survive in zoos as relics of a better past, it is a sad compromise. The mountains gave man soil, provided him with food, and stored his water, but he has taken almost everything, leaving the earth's bones bare. The snow leopard might well serve as symbol of man's commitment to the future of the mountain world.

Beyond the Ranges

I was usually out of harmony with the winter peaks in Chitral. The mountains remained remote and passionless, providing no moments of liberation, of personal illumination, and I tended to view them as local people do, as places to visit out of need, not pleasure. Perhaps my thoughts dwelled too much in the distant past before the slopes had been denuded by man, striving to return to an age that I could never share. I needed to find the lonely world beyond the ranges. Chitral extends eastward like a crooked finger, encompassing the Yarkhun River drainage which on the north is flanked by the Hindu Kush and on the south by the Hindu Raj. The headwaters are at Karambar Pass, just south of the Russian Pamirs. A trip to the area would provide a happy combination of personal quest and scientific endeavor. Also, a wildlife survey was needed there, for it was said that brown bear and Marco Polo sheep, both rare species in Pakistan, frequent the upper Yarkhun.

Pervez Khan and I reached Dir in the evening of July 19, 1973. Although wildlife watching is an individual experience, not one of fellowship, I prefer to have a companion on long journeys; I like solitude, not loneliness. Pervez worked for a rubber company in Lahore on a job that somehow permitted him to vanish for weeks. Like many middle-class bachelor males in the city, Pervez spent almost all of his free time within a circle of male friends, going to movies, cruising the streets in cars, and talking, talking of what they might do and what should be done, talking in their homes, in restaurants, talking through the night into the early morning hours. "All of us are useless chaps," he once commented. But Pervez indulged in more than what passed for merry nightlife in Muslim society. As a competent photographer and dedicated outdoorsman, he had been on several mountaineering expeditions. Few Pakistanis know their own country, especially the mountains, and to this Pervez is a happy exception. I was fortunate to have him join me on this trek.

At Dir we rented a jeep for the five-hour trip to Chitral town. The road, we were told, was open. However, experience had taught me never to expect a routine trip in the mountains. Approaching the Lowari Pass, we commented on the complete absence of traffic from Chitral, and soon the reason became apparent: landslides, boulders, and uprooted trees blocked the road in many places, the result of a cloudburst the previous day. After digging and rolling debris aside, we finally surmounted the last obstacle, reaching the town eight hours later than planned.

However, physical obstacles are easier to overcome than political ones. Bordered by an unfriendly Afghanistan and within a few miles of Russia, northeastern Chitral is politically sensitive. The Yarkhun Valley was once a strategic land route between the Indus Plain and Russia and China. For centuries various travelers, peaceful and otherwise, crossed the Baroghil Pass on their way to and from the Pamirs and Sinkiang. The Chinese maintained an interest in Chitral until the eighteenth century, in the 1880s a detachment of Russian Cossacks crossed into Chitral, and in 1886 the area came under British influence. From that time until 1947, the British explored every corner of the state; they hunted in every valley, mapped the mountains, and described its people and resources, giving the area a new reality, a written history. After the British departure in 1947, the state withdrew into itself again. Frontier areas became off limits. Although mountaineering expeditions conquered the highest peaks—Tirich Mir was first climbed by the Norwegians in 1950—the days of carefree travel were over. A German-American climbing party reached the Karambar Pass in the early 1960s, to my knowledge the last foreigners there. With some trepidation we approached Deputy Commissioner Gul Khan for permission to go to Karambar Pass and beyond. A stocky, decisive person, he had earlier on his own initiative banned all hunting of large mammals in Chitral, and now, to our delight, and to the surprise of several local officials who viewed me with suspicion, he gave us a permit.

Sher Panah agreed to accompany us as cook, and so did his brother Said. We left at dawn, our rented jeep piled with provisions for a month. A road follows the Yarkhun, or Mastuj as the river is called along its lower reaches, for fifty-two miles, as far as the village of Buni. Narrow and hewn into the side of a gorge, with the silty Yarkhun far below, it was not a road to inspire confidence. And suddenly, at a bend, it was gone, a section of it having slumped. After carrying our belongings across the gap we were fortunately able to rent another jeep. Soon the precipices retreated to reveal a wide, rather desolate valley, a bare sepia expanse. It was midafternoon by the time we reached Buni and at the edge of the village we made camp.

Hiking through mountains with a pack on my back, dependent on no one, is pleasure, but a need for transport, whether it be porters or beasts of burden, frequently turns a trip into tedium. My journals are full of private tirades against unwilling or rapacious porters and reluctant donkeys, horses, yaks, or camels. A journey all too often

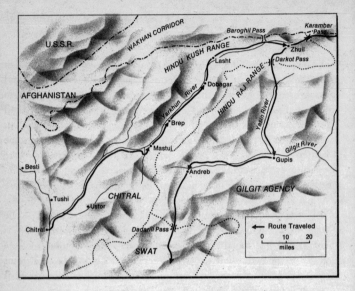

becomes a daily struggle just to keep moving instead of a joyful quest into the unknown. Endless delays and arguments produce a certain stoicism, a submission to the local law that time is of no consequence; sooner or later all problems solve themselves. *"Insha Allah,"* the Muslims fatalistically say, "God willing."

At first we tried with little success to obtain porters at Buni. "We are contented; we don't need work," said one villager, leaving us with a shrug of his shoulders. His attitude was a preview of the days ahead. No one wanted to leave home. Each day we had to find new transport, sometimes porters, sometimes donkeys, and we advanced slowly, seldom more than ten miles a day, from village to village.

We left Buni at 7 A.M. with several reluctant porters and a donkey.

It was harvest season and women were already in the fields of golden wheat, carefully cutting the precious stalks with sickles. From behind a hazy veil sun scorched the land until it pulsated; temperatures were close to 90° F. even at 7,000 feet. Each footstep kicked up dust until a pall hung over our little caravan. We were among mountains but not part of them. Mountains must offer some kind of intimacy, some personal identity, before I want to explore them, but here only bare hillsides sloped endlessly up toward walls of shale and limestone summits so remote as to be of no positive color. In the sun's white glare the peaks offered no pleasing retreats, no invitation to linger. I, who had sought this remote world, remained bound to the valley, to the sporadic hamlets and deserts of silt and stone.

We often tarried in the villages, in the shade of walnut and willow and apricot trees. Most trees grew on irrigated land; glacial streams have been diverted into sluices, and by gravity alone, the water is gently coaxed along a hill's contours to the fields.

It was the fruit even more than shade that attracted me to the villages. Mulberries, sticky and syrupy-sweet, pebbled the ground, and boughs laden with apricots arched over the paths. A boy sold us a bowl of apricots for the equivalent of ten cents. I gorged on the delicious fruit. The almondlike seed in each apricot pit is rich in oil and such a nutritious addition to the diet that locals treasure it more than the fruit. Like them, I occasionally broke the monotony of our trek by smashing a handful of pits to extract the seeds. With other travelers having done likewise, small caches of shells littered our route, like the leavings of a phantom squirrel.

Spying several pairs of ibex horns nailed to the earthen wall of a house, we stopped to talk to their owner, the local shopkeeper, who from a small stall on the main trail sold such items as matches, tea, and cigarettes. With typical mountain hospitality he invited us in to chat. We sat on green grass in the shady courtyard of his home and ate more apricots and mulberries. Tea was brought and an omelet. The mountains are so immense that it is impossible to check every valley for wildlife during a brief survey. But at least we could obtain some idea of the status and distribution of species by interviewing hunters such as our host.

"Are there markhor here?" I asked, knowing that these goats ranged only as far upriver as Barenis but wanting to test our informant's reliability.

"No. Some are on the cliffs a day's walk downstream."

"Ibex?" I queried.

"Still a few. Sometimes in winter they come close to the village," he answered, pointing at the sagebrush slopes nearby.

"Brown bear?" I continued.

He shook his head. "Twenty years ago, when I was herding goats high up, we saw one and shot it."

I measured the trophies, and then we thanked our host and reluctantly left his cool retreat to continue up the dusty trail.

Toward noon the following day we reached Mastuj, a large village at the confluence of the Mastuj and Yarkhun rivers. Chinese chronicles of the eighth century A.D. mention Mastuj, or Shang-mi as they called it. Late in the seventeenth century the Khushwaqt family made the village its base and through war and intrigue extended its rule over the Yasin Valley, as well as other parts that now belong to the Gilgit Agency. Pervez and I examined Khushwaqt fort, an inhabited ruin with crumbling walls and sagging roofs, already an ancient memento though the age that produced it has barely passed. A ruin is not just something that happened long ago to someone else; its history is that of us all, the transience of power, of ideals, of all human endeavors. A fragment of a Shelley poem came to mind as a fitting epitaph:

> "My name is Ozymandias, king of kings:
> Look on my works, ye Mighty, and despair!
> Nothing beside remains."

At dusk we reached Chuinj, where we slept on the grassy polo ground. Polo originated in this part of the world and most villages have a polo field though few can now afford to keep the horses necessary to play. I watched several polo matches in Chitral, rough matches like wild cavalry charges which bore only casual resemblance to the rather tame games now practiced in the rest of the world. As usual the only spectators were men, although, confined to their homes, the women could still determine the score by listening to the music of flutes and drums which signaled every goal. Each prominent player has his personal tune so that all those within hearing know not only that a goal has been scored but also by whom.

Several villagers had an animated discussion with Sher Panah. The word *niki* meaning "no" was as usual prominent in their conversation. It seemed that the trail ahead was impassable and no one was willing to be a porter. Knowing of the Chitralis' proclivity to consider the possible as quite impossible, I insisted on making an attempt the next day but without donkeys. The trail was indeed bad; in fact, it was gone, washed away by the river's turbulent waters. A sheer cliff faced us. But by inching along ledges and clambering up clefts we surmounted the obstacle. There the valley widened again and three large springs, their waters clear and cold, welled up at the base of a slope. And just beyond, on an alluvial fan, was the village of Brep. The Chinese once had a fort here, but the ramparts have turned to soil and now a school dominates the site.

At noon we reached Bang. The porters refused to continue so we paid them. Disgruntled, I sat in the shade of a walnut tree at the village edge guarding our gear while Sher and Said were off collecting firewood and Pervez looked for new porters. Potatoes, barley, and peas grew around me, as did fields of poppy and hashish. The hashish of Chitral is renowned for its pleasing effects. The dried leaves are first pounded into dust, and then crushed with heated pestle stones until there is a black doughy mass. Shaped and dried in sticks resembling whetstones, this hashish becomes a coveted item of trade far beyond the confines of Chitral.

Several goitered men and a few boys hunkered in a semicircle around me, staring mutely without friendliness or antagonism, just vacant looks that seemed to deny me existence. I wanted to shout, to rush among them, anything to elicit a response. Yet I also knew that I should reach out to them as a friend, that my strangeness inspired fear just as their bovine scrutiny produced uneasiness in me. But my own reticence won, and I avoided the issue by writing the day's events in my journal. A boy brought me a *Plecotus* bat, a small animal with huge ears, pale and translucent like an insect's wings. As I examined its furry body my irritability vanished.

Just beyond Bang a bridge spans the Yarkhun where it emerges from a gorge. From this point the character of the valley changes. Mountains crowd the river, and glaciers hang low on the slopes. In spite of their crumbling forts and forgotten polo fields, villages in the lower valley convey an aura of permanence, a knowledge that though conquerors may come and go they have endured for centuries and will continue to do so. But villages in the upper valley seem tentative, their inhabitants desperately defying the elements to wrest but a scanty crop from barren soil. In this new environment the first village is Dobagar. Lying at 9,000 feet, it consists of only a few miserable huts and stony fields, and the last fruit trees in the valley. Camped in a grassy hollow, we crowded around a juniper fire for warmth, and there several local men joined us to offer their services as porters.

The porters came promptly at 5:30 A.M.; there was no haggling about price, no complaining about the size of the loads. Cheerfully they burdened themselves with our food, tents, and personal things, and smartly headed upvalley. They were unusual porters indeed! That evening we camped near the village of Lasht, and the following dawn we continued, across alluvial fans covered with sparse stands of juniper and aspen, and where the slope dropped abruptly to the river, along crumbly slopes of talus. The valley narrowed beyond the village of Kan Khun where a trail, just wide enough for one person, traced the contours of the slope. Yet this modest path had served as a highway through these mountains for thousands of years. To the south, across the river, forbidding peaks, pitiless walls of ice and toothed crags, flung themselves up, some to a height of over 20,000 feet. Contorted glaciers protruded from the canyons, and blocks of ice floated in the river. It was a savage scene, superbly disdainful of us, yet somehow deeply satisfying. Along the lower reaches of the Yarkhun the mountains and valleys seemed tired and worn, a resigned landscape wearing the history of man on its surface. Here everything appeared young and whole.

Once more the valley widened and in the lee of a glacier were nine huts, the village of Pechus. In a mighty cataract the Darkot Glacier swept into the valley to halt abruptly at the river's edge. There the dark and violent waters attacked the crevassed flanks of ice, tearing off and carrying away huge pieces. Most mountain glaciers have been receding in recent years, but the Darkot has resisted this trend. When Lord Kitchener passed here in 1903 he noted that, as today, the river washed the glacier's snout. Three years later Sir Aurel Stein found that ice bridged the stream. It was almost dusk as we climbed wearily up a slope beyond the river where at 11,600 feet we found a lone hut surrounded by small plots of barley and peas. We camped nearby, spending the night in the open. As I lay under the stars, watching them glitter red and gold, an icy breeze passed over my face like a breath from outer space.

We were in a new world, the mountains no longer crowded and vistas wide. Ice and wind had worn away the rugged spurs, smoothing many summits and giving them a gentle warmth. We had reached the southern edge of the Pamirs. After an hour's walk we topped a rise and below saw a fort, a mud-walled square almost hidden in the folds of the Hindu Kush. For four months each summer some forty-five Chitral Scouts live here, guarding the Baroghil Pass. We paid our respects to the commandant, a Captain Afridi. Like most Pakistani officers, he was intelligent, pleasant, and helpful; he was also bored in this lonely post and delighted to have visitors. Proudly he showed us the 17-inch horns of a young ibex which a villager had killed on the crags above Pechus. These puny horns instilled in him atavistic dreams of glory, and he now wanted to collect trophies of all the different species.

We erected our tent about a mile from the fort. Then leaving Sher and Said to organize camp, Pervez and I hiked toward Baroghil Pass. After crossing the Yarkhun via a bridge where the river lunges over a fall, we ascended to Baroghil village where some twelve families of Wakhi tribesmen live in stone huts. Originally they grazed their yaks and goats on these pastures only in summer, then retreated into Afghanistan for the winter, but since the turn of the century they have been permanently settled on the upper Yarkhun. A broad valley rose imperceptibly to the divide where a stream forked, one draining into the Oxus, the other into the Indus. We turned toward home. The whole pass was illuminated: ripe grass heads glittered on upland meadows, and the sky was brilliant blue; just ahead, bridging heaven and earth, stood a pure ice peak. There was no sound other than the shrill calls of marmots, sitting upright like golden sentinels beside their burrows. There are many ways to enjoy mountains: some persons engage their passion by cutting steps into impossible ice walls, others entrust their lives to one fragile piton in a rocky crevice, and still others, I among them, prefer simply to roam the high country.

Although the mountains around Baroghil Pass were lovely, they contained little wildlife now. More of it survived at Karambar Pass, the Wakhis told us, and we arranged for three horses to carry our equipment upriver at dawn; I could have hired a horse for myself too but I preferred to walk—it is impossible to observe things closely and at leisure on horseback. At dusk I set a few mousetraps around camp to find out what night creatures lived in these uplands. The next morning my traps yielded two rodents, one a fluffy gray and white hamster, *Cricetulus migratorius,* and the other a nondescript brown and gray vole, *Pitymys carruthersi,* which, according to Tom Roberts, author of *The Mammals of Pakistan,* "constitutes a new record of a new species for the sub-continent," its usual haunts being in Russian Turkestan.

In the afternoon we reached Zhuil, at 12,300 feet the last Wakhi village in the valley. Here, four huts of glacier-worn stones nestled among limestone knolls, and over a nearby rise the Chiantar Glacier snaked some fifteen miles into the depths of the Hindu Raj. Several men came to our camp, among them Meerza Rafi, by virtue of his wealth and personality the most prominent man in the area. Quietly forceful and with a kind of feral magnetism, he inquired about our business. Satisfied that our interests were harmless, he ordered some boys to bring us bowls of refreshing yak curd. Meerza Rafi is a Tazhik from Sinkiang married to Wakhi women. In 1933 his uncle traveled through the area on a pilgrimage to Mecca, liked this high valley, and with the mehtar's permission, settled here with his family. In 1942 Kirghiz raiders from Afghanistan attacked Zhuil, killing Meerza Rafi's father and sister, among others. His knowledge of wildlife was precise and to me the information was disappointing: ibex scarce, snow leopard and brown bear very rare, Marco Polo sheep absent. The majestic Marco Polo sheep occur just to the north in the valley of the Oxus. It puzzled me why this species of sheep failed to colonize the upper Yarkhun. The wide rolling valley should be to its liking and forage is plentiful. Indeed, the terrain looks much like that of the Pamirs where Marco Polo first found evidence of the animal, when on his way to the court of Kublai Khan in 1273, and noted:

> And when he is in this high place he finds a plain between two mountains, with a lake from which flows a very fine river. Here is the best pasturage in the world . . . wild game of every sort abounds. There are great quantities of wild sheep of huge size. Their horns grow to as much as six palms in length.

Unable to cope well with deep snow, Marco Polo sheep possibly find winter storms too severe in the upper Yarkhun.

Just before the sun slipped behind a ridge, two barefoot girls drove a yak herd thundering down a slope and into the village. There some

Marco Polo sheep

dozen calves with woolly coats and bulging eyes stood tethered in a row, waiting for their mothers. Each was allowed to suckle about three minutes, and when the milk flowed well, a woman pushed it aside to do the milking, leaving only a little for the youngster. Unlike other Muslim women, these Wakhis permitted us to observe their routine. In fact, because of our presence they had replaced their usual drab homespun with holiday finery. Their dresses were brightly colored and decorated with silver buttons; silver necklaces tinkled as they nudged the stolid yaks into comfortable milking positions, and they wore turquoise rings on their fingers. They went about their task gaily, in a festive mood, somewhat shy of us, yet pleased by our interest.

At dawn Pervez and I left for the Chiantar Glacier to look for ibex. Along the glacier's edge was a chaos of delicately balanced boulders, and beyond that a labyrinth of crevasses. Most crevasses were mere slashes in the ice with rivulets gurgling cheerfully in the bottom, minor obstacles that were easy to cross. But there were deep chasms too, filled with sinister darkness, around which we had to make long detours and which taught us to move fastidiously. After a while the glacier's surface became less broken. In places huge boulders rested on its surface, some on ice pedestals like giant mushrooms. At intervals I glassed the slopes for ibex, searching for them on tiny meadows among the expanses of rock. Pervez was far behind, his red sweater a mere moving dot. We do not walk well together: I forge impatiently ahead, he moves steadily along. For an hour I had been angling across the mile-wide Chiantar toward the confluence between it and the Garmush Glacier. After scrambling over a lateral moraine, I once more stepped on firm ground. Meltwater from the snows above had made the slope intensely lush, ablaze with flowers. Full of delight, I walked in my mountain garden, among the cinquefoils, asters, louseworts, roseroots; there were orange poppies and clusters of forget-me-nots. It all seemed so familiar, and then memory took me to the alpine meadows of Alaska where long ago I had climbed on similar slopes among similar blossoms. I sat on a boulder, its surface sensuously warm from the sun. Above, I heard cackling and looking up saw two snowcocks, large gray partridges, stripping the rich grass heads. Farther on, the slope's gentle curve ended in the ice wall of Garmush Peak. Mint perfumed the air. I looked around this wilderness garden with an owner's eye, knowing that it was I who was possessed. I longed to remain, wanting to prolong such peace and tranquil beauty, almost forgetting the violence that lurks among the peaks, and the cold.

Descending the slope's steep pitch, I continued to the glacier where I met Pervez and we stopped for a lunch of crackers and cheese. In a swale near camp, we found the remains of an ibex, just a few bone chips and tufts of wool softer than the finest down. Ibex wool, or *pashm,* was once an article of trade, famous for its lightness and warmth. Wolf droppings at the site attested to the cause of this animal's death. Driven by deep winter snow into the valley, away from the safety of cliffs, it had fallen easy prey.

Morning saw us on the way to Karambar Pass and beyond with two yaks carrying our luggage. I like yaks. Bulky, black, and shaggily clad, yaks convey a rugged elegance; they belong to bitter storms and barren uplands. They are far superior to horses as pack animals in mountains, the latter being excitable, capricious, clumsy, and given to mindless energy in dangerous situations, very different from the stolid yak. A Zhuil man and boy each led a yak by the rope tied to a ring in the animal's nasal septum. Following the U-shaped valley steadily upward, we reached the gentle divide within three hours. Here at 14,200 feet we were at the source of the Yarkhun. Leaving our caravan behind, I strode ahead toward a large lake, silent and blue. Karambar Lake lies at the head of the Ishkuman Valley, which extends east and then south and finally joins the Gilgit Valley. The slopes to my left were barren, utterly desolate, whereas those to my right were clad in green, and in each valley a glacier nestled.

The most memorable wildlife here were the horseflies, each an inch long. They swarmed around in their determined quest for a bloody lunch, but once settled they were slow to flush and a quick slap killed them with a satisfying crunch. Once in an idle moment I watched a horsefly examine the back of my hand with its proboscis; two houseflies landed immediately and scurried around their massive relative, ready to scavenge food like jackals circling a lion kill. Later, in camp, I bared my arm to continue the observations, noting that the small flies scavenge blood directly from the proboscis of the horsefly. Looking up I met Said's nervous gaze. Said was a simple fellow with an inanely cheerful smile and rubbery legs, each with a will of its own. I grinned at him as I wiped the blood off my arm but he remained disconcertingly serious, as if uncertain of my sanity.

Along the lake shore, among tussocks of sedge, I found a pile of droppings composed of roots and grass. Nearby were three crudely excavated holes beside which were torn and plundered vole nests. Brown bear. And the spoor was only a few days old. That day, and on those that followed, I hopefully investigated all brown spots on the slopes, almost willing them to move, and I searched for fresh tracks. But to no avail, for the brown bear in Chitral is virtually extinct. One was seen in the northeastern corner that summer, and the animal whose spoor I found no doubt strays over the Karambar Pass into Chitral. An inhabitant of rolling uplands, the brown bear is ecologically separated from the forest-dwelling Asiatic black bear. Once brown bear were abundant in the Himalaya; in Kashmir during the 1880s, the hunter Alexander Kinloch saw twenty-eight in one day—and shot seven of them. Now the bears are more seriously threatened in Pakistan than snow leopard. Herdsmen shoot adults and capture cubs to sell to itinerant entertainers. Selling for two hundred dollars or more, the profit from a cub equals a year's salary for a local person. With canine teeth smashed to blunt stumps and a rope threaded through mutilated nostrils, the bear plods behind its owner on burning city pavements far from the cool heights of its mountain home. For a few coins the owner plays a flute and the bear rises on its hindlegs to sway and shuffle to the tune, a desecration of a magnificent being. I saw bears on the streets of Lahore and Rawalpindi and Peshawar, but never free among the shining peaks.

A few miles east of Karambar Lake, just beyond a stone corral at a place named Shuinj, a glacier spills into the valley and the mountains close in to form a gorge. A torrent cut across our path. Originally we had planned to descend the Ishkuman River but Meerza Rafi told us that the gorge is impassable until September when the river has less water. Here we camped to explore our surroundings. The day's notes were unspectacular but quietly pleasing, an inventory of wild-life. I watched marmots, noting that they were not as brightly golden as those around Dorah Pass in northwestern Chitral. Probably a different subspecies. I recorded a snow pigeon, a hoopoe on a moraine at 14,000 feet, and a fledged brood of Gyldenstolpe's redstart. There were two kinds of rosy finches too, but I was unable to identify them; no field guide exists for this part of the world. I found several wolf droppings and tucked them into the pocket of my parka, and later in camp I examined them to see what the wolves had eaten: there was the soft, dark wool of ibex, the monkeylike paw of an unwary marmot, and some coarse black hair, probably domestic goat from Zhuil. The residents of Zhuil have some 250 sheep and goats of which they expect to lose about 15 to wolves each year.

The following day we retraced our steps and camped near Karambar Pass, where Pervez and I climbed the northern flank of the valley to the Afghanistan border. The slope was a vast pile of loose rock, and, above, a black-fringed skyline. We toiled upward to the crest. To the north a glacier swept steeply down and beyond, across the

Hoopoe

Wakhan Corridor, range after range of long, flowing ridges receded into the Russian Pamirs. Climbing to the head of the glacier, we followed the base of a huge cliff, and stopped on a mound of black shale. My altimeter read 16,900 feet. At extreme altitudes the lowered barometric pressure results in less oxygen being driven from the lungs into the blood. Insufficient oxygen makes people irritable and evaporates their mental energy. But here, at only about 17,000 feet, "the capacity to submit to impressions; to be delighted, touched and exalted," as Goethe phrased it, remained intact. To the south was the formidable wall of the Hindu Raj with its sullen canyons and whorled peaks. Clouds had appeared for the first time in days. Mountains constantly change their appearance, mere translucent vibrations in the haze of noon, lucid and stark in the westering sun. This is especially so when cloud shadows move restlessly over the slopes. Clouds add motion to the resistant form of the peaks, imparting a jostling pattern of light and color. When clouds and mountains combine, one ethereal, the other impregnable, the landscape attains a new dimension. I stood entranced by this view of illusion and substance, until Pervez called to me. It was time to return. We hurried toward our tent far below. As we approached camp, Captain Afridi from the Baroghil fort rode up with a companion from the intelligence service.

The latter quizzed Pervez about me. Disgruntled by this manic intrusion from the outside world, we returned to Zhuil.

We had been trekking for sixteen days and nearly half of our planned journey lay ahead. We wanted to cross the Hindu Raj into the Gilgit Agency and then continue southward into Swat. The villagers of Zhuil agreed to help us across the glaciers of the Hindu Raj, and at dawn we lashed our belongings, packed in tidy bundles, onto the backs of three yaks. First we had to traverse the Chiantar Glacier. Led by our guides, the yaks stumbled through the lateral moraine and then zigzagged along crevasses where the slip of a hoof might plunge them into the depths. From there we traced the edge of Yarkhun Valley, but a swift stream soon barred our way. The guides straddled their yaks, and crossed in belly-deep water, leaving the rest of us to fend for ourselves. The water was murky and stones rumbled in it. Facing the current, I inched to the other side. Pervez, who is suspicious of water, usually has someone carry him across streams, but this time he found a shortage of volunteers. Unsure of himself, he was soon bowled over by the current, but with a helping hand from Sher he reached shore. We halted. While Sher brewed tea, Pervez spread his soaked clothes in the sun and two of our guides huddled beneath a blanket to share a pipe of opium. Then, refreshed, we continued up the Zindikharam Valley directly toward the bastion of the Hindu Raj. In a stand of willows we stopped again to collect three bundles of twigs which we would need as fuel on the glaciers ahead. A patch of fireweed in a moist hollow added a cheerful note to our departure from this human world for the alien one of rock and ice.

The sun had vanished. Deprived of its radiance, the slopes were somber, their summits again hidden in clouds; winds warred with us and sleet whipped our faces. We camped in the lee of a spur and on a sparse fire heated some soup. Later, lying in my sleeping bag, I could hear snow falling heavily on the tent. At first light we toiled on, now through a white void of cloud and ice. One guide walked ahead to probe for crevasses with a pole. A yak suddenly sank through the snow, its legs dangling in a crevasse. Quickly we unloaded the ponderous beast and, with all of us pulling and pushing, it finally struggled to more solid ground; then, impassively, it continued the journey. Wind began to sweep away the cloak of mist, slowly at first, only dark fragments of rock appearing briefly, but finally, in one dramatic gesture, it cleared the peaks. Yesterday the mountains had threatened us with storms and sullen crags, while today, just as indifferently, they revealed to us the beauty of their untainted grandeur. Around noon the ice became more level and the Darkot Glacier joined ours from the east. We were at Darkot Pass, at 15,400 feet. Our route now lunged with one violent leap into the Yasin Valley 6,000 feet below.

Long ago other travelers had looked at this steep descent with dismay. The Tibetans expanded their influence as far as the Pamirs early in the eighth century and thereby came into conflict with Chinese interests. In A.D. 747 a Chinese general, Kao Hsien-Chih, defeated the Tibetans on the Oxus and that same year he took 3,000 troops up the Darkot Glacier, the first time an army had climbed these remote heights. After crossing Darkot Pass he descended into the valley and conquered the village of Yasin. Moving downstream to the confluence of the Gilgit and Yasin rivers, General Kao destroyed a bridge across the Gilgit River near Gupis. This prevented Tibetan reinforcements from reaching the shattered forces on the Oxus— but it also stopped the Chinese march on Gilgit. General Kao then retreated back over the Hindu Raj, leaving only a garrison at Yasin. He was defeated by Arabs in 751, and thereafter Chinese power declined in Central Asia. Yasin still paid tribute to the Chinese as late as 755, but after that date the mountains retreated into obscurity and over a thousand years were to pass before this area appeared in historical records once again.

Descending from the heights we met the first blade of grass and the first flower, and finally the slopes were hairy with sagebrush.

Perhaps our passage from the cold upper reaches to the familiar earth had been too rapid; as I looked back at the lonely peaks, then at the huts and fields below where people groped their whole lives away, the raw contrast between the two filled me with sadness and anxiety. Torn between contentment and longing, caught between two worlds, one that had possessed me, yet could never be more than a passing phase, and that other which is a part of human existence, I yearned to retain my dual destiny. I stopped walking, and the yaks passed me by, and the men. Pervez asked if anything was the matter. I replied that all was well, I was just admiring the scenery.

Although the trip was not yet over, a feeling of having fulfilled some purpose also pervaded me. Our efforts so far had been considerable but the achievements negligible. I knew that in the days ahead, among the villages, I would learn little about the mountain animals. This wildlife survey had been a failure, for in all these miles of walking, I had seen only four ibex. The end of an era is swiftly closing in. Europe began to discover and conquer the world in the fifteenth century. Five hundred years later, with the end of the Second World War, the colonial empires crumbled and a new civilization is in the process of emerging. But political realizations have tended to obscure an even greater world revolution occurring at the same time, that of an explosively expanding human population destroying its finite resources. There is now a great dying as man exterminates species and otherwise reduces the earth's complexity. My surveys in these mountains are thirty years too late, only thirty years. In this brief span of time, in this fleeting moment of history during which the persistent assault of wind and snow has barely been able to affect the crags, man has seriously decimated wildlife in the Himalaya. In recent years he has created a design for coexistence with the natural world; he now has the necessary ecological guidelines, and needs only to live up to his moral imperatives, to discard the conceit that he stands apart from nature. As Ezra Pound expressed it:

The ant's a centaur in his dragon world.
Pull down thy vanity, it is not man
Made courage, or made order, or made grace,
      Pull down thy vanity, I say pull down.
Learn of the green world what can be thy place. . . .

I hurried after my caravan, down toward the villages, back to my human bondage.

It took us two days to descend the Yasin Valley to Gupis, two days of plodding through hamlets and wastelands behind pack donkeys that had all the faults of their race, as well as a few of their own. Once again the peaks were pale and impersonal in a sun-leached sky.

Finally we reached Gupis on the banks of the Gilgit River where we waited for a jeep to take us forty miles upriver. But drivers dislike the rough and winding track and none wanted to go. We waited for transport in the local rest house which had been built here, as in most large villages, by the British to accommodate traveling officials. The Panah brothers left for home, there being a good foot route to Mastuj over the Shandur Pass. There was little for us to do. We had tea with the telegraph operator. His living quarters had the camped-in look typical of those used by officials—the room was almost bare, its walls splattered with tobacco juice and cracked from an earthquake the previous year. After two years in this dismal post he felt forgotten.

The Raja of Gupis was rumored to know much about the local wildlife, and I sent my card, asking for an interview. He met us in his garden, a tall, erect old man with a Mongolian cast to his eyes and a neatly trimmed white beard that made him look like an aged Joseph Conrad. Raja Hussain Ali Khan's family came originally from Skardu where it settled in 1225, he told us. Once powerful, the family's realm extended from Ladak to Chitral in the early 1600s, but thereafter the influence of the House of Khan declined. His grandfather had four sons and in 1910 the Maharaja of Kashmir gave each an area to rule, his father receiving Gupis. As he was an outsider without ties to the people, few mourned when in 1972 the government abolished all titles and feudal privileges and the raja retired to his modest bungalow. He seemed pleased at our interest in his past.

As a hunter who had lived for over half a century in Gupis, the raja knew its wildlife well, and with precision he outlined the past and present status of each species. Two populations of Ladak urial just downstream of Gupis are now extinct, and farther down it is rare. Thirty years ago markhor were abundant on the cliffs for ten miles up- and downriver of Gupis, as well as for a few miles up the Yasin and Ishkuman valleys. Now, all but a few have been shot. No black bear survive in the Gilgit Valley, the last ones having been killed in 1910 in a riverine thicket near the village of Gakuch. Until 1947 musk deer occurred in all ravines south of the Gilgit River. The last time the raja saw snow leopard was in 1952. A few wolves still hunt the valley; last winter they captured a donkey here, and villagers put poison in the carcass, not only killing several wolves, but also foxes, dogs, and crows.

"Between 1934 and 1954, I shot thirty-six animals—ibex, markhor, urial—just along the road between Gupis and Gilgit. I was not even hunting. Animals were so abundant then." The raja said this with infinite sadness, thinking, I felt, not just of the vanished fauna but also of his past, of a way of life that will never be again.

After two days of waiting, late in the afternoon, a jeep driver agreed to take us upriver. When we left the sun had already deserted the valley. It grew dark and then a full moon appeared, suffusing the cliffs towering above us with a soft, primordial light as in the depths of the sea. We slept at a rest house in Pander where, centuries ago, two giant landslides had blocked the valley and created a deep lake. Ultimately the waters cut their way out, but a small lake remains and in British days it was a well-known place for duck hunting and trout fishing. The following morning, a few miles upstream from Pander, we paid off the jeep driver. The Gilgit River is shallow here, and we waded across it to the village of Andreb at the mouth of the Shuinj Valley hoping to find porters for the trip south. It is a three- to five-day walk to the nearest town in Swat, the length of the trip depending on weather and urgency. The local men hesitated to accompany us, saying that the mountain people of Swat are dangerous robbers and murderers, but we offered five days of salary for a three-day trip and several reluctantly accepted. We left in the early afternoon and halted at dusk at an altitude of 11,200 feet. A storm blackened the sky to the south and then it rained.

Dawn sees a ritual repeated in our tent.

"Pervez. Hey, Pervez! Time to get up," I call while rising and slipping into my clothes.

"Urghh," grumbles Pervez, and slides farther into his sleeping bag, pulling down his wool cap so that it covers his face.

I go in search of a cup of tea and check on the porters. Ten minutes later, as I pack my rucksack, I nudge him again:

"We're leaving soon, Pervez."

No response.

After rolling up my bedding and clearing my belongings from the tent, I give him a final warning.

"Pervez! The porters are ready." He sits up, moodily staring somewhere in the vicinity of his knees, and, still sitting, slowly begins to stuff his things into various bags. Meanwhile, the porters, their loads ready, gather by the tent. Pervez emerges on all fours as the porters collapse the tent behind him.

Lonelier and wilder grew the valley as it narrowed and we ascended rubble fields against an icy wind. Amid sleet we made camp that night on a tiny alpine meadow. The next morning took us first up over moraines and then up a small glacier to the top of the Dadarili Pass, which at 15,700 feet is the same altitude as Mont Blanc, the highest point in Europe. We rested beside the skeleton of a horse before descending into the Ushu Valley, a tedious and tiring two hours of crawling, leaping, and balancing over a vast boulder field, a cloudburst of stones. Finally we reached a meadow ablaze with pinkish *Polygonum* above a turquoise lake. There being no firewood here, we continued down the valley until at dusk some

willows provided fuel. We were now in Swat, a hill district bordering the Indus Plain. In 1926 the British consolidated the various
tribes of Swat into a princely state and placed them under one ruler,
the Wali, but in 1969 the area was merged with the national government. Although southern Swat has seen civilization for thirty-five
centuries, the high valleys retain their wildness, both in landscape
and in people.

It drizzled in the morning. This area receives some of the summer
monsoon which sweeps across India and penetrates the southern
flanks of the mountains, making them quite lush. Today, twenty-
seven days after leaving Chitral, we planned to reach Matiltan, the
end of our trek. Huge granite cliffs, broken by stands of birch and
tongues of spruce, flanked us as we hiked down the valley. The
stream we followed was clear, meandering placidly among sparkling
meadows or tumbling in white cascades through gorges flanked with
pine. Crude log cabins, the homes of herdsmen, imparted an aura
of the Rocky Mountains. After the austere landscape beyond the
ranges, the trees and soft meadows were soothing to eye and mind.

It seemed strange that in this lovely valley, where livestock was
sleek and environment benign, where life was easier than anywhere
in these mountains, the people were disagreeable as nowhere else in
Pakistan. Men stopped us in a peremptory manner to demand money,
cigarettes, or medicine. When we inquired about wildlife, we received
either an insolent look before the man turned rudely away or a
blatant lie. Tired after walking twenty-five miles, we finally entered
Matiltan. Men hunkered in rows on low stone walls, watching us
sullenly and ignoring our greeting. When a boy threw a rock at
Pervez they jeered.

A bus for the plains left Matiltan in the morning and we were
on it.

Karakoram

Karakoram: a solid name, hard as rock and ice, a name with the primitive ring of howling storms and desolate valleys, a fitting name for the most rugged range on earth. Stretching some three hundred miles north of the Indus, from the Ishkuman River in the west to the upper Shyok River in the east, the Karakoram contains nineteen peaks over 25,000 feet, including K2, which at 28,741 feet is the second highest mountain on earth. The longest glaciers outside the subpolar regions crowd into these peaks, among them the Siachen, forty-five miles in length; the Baltoro, thirty-six miles; and the contiguous Hispar and Biafo, seventy-six miles.

Driving upstream from Skardu along the swift Indus and continuing along the Shyok, one soon reaches a large green oasis, the village of Kapalu. With the mighty ice fortress of Masherbrum to the north, one crosses the Shyok by raft or on swaying logs, depending on the season. Ahead, dividing the Shyok and Saltoro valleys, is a desolate ridge. I climbed it one day in May when snow still lingered in the couloirs and marmots were just venturing forth after their winter sleep. Standing on top, I experienced the landscape as do the griffon vultures: the slope drops abruptly for 5,000 feet to a gray ribbon that is the Saltoro River, and there on an alluvial fan is a village—like a small green blight on the earth's dead crust. Behind the village rises a bristling mass of peaks, a gigantic disorder of sheer and naked rock, of raw creation. The crowded summits fade into gloomy clouds, withdrawing from life. It is incongruous that the infinitesimal spot of green at their base can be a village, that humans have struggled and won there without being swallowed by the elements. Yet mountains such as these have forged the ibex and snow leopard, the energy in their bodies, the luster in their eyes.

I made three trips to the Karakoram to study wildlife and to look for areas that might make suitable national parks. Hardship and disappointment marked these journeys—they contributed little to my knowledge of wildlife—but now I think they fulfilled a need, both scientific and personal. During my first journey, in the summer of 1973, I drove over many roads to become familiar with the area and its problems. Major Amanullah, the administrator of World Wildlife Fund Pakistan, was with me, as were my sons, Eric and Mark, both then in their early teens. We had an exciting trip, exploring this new world. But mountains should not be viewed from a car, they should not be traversed hurriedly; there is a kind of satisfaction that only effort and endurance can provide.

Mountains become an appetite. I wanted more of the Karakoram, but over a year passed before I was to return. In the summer of 1974, I had taken my family back to our farm in Vermont and there I spent several sedentary months writing reports. A part of me was content with this easy life, but another yearned for the mountains, for the chance to test again the limits of strength and will.

Many people, I suspect, have visions of a secret home, which they seek in deserts, at sea, or in mountains.

The political problems of working in the Karakoram were more serious than the physical ones; they are the direct result of that area's turbulent history during the past hundred and fifty years. From 1830 until 1842 the Raja of Jammu, Gulab Singh, extended his control over Kashmir, which included some 82,000 square miles extending from Tibet in the east to the Chitral border in the west. Then, in 1846, the British absorbed Kashmir and promptly sold it back to Gulab Singh for one million pounds. In 1859 the British established the Gilgit Agency and became *de facto* rulers, although the various local rajas retained some of their feudal power. When independence came in 1947, the subcontinent was to be partitioned and Kashmir had a choice: join Hindu India or Muslim Pakistan. For over a hundred years a Hindu maharaja had subjugated a Muslim population until "the Kashmiri has come to hug slavery to his bosom," as the poet Muhammad Iqbal phrased it, and the choice of the people was obvious. But the Maharaja of Kashmir, Hari Singh, was a weak man, more interested in duck-hunting than the well-being of his people. He intended to attach himself to India. Hearing reports of this, Pakistan encouraged a private army of Afridis, Mohmands, and other Pathan tribesmen from the Northwest Frontier to invade the Vale of Kashmir and occupy the city of Srinagar and its airport before India could absorb the area. Since Pathans are hard and dangerous fighters, used to blood feuds in a barren and rugged homeland, they seemed ideal for the task. However, they are also undisciplined, individualistic, and, as Frederick Mackeson noted in the 1850s, "a most avaricious race, desperately fond of money." The road to Srinagar, only 135 miles away, lay open when one October night the Pathans crossed the frontier in trucks. But instead of rushing toward the goal that they could have reached in a few hours, they paused two days to loot and rape. When they reached the outskirts of Srinagar, newly arrived Indian troops repulsed them. The weary Pathans had lost Kashmir for Pakistan. A mountain war which raged that winter

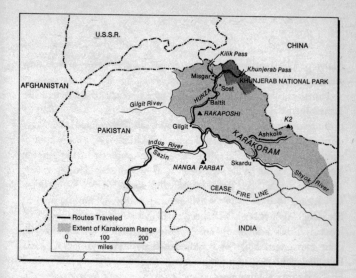

ended in a stalemate along a crease-fire line dividing Kashmir. Earlier, India had agreed to a provision that a plebiscite would decide the ultimate fate of the Kashmiri people, but she refused to honor this agreement, and the dispute died in the United Nations. Continued discord over Kashmir caused two more wars, in 1965 and 1971, and in the end the cease-fire line was much as it was in 1947, with India holding Ladak and the Vale of Kashmir, and Pakistan most of the rest.

These wars changed the mountains. Roads began to penetrate remote valleys for strategic reasons, roads hewn into rock where only markhor and ibex had once ventured. Where bridges spanned gorges, the roar of water mixed with the roar of trucks hauling supplies. By the late 1960s the Indus Highway was completed, and so was the Karakoram Highway from Gilgit through Hunza to the Sinkiang Province of China. Large stretches remained closed to foreigners, but in 1973, for the first time, the whole Indus Highway was opened, and I took immediate advantage of this. In the spring of 1974 the Karakoram Highway permitted foreigners, briefly. By summer of the same year both roads were closed again because the Chinese had been hired by Pakistan to widen them.

In spite of this political confusion, I was determined to make a status survey of Marco Polo sheep in Pakistan. The sheep itself is not threatened with extinction, being fairly common in the Russian Pamirs and in the Wakhan Corridor of Afghanistan. However, it is rare in Pakistan. I had failed to find it in northeastern Chitral, but it was known to exist in two small areas of northern Hunza adjoining Sinkiang. Also, Marco Polo sheep intrigued me. Though only a subspecies of *Ovis ammon,* a large Asian form generally known as argali, it has the longest horns of any sheep. These horns form open, graceful spirals with the tips arcing up, out, then down again. The record head measures slightly over 75 inches and the next largest one 72½. Both heads were found up in the hills, and possibly the animals were killed by wolves; I like knowing that they escaped a hunter's gun. The quest for such trophies drew hunters to the uttermost parts of the mountains, and incredible hardships were endured by those who wanted horns just a fraction larger than all previous ones. As Rudyard Kipling wrote:

> Do you know the long day's patience, belly-down on
>   frozen drift,
> While the head of heads is feeding out of range?
> It is there that I am going, where the boulders and
>   the snow lie,
> With a trusty, nimble tracker that I know.
> I have sworn an oath, to keep it on the Horns of Ovis Poli,
> And the Red Gods call me out and I must go!

Marco Polo was not the first European to write about argalis. Some twenty years before he crossed the Pamirs, in 1273, William von Rubruck, a friar from Flanders, carried letters from St. Louis of

France to Kublai Khan, a journey that took him from 1251 to 1254. Crossing the Tien Shan, where the argali is so similar to the one in the Pamirs that some biologists consider the two identical, he saw a "kind of wild animal which is called 'arcoli,' which has quite the body of a sheep, and horns bent like a ram's but of such a size that I could hardly lift two horns with one hand; and they make of these horns big cups." Had the friar's journal made a greater impact we would today speak rightly of von Rubruck's sheep.

To visit the home of this grand sheep, the greatest obstacle was obtaining a permit to enter northern Hunza; weeks of dealing with the creative inefficiency of government bureaucracy were required before I managed with the generous assistance of Dr. S. M. H. Rizvi and Major-General Imtiaz Ali to receive permission directly from the prime minister. I shall not dwell on our seven-hour journey by Land Rover from Islamabad through the hills to the first guardpost on the Indus only to be told by a nervous captain that a special road permit must also be obtained from the Northern Frontier Force Headquarters back in Islamabad; the next day, after a night's drive, we were informed at the headquarters gate that no foreigner might enter for any purpose, not even to get a permit, and anyway, permission must first come from the Defense Ministry, where visits are by appointment only, and besides, the man in charge is out of town, the day of his return unknown, and a prior permit from the Interior Ministry is essential. In such a situation one either becomes a stoic—or has Pervez to activate his friends and friends of friends. In one day he had the permit; on November 9 we finally began our journey.

The road swept down out of the hills into the Indus Valley near Besham Quila, a typical roadside bazaar with tea shops and scabied dogs snuffling through garbage. The gasoline pump here was the last one until Gilgit. An officer of the intelligence service interrogated us at the checkpost and then gave us information about road conditions ahead which proved to be wholly wrong. Our road followed the gorge of the Indus northward, one moment tracing the river's edge, the next climbing high up some cliff face, leaving the roiling waters far below. At dark, our world grew very small, limited to the headlights' beam. Occasionally, on the sharp turns, the lights carried past the road into the void of the gorge beyond, fleetingly illuminating the walls across the river. Steep, winding, and narrow, the road was so dangerous that we averaged only ten to fifteen miles an hour. After seven tense hours, relieved only by the sight of a leopard cat and several red foxes, we reached a widening of the road at Sazin. We slept there by the side of the track while convoys of trucks rumbled past all night.

At Sazin the river curved sharply, coming now from the east. Here the valley broadened, filled with sandy river terraces, gray and sienna in hue, and high above, the season's first snow whitened the slopes. Within this great bend of the Indus lies the home of the Chilas tribe. The previous year I had seen many tribesmen in the Chilas bazaar and in the village of Khe, tucked into a hidden valley. They were unprepossessing, little different from other hillmen, but protected by the fastnesses of their mountains and their unrelenting aggressiveness toward outsiders, these tribesmen had a unique distinction: conquering armies had subdued the tribes of Chitral, Yasin, Hunza, and others, but Chilas had repulsed them all. Raiding far and wide, Chilases killed men and carried away women, crops, and cattle to such an extent that the Astor and other valleys were almost depopulated. A Sikh army sent to punish them in 1852 was annihilated. The British fared little better, for as A. Neve noted in his book *Thirty Years in Kashmir,* "even English sportsmen in those days, if shooting markhor in the *nullahs* bordering Chilas, would have to take precautions against sudden night attacks, shifting their tents after dark and avoiding lighting fires. . . ." To this day, to my knowledge, no foreigner has crossed Indus Kohistan, homeland of the Chilas tribe.

After crossing the Indus on a massive bridge and gaining high

Chough

ground again, it is wise, if the day is clear, to halt and look down-valley. There is the river, deep within the earth's crust, and border-ing it the desiccated landscape, its color burned to soft tones by the fierce heat of summer. It is a bitter scene, seemingly lifeless except for an occasional tuft of coarse grass or creeping *Capparis,* and over-head perhaps a lingering flock of choughs. But up the sere slopes, beyond where the last shrubs die out, upward until even the moun-tains are mere anthills, a brilliant peak of ice illuminates the sky, not just a mountain but a focal point of the universe. *Nanga parvata,* "the Naked Mountain" as the ancients called it, rises in one gigantic sweep for 22,000 feet above the Indus to a height of 26,660 feet. A Sanskrit proverb states: "A hundred divine epochs would not suffice to describe all the marvels of the Himalaya." Nanga Parbat alone transcends description.

Nanga Parbat is more than rock and ice, but like most mountains it does not reveal its intimate side until one climbs into its valleys. In the summer of 1973, I hired two baggage donkeys and with my sons, Eric and Mark, wandered through the upland forests. It was soothingly cool there, and the air was fragrant with pine and fir; far away a cuckoo called, reminding me of a German childhood. High up, beyond the last conifers, where only bent birches shivered in the wind, we reached Rama Lake and there on a flowered meadow pitched our tent. The meadow and copses had a civilized look, as in a park, except for an ice wall looming at the head of the valley.

At the confluence of the Gilgit and Indus rivers the road swings northward to Gilgit, which Pervez and I reached after nine hours of steady driving from Sazin. Lying at an altitude of 4,800 feet, Gilgit has mild winters; in mid-November the sycamores and mulberries were still in yellow leaf and temperatures were in the fifties. The bazaar is the largest in these northern mountains, and goods fill the shops—dried apricots, fox skins, felt bakhols, and other local produce, bolts of cloth from the plains, and imported blocks of black Chinese tea and German kerosene lanterns smuggled in from Afghanistan. Sharp-faced Pathans, Baltis in peaked caps, and herdsmen with Mongolian features loiter in the streets.

For a moment the present receded and once again Gilgit was a famous trade center on the Silk Route that linked the subcontinent with Central Asia. Agents of the Han emperor Wu-ti first opened the Silk Road in about 120 B.C. and then patrolled it, protecting it from bandits, as caravans carried silk and other luxuries to the West. It was a difficult route, of "dark and gloomy mountains," in the words of the Chinese traveler Fa-Hien in the third century A.D., but it persisted. For two thousand years the caravans struggled over the rugged Mintaka Pass in Hunza, on their way to and from Sinkiang. Then in 1949 Communist China closed its borders, ending an era, and Gilgit was reduced from an international trade center to a local one. Today modern soldiers and government officials mingle with the ancient tribal throngs, the ages of man persisting here like geological strata.

The resident of the Gilgit Agency, Ijlal Hussain, lived in a large bungalow overlooking the town. As the highest-ranking official in the northern region, his permission was required to visit Hunza. I had met him the previous year when he allowed me to measure the Marco

Polo sheep, ibex, and other old trophies that lined his bungalow. The virtues of previous generations are the faults of this one, and so it is with trophy hunting. Today, when many species cling to a vestige of their former range, to kill merely for some trophy is anachronistic. But the hunters of the past, who lived when ethics were different, who for months braved remote ranges and treacherous tribes, seem of a more heroic mold than the pleasure killers of today.

The resident received us cordially, and assigned Ghulam Muhammad Beg, a man in his midthirties, to be our liaison officer. With his long, austere face, erect posture, and his habitual Jinnah cap of Karakul wool, Beg had the mien of a schoolmaster. Belonging to an old Hunza family that traced its history back for a thousand years, he knew the valley intimately, and, in fact, had been on the commission that settled the current border with China.

In one gigantic swath from north to south, the Hunza Valley slashes for eighty miles through the Karakoram. Guarded by formidable canyons and high passes, the Hunza and Nagar people—the former live on the west bank of the Hunza River, the latter on the east bank—could with impunity issue from their natural fortress to raid the surrounding areas. They pillaged incessantly, roving as far as two hundred miles from their valley. Caravans traveling from Yarkand to India over the Karakoram Pass were favored victims, and one raid netted fifty laden camels and fifty ponies. As recently as 1888, eighty-seven Hunza men attacked a caravan near that pass and for good measure took home some Kirghiz herdsmen as slaves. Although Hunza paid an annual tribute to the rulers of Kashmir—twenty ounces of gold, two horses, and two hounds—this did not preclude freebooting. Gilgit dreaded the continual attacks and retribution was difficult. In 1848 the Governor of Gilgit and his army were massacred, and in 1866 the Maharaja of Kashmir's troops were repulsed. When not attacking neighbors the people fought among themselves. In 1886 Safdar Ali Khan murdered his father—who had himself murdered his father—and usurped the throne, and he also put his two brothers to death. Not to be outdone, the heir-apparent in neighboring Nagar killed his two younger brothers. In 1973 the Mir of Hunza had no such worries: his son was drummer in a rock band in Lahore.

Being orderly people, the British could not tolerate such restless behavior among people they ostensibly governed. Hunza's ruler was also making overtures to the Russians, who were exploring the border regions at that time. In a treaty of 1889, the Hunzas and Nagars had agreed to stop their raiding, but when they broke this agreement two years later the British used the incident as a pretext to send troops from Gilgit. Several vigorous but inconclusive clashes were followed by a decisive one at the fort in the village of Nilt. The British, who had 3,000 troops, sent 100 Gurkhas to storm the outer gates, which they hacked to pieces with their sharp kukries. Then an explosive charge shattered the main gate and

> three British officers, with the six men at their back, clambered through the breach and were within Nilt Fort. Enveloped in dense smoke and dust, their comrades, who had been cutting their way through the abattis, could not find the breach. . . . Having gained this position, they held it resolutely, but soon two were killed and most of them wounded.

But then

> the Gurkhas poured into the narrow alleys of the fort and fought as they always do fight. The Kanjuts defended themselves like fanatical dervishes at first, but soon lost heart before the fierce attack.

So wrote E. Knight, a participant, in his book *Where Three Empires Meet*. The ruler of Nagar was killed, the towers of the fort blown up, yet the fight continued for eighteen days that December before all the defendants were subdued. Hunza's ruler fled to China, and in March 1892 the British installed his pliable half brother, Nazim Khan, as mir.

Over eighty years later, in 1973, I met Mir Muhammad Jamal

Khan, grandson of Nazim Khan, at his residence in Baltit, the capital of Hunza. Major Amanullah, my sons, and I had asked for an interview to inquire about wildlife conditions. An elderly man with short-cropped white hair, craggy face, and a hint of Mongolian blood around his eyes, he served us tea and cherries. Little wildlife, he told us, survived in the main Hunza Valley. Ladak urial had vanished, but there were still a few ibex, and downstream of Chalt, some markhor; snow leopard were rare, but one was recently shot at Dhi, in the Khunjerab Valley. I commented on the three Marco Polo sheep trophies on his wall, fine heads with gleaming white neck ruffs and elegant horns spiraling outward for some 50 inches. Marco Polo sheep had suffered much in recent years, the mir continued in a weary voice. In 1959 an American hunter, Elgin Gates, met a large herd of rams at Khunjerab Pass. "The man lost his head," sighed the mir. "He shot and shot. He could not be stopped. My shikari said he killed at least seven, and many were wounded." The son of President Ayub Khan came by helicopter and shot five head; a German industrialist with his two sons shot nine. And then the army engineers killed many while building the Karakoram Highway: in 1968 one officer is said to have killed fifty to feed his men. The mir's sad words were more than a recitation of other people's misdeeds; they were a tacit admission of his weakness as a ruler, of being unwilling or unable to enforce the laws of his own state.

In his grandfather's time, until the late 1930s, the sheep had been rigidly protected. Animals flocked to the safe haven of Hunza, for in neighboring Sinkiang the Kirghiz tribesmen drove them with dogs into narrow valleys where hidden hunters shot them. Then conditions changed. Communist China tried to protect its wildlife, whereas Hunza, under its present ruler, neglected it. Marco Polo sheep trophies became status symbols in middle-class homes, and were sold in the Gilgit bazaar. The mir died in 1976, two years after the government annexed his state.

Despite the mir's gloomy assessment of the wildlife situation, I was back to continue the search. It took Pervez, Beg, and me all day to drive sixty miles from Gilgit into the Hunza Valley because thousands of Chinese workmen labored to widen the road. Every few miles one would wave us to a halt and yell, "Boom-pow." Within minutes the mountains vibrated and thunder rolled down the gorges. As the dust cloud from the blast settled over the river below, we settled down to a long wait. Dozens of workmen, dressed in blue, milled around the blast site. Usually lacking bulldozers or other earthmoving equipment, they attacked the heaps of rubble with shovels and pickaxes. And they worked with unbearable patience, so much so that we sometimes helped them clear the road; at one site we had to wait while all workmen vanished for a three-hour lunch. Our Land Rover carried the panda emblem of World Wildlife Fund on its door, and intrigued by this display of an animal they recognized, calling it *"shumao,"* the workmen tried to find out the reason for our presence. We had, however, no means of communicating about abstruse matters, and anyway they were even more interested in our watches. Those who had watches—and one worker had a Swiss-made one— eagerly showed them to us and gestured to see ours. Pervez and Beg had wristwatches fine enough to elicit respectful nods, but I, with a cheap pocket watch inferior to anything on this road, lost completely in the game of international one-upmanship.

It was dusk when we approached Chalt. Here the road made a sharp turn out of a gloomy gorge, and suddenly the ice spire of 25,550-foot Rakaposhi filled valley and sky. The road turned again and the valley widened, now crowded with villages and terraced fields, brown and bare in the winter evening. Blocked by yet another blast site, Beg arranged for us to spend the night in a nearby home. Belonging to a family which traditionally has had one member as minister in the mir's assembly, and being himself a member of the Ismaili council—most people in Hunza venerate the Aga Khan—Beg had an entrée everywhere. Since the average Hunza man hides his suspicion of strangers behind an extreme dourness, Beg's presence was solely responsible for the hospitality that was always extended to us.

Our Land Rover would not start in the morning. We tried pushing it, then a jeep owner worked on the engine for two hours to no avail, but finally, two army mechanics from a nearby road camp brought the engine to life. The distributor points were bad, they said. We had barely gone a mile when blasting halted us for another two and a half hours. By the time we passed this obstacle it was late afternoon, and Beg found us another home for the night, this one in the village of Hyderabad. I walked out into the garden among bare apricot trees. Downstream the shining mass of Rakaposhi pervaded the valley, barring, it seemed, all access to the outside world. Behind me, high above, was the whitewashed fort of Hunza's rulers looking down at the huddle of drab huts and fields. It is a typical Tibetan fort, vaguely ominous with its high walls and narrow windows; wild, dark crags tower above it. Only the rows of poplars along irrigation canals add a touch of gentle elegance to the stark scene. I found it easy to see why Western visitors imbue this valley with a romantic aura, infusing a scenically lovely spot with their dream of a Shangri-La where everyone possesses the secret of health and tranquility and lives to extreme old age. Yet the people of Hunza differ little from those in other valleys, neither happier nor sadder, healthier nor wealthier. Men and women toil in their rocky fields barely to subsist on a sparse diet of unleavened bread, potatoes, and dried fruit. Foreign visitors are generally entertained in the wealthier homes where they are served such delicacies as meat and yogurt, which seldom appear on the daily menu. Desperately poor, many men leave their homes in winter hoping to earn money in the world beyond. Respiratory diseases are common. Perhaps a disproportionate number of persons do become centenarians, but when I asked Beg about this he scoffed at the idea. At any rate, accurate records do not exist, and other peoples in other valleys have not been surveyed adequately for comparison.

In the morning we headed northward and soon entered canyons again. The previous year I crossed the Hunza River via the Pakistan-China Friendship Bridge, but a few months later thousands of tons of silt and rock suddenly rushed out of a side canyon, damming the river. Now a lake, one and a half miles long, filled the valley, and barely visible in its bluish waters stood the submerged Friendship Bridge; we crossed on temporary pontoons. There were few villages here because rubble-covered glaciers—the Gulmit, Ghulkin, Pasu—crawled off the desolate peaks almost to the road. Toward noon we reached Pasu, a military checkpoint past which I had not been able to pass the previous year; eagerly I entered new terrain. Ahead, the peaks were rough, and to the east the Shimshal Canyon opened its jagged jaws. Incredibly, the road was paved here all the way to Sinkiang. Smoothly we drove past pinnacles, broken cliffs, and vast eroded slopes that looked as if a monstrous cat had clawed them in fury. Each turn of the road revealed more barren vistas and sullen clouds beat against the slopes. We stopped at the village of Sost. Here we would leave the Land Rover and proceed by foot to Kilik Pass. Beg found us lodging in the low flat-roofed home of a Wakhi who had emigrated from the west. Like all Wakhi houses, it had a large main room with an open clay hearth in the center, and lining the walls were wide sleeping platforms made of planks piled high with bedding, as well as wooden storage chests for grains, clothing, and other items.

Just beyond Sost the main road swings eastward into the Khunjerab Valley while a track turns westward to Misgar, five miles away. Lying at 10,000 feet, Misgar is the last village on the old Silk Route before China. It is a large village, containing some eighty huts, and its inhabitants are considered argumentative and devious even by local standards. Our host for this night was Kourban Ali Khan, a powerfully built landlord and trader. Like many Hunza men he is cosmopolitan, having traveled widely in Central Asia, and speaks several languages, among them Burushaski, Wakhi, Turki, and Urdu. As we sipped tea and ate bits of roasted yak by a crackling juniper fire, conversation roamed over many topics of local concern. Here, as elsewhere, taxation worried the populace. Since Hunza had just been reduced from a princely state to a district, the mir could no longer collect his usual taxes of goats, butter, and a percentage of the crop. What would the future bring? The new government had not imposed taxes yet. As usual I queried our host about wildlife and local history, trying to understand a little of the past and the present in order to obtain some intimation of the future. Every summer the Misgar people take their four thousand or so sheep and goats to the upland ranges around Kilik Pass, Kourban Khan told me. There on the border, they still trade a little with shepherds from Sinkiang and Afghanistan. However, contacts with other tribes had not always been this friendly. Once, long ago, Misgar men raided northward and there was a battle on the pass in which fifty were killed. Since that time the place has been known as Kilik, *ilik* meaning fifty in Turki. With luck we might see Marco Polo sheep at the pass, but since they are often killed for food most now remain in Sinkiang. There were still some ibex, although the Gilgit Scouts in a nearby post had killed at least sixty in the winter of 1972–73 to supplement their rations.

"Do you know," I asked Kourban Khan, "how much Afghanistan and Mongolia charge a foreign hunter for a license to kill just one of their big sheep? At least 50,000 rupees or $5,000. Outsiders come into your valley to kill ibex and sheep for nothing. Your own people kill females and young just for a little meat. The last animals will soon be gone. And you will have lost a valuable resource."

With Beg and Pervez translating, I suggested that the people of Misgar should protect the wildlife in their valley for a few years until populations had increased. Then, for a healthy fee, they could permit outsiders to shoot occasional trophies. In an area where the monthly wage is thirty United States dollars, the income from even one Marco Polo sheep would have a considerable impact on the village economy. And after ibex are abundant again, a percentage of the population could be cropped each year to provide meat for the Misgar households.

"Yes," Kourban Khan agreed, "it could be done. The village council would cooperate. But would the government?"

The government would have to be involved in such matters as promoting hunts and providing necessary permits. Would the village ever see any of the license money? Would the military abide by rules? Our conversation floundered on these intangibles.

Hemmed in by gray slopes, the trail wound steadily upward;

Qurban Shah, our guide, warmly dressed for the trip to Kilik Pass in coarse wool pants, a thick *choga,* and leather moccasins, led the way. After two hours we passed a Gilgit Scouts post and after four more hours reached Murktush where the valley forks, one trail going to Mintaka Pass, the other to Kilik Pass. We moved into an abandoned shepherd's hut.

Night still tarried in the valley when I reached for the thermometer near my sleeping bag. It was 10° F. Pervez grunted like a torpid bear when I nudged him to get up, but he did not stir. So Qurban and I left him behind to follow with Beg and the sun. Hunched against an icy wind we trudged up the valley, occasionally halting to glass the slopes for ibex. Qurban was quick to spot the tiny moving dots on rock and snow. Each time I had to set up the tripod, adjust the scope, and with numb fingers scribble a brief note about herd composition and activity: 0815. 5 ♀ 3 yg, 1 ♂ 2.5 yrs., 14,300 ft, w-facing slope, feeding on avalanche path, upper edge of scree.

Shortly after 11:00 A.M. we reached Haq, a level place at the junction of the Harpuchang and Kilik valleys. Here we moved into a hut of stone with a sod roof so low I could not stand upright; the hut had the practical simplicity of an animal's lair but none of its comforts. At Haq the topography changed, deeply cut valleys and jagged peaks giving way to smoothly rounded hills where only some of the highest reaches turned to rocky ramparts and glaciers. While waiting for Pervez, I explored the surroundings on my own for a few hours, and checked the vegetation on snow-free patches. Besides tiny sedge meadows, there were sagebrush, *Ephedra,* saxifrage, all plants resistant to aridity and cold; livestock had cropped all of them heavily. I noted marmot holes, and on a slope above, the snow craters left by a herd of feeding ibex, but there was no sign of Marco Polo sheep. Still, my day was a success—loping steadily along the ibex trail were two gray-brown wolves.

That evening in the hut was dismal. Yak dung smoldered, filling the room with a layer of acrid smoke so low that we either had to cower down or lie flat in order to breathe. But the fire also provided heat, and in this icy tomb of a hut warmth was life.

It was 0° F. as we left for Kilik Pass, but soon the sun glissaded down the hills and its coming put heart into our climb. Descending from the pass were pugmarks of a snow leopard, and then tracks where another leopard had joined the route of the first one, following it down a gentle ravine before going off alone. It pleased me to know that they were somewhere in these hills. Climbing steadily, we surmounted a final steep patch of scree and reached a plateau in the middle of which stood a cement pillar with the inscription PAKISTAN 1964. Here at 15,600 feet, on this sweeping expanse, among these desolate hills, four empires meet. I stood with one foot in Pakistan, one in China. A ridge to the west belonged to Afghanistan, and beyond, across a valley, the snow-bare slopes were in Russia. The only sign of life was a fox track.

The next morning Qurban and I hiked up the Harpuchang Valley in a final effort to find Marco Polo sheep. Although the north-facing slopes were deep in snow, the south-facing ones, exposed to sun, were mostly bare rock. There Qurban spotted a herd of seventeen ibex, bringing our tally for the Kilik area to sixty. Later, we spotted the tip of a Marco Polo sheep horn protruding from the snow. It was a fine head measuring 51½ inches in length, and a count of the horn rings revealed that the animal had been seven years old when it died. But the find only accentuated my disappointment in not having found live sheep.

Twenty-five domestic yaks lived in this remote valley much as their wild ancestors might have done. On the basis of morphology some zoologists have suggested that yaks are not just a type of wild cattle, but connecting links between cattle and bison. Could behavior help clarify the matter? I settled myself on a knoll and watched the animals for a while, waiting for something to happen. Most grazed peacefully except for three that reclined in separate dust wallows. Occasionally one rolled over on its back, throwing up a cloud of dust with its legs. Then, walking along the streambank, came a huge, lone bull. He held his swaying head low and his dust-mop tail was raised high. Seeing his ominous approach, the animals at the wallows casually drifted away. The bull grunted hoarsely, giving reality to his scientific name, *Bos grunniens*, the grunting ox. Two times he rubbed his face on the embankment before striding with grinding teeth to a vacated wallow. Digging a horn repeatedly into the earth, he twice rolled in the dust, as if claiming the site by impregnating it with his personal odor, then horned a second wallow before standing in it, head raised and very erect, displaying his imposing physique. Even this one incident taught me something of the species. Several aggressive displays, such as loud grunting and horning of objects, are widespread among the yak's close relatives, but tooth grinding seems to be a unique trait. Its habit of wallowing was of particular interest, for other members of the genus *Bos*—domestic cattle and gaur for example—do not wallow, in contrast to *Bison,* which do. Yaks thus are behaviorally linked to both cattle and bison. With so little to show for my efforts on this trip, any new insight pleased me.

Three days later we were back at Sost, ready to proceed by car to Khunjerab Pass. Khunjerab is a Wakhi word meaning Valley of Blood, so named because of the fearful toll it exacted of animals and men. No Westerner penetrated the valley until Sir George Cockerill did so in 1892. Now there is a paved road which, for over forty miles, snakes up a canyon flanked by rock skeletons without identity and endless slopes of slate and shale. Scattered groves of birch and willow once provided a feeling of intimacy, but a military contractor recently cut most of them, his act a negation of life. Although the road had been finished only two years before, it was already disintegrating from lack of maintenance. Poorly aligned beneath unstable slopes, encroached on by landslides and boulders, it was also being gnawed at by the river.

We passed the military checkpost of Dhi and drove on, the car now laboring with the altitude. Ahead the valley divided and our road became a series of switchbacks as it climbed up a mountain until the canyon was left below and rolling uplands stretched ahead. At 14,000 feet the Land Rover moved so slowly that we helped it by pushing. We had brought three men from Sost, a hunter who knew the Khunjerab, a camp hand, and a driver who would take the car back to a lower altitude to prevent it from freezing. Suddenly the engine stopped, three miles from our goal: the driver had turned it off because he wanted to relieve himself. At times expletives provide a useful alternative to physical assault. Naturally the car refused to start. So unloading our gear, we sent car and driver rolling back down the road with instructions to return in a week. It was dusk, and the bleak glow of a half moon gave the landscape a hard, bitter look. Windblown snow flayed our faces as we carried our bedding and a little food and firewood to the abandoned huts of a road camp. Our two helpers could retrieve the rest of the baggage tomorrow and move us to a more comfortable shepherd's hut nearby.

It was barely light the next morning when I toiled alone up a steep slope behind the camp, eagerly looking around for Marco Polo sheep or their spoor. Two hours later I reached the 17,000-foot crest where an icy wind whipped snow over the surface of the plateau and clouds moved restlessly around the peaks. Except for the wind there was no sound, no life, only emptiness. Usually there is a pervasive contentment in climbing and joy in seeing yet another slope beyond, but that day I was intent only on Marco Polo sheep. I swung eastward along a glacier toward the Sinkiang border where far below some ridges were fairly free of snow. On a high knoll, in the lee of an outcrop, I set up my scope. Slowly I searched the terrain, each gully, each stone field, and I did so again, and once more. I saw the Chinese borderpost down where the valley narrows and turns northward again before opening onto the Taghdumbash Pamir. And I watched a convoy of dark blue Chinese military trucks creeping over the pass into Pakistan, heavily loaded not with secret armaments, but with Chinese cabbage and turnips to feed the road crews. Again there was no sign of Marco Polo sheep. Villagers had assured me that November was a good time to meet the animals here, and in 1959 an American hunter had seen a herd of sixty-five rams. I felt utterly dejected; it was my nadir on this trip. I descended to the road, to the top of the pass at 15,600 feet, where red signs proclaimed: *Pakistan Drive Left* and *China Drive Right*. For mysterious reasons both signs were in English.

The temperature was $-3°$ F. when the guide and I left the following morning. No longer anticipating sheep, I could enjoy my walk. We wandered from one snow-free patch to another, receptive to whatever came our way. A brown bear had torn the rocky soil in pursuit of marmots; a red fox flushed from behind a boulder; a wolf dropping on a lichen-covered slab contained the coarse white hair of Marco Polo sheep. Here and there we found sheep horns, sometimes just a single hollow horn, at other times a complete skull. I measured each find and noted that horn growth is impressively rapid. By the age of a year and a half a ram may have 15-inch-long horns, and in each of the two subsequent years they may grow another 9 to 10 inches. The annual increment becomes progressively smaller thereafter, but a ram may still reach a horn length of 65 inches by the age of eight

Marmot

years. Although the horns are long, they are not massive and the head of an adult ram weighs only about twenty-five pounds. The animals have a surprisingly short lifespan, seldom reaching an age beyond ten years, whereas American sheep commonly survive for fifteen years or more in the wild.

Aferd Khan, a friend of Beg's at Sost, arrived that afternoon as passenger on a Chinese truck. Since our Land Rover had not returned, he became worried and went in search of it, finally finding it stalled at Ghoskil, a Frontier Works Organization camp. Leaving the others to guard our belongings, Pervez and I walked to Ghoskil, eleven miles down the road. It is an awful spot. Lying in the depths of a gorge at 12,800 feet, it receives only an hour of sun a day. A major there invited us to his quarters, a cement room with soot-blackened walls that radiated cold. Huddled around a tiny kerosene burner we discussed means of getting the others off the pass. He had no transport, the major said, except for an ancient truck with a broken fanbelt. Lacking a radio, the only means of obtaining a new belt within a reasonable period of time was to ask a passing Chinese truck for one, and the Chinese never stop if they can avoid it. However, he knew of an effective way to force them to halt: he ordered his men to block the road with his truck. Within hours a new fanbelt was installed and by evening our group was together again. Surely a small push would now start our Land Rover, especially since a local mechanic had preheated the engine by building a fire beneath it. The truck pushed us two miles without effect. The truck driver then said that he had only enough gasoline for his return to Ghoskil. One more push, we begged, and a push we got. He backed up 150 feet and now came at full speed, hitting us with a thud that caved in the back door and shattered the window. After that parting gesture we were left to fend for ourselves. It was dark and cold. Our best hope for assistance was at the Gilgit Scout post at Dhi, twelve miles downvalley. Pushing a loaded Land Rover by hand twelve miles through the Karakoram is surely not the most ideal way to spend a winter night. Luckily the gradient of the road was level or downhill and we reached Dhi after five hours. As we sipped a much-needed cup of hot tea, the commanding officer explained that he had no transport, that the nearest mechanics were at Baltit, but at least he could radio Misgar and find us a private jeep.

To describe our humble retreat down the Hunza Valley would be monotonous. Suffice it to say that we could not find a mechanic willing to retrieve the Land Rover, that Pervez almost tumbled into a gorge when the army truck on which he was riding skidded on ice, and that our hired jeep broke an axle just after traversing a particularly dangerous part of the road. Our tribulations continued in Gilgit. No mechanic would brave the heights and the car would have to remain at Dhi until spring. All seats on flights out of Gilgit were taken for the next two weeks but the deputy commissioner generously gave us a priority booking. The plane arrived and departed virtually empty the following day, leaving us and dozens of others stranded at the airfield because the military had preempted the scheduled flight to show Gilgit briefly to an Iranian general. Clouds now settled into the valley. When three days later the weather showed no sign of improving, we decided to go by road. Truck drivers returning empty to Rawalpindi take passengers for a small fee, and we readily found transport. As is customary in South Asia, the wooden body of the truck was gaily decorated with paintings of lions and scenes from the Alps, like someone's visible dreams of animals and places he would never see. The trip was scheduled to take two days, driving round the clock, but near the village of Patan a Chinese crew had obliterated the road with a dynamite blast. One day's wait, we were told. A night passed and much of the next day as the Chinese worked slowly and steadily, impervious, it seemed, to the traffic jam of about a hundred trucks, their drivers increasingly impatient, that now lined both sides of the obstacle. By late afternoon the impassive workmen prepared to withdraw into their camp, and I was resigned to waiting yet another night and day. But then a Chinese official arrived who needed to get through, and within an hour and a half the road was clear. Fate seemed against us throughout this trip; our tribulations had been of the kind that rob a journey of pleasure. Yet we were lucky, for later that month an earthquake along the Indus killed several thousand people and destroyed many villages, including Patan where we had waited for the Chinese to clear the road.

The visit to northern Hunza added little to scientific knowledge; nevertheless we accomplished something more important than collecting a few esoteric facts about a wildlife species. To define the significance of such a survey trip one first needs to consider the Himalaya as a whole. To me the most startling discovery was the extent to which the mountains have been devastated by man. Forests have become timber and firewood, slopes have turned into fields, grass has vanished into livestock and wildlife into the bellies of hunters. The future of some animals and plants is now in jeopardy. However, the earth is remarkably resilient, and habitats can recover if species have not been exterminated. Some day man may want to rebuild what he has squandered, and to do that he must save all species, he must maintain the genetic stock. This can best be done in reserves where the fauna and flora can prosper with little or no interference from man. In the not too distant future much of the world's biological endowment may well be found in reserves, in islands of habitat surrounded by biologically depleted environments. However, species cannot always be maintained in a reserve: it has been found that the natural extinction rate in small, isolated habitats is remarkably high, that a Noah's Ark in which species are saved two by two is not possible, for chance alone would eliminate some. Large reserves are needed, especially for such animals as markhor, which migrate seasonally, and for snow leopard, which roam widely in search of prey.

One might think that many areas in the vast mountain tracts of northern Pakistan would make suitable reserves. However, a reserve is not just rock and snow, which will survive no matter what man does to the living world, but birches, forget-me-nots, horseflies, marmots, and all the pieces that are needed to maintain a harmonious ecological system. People have penetrated to the most remote valleys, whether to live permanently or only to graze livestock during the summer months. Any new reserve will automatically conflict with local human interests, and one can but hope to find areas where such interests are minimal. The traditional rights of the local people must thus be considered. Villagers cannot be evicted unless alternative means of earning a living are provided.

I felt that northeastern Hunza would make a perfect national park. On a map I drew a line from the Sinkiang border southward past Dhi and across the mouth of the Ghujerab Valley, then eastward to by-pass the village of Shimshal, and again southward as far as the crest of the Shimshal drainage, and finally eastward to the Sinkiang border. This mountain block, 877 square miles in size, is scenically spectacular, biologically complex, and contains some rare wildlife. Aside from snow leopard, brown bear, and Marco Polo sheep, it harbors the country's only population of bharal and is visited by kiang or Tibetan wild ass. The Karakoram Highway provides access, but there are no permanent villages within the proposed area. The fact that people from several communities graze their livestock for about three months each summer at Khunjerab, Shimshal, and other uplands poses some problems, for by definition a national park should be free of such disturbances. However, I felt that such details could be resolved later. Herd owners, for instance, could be encouraged to reduce or sell their herds in exchange for jobs connected with maintaining the park. The important point was to protect the area now, for within the past five years most Marco Polo sheep had been killed and most trees cut. What of the next five years?

There is a tendency to think of ecological problems as scientific and technological when they are actually social and cultural. Would villagers accept the reality of a national park? At Dhi I had hiked up a valley pleasantly wooded with willows and junipers, uncut because they belonged to the mir. There was a hut surrounded by ibex bones and the owner was just returning home with a red fox he had shot. Would he honor the rules against shooting in a park? I talked to Aferd Khan, Kourban Ali Khan, and others about this problem. The help of such prominent men in their respective communities would be essential to the success of any conservation effort. We agreed that the local people must somehow benefit financially from a park, especially in the form of permanent jobs as guides and guards. No one could afford to preserve an area out of compassion. The concept of ethics—the ideas one has about good and evil—rests upon a main premise that everyone must live in harmony within the natural community. But such an argument has no effect on those concerned solely with surviving, it being difficult to explain to villagers that they are consuming themselves and their descendants into oblivion.

On my return I wrote a report to the government in which I proposed the establishment of the Khunjerab National Park. Dr. Rizvi, who first helped me to obtain permission to visit northern Hunza, now made certain that my report reached Prime Minister Zulfikar Ali Bhutto. The prime minister read my notes, agreed with the concept and the proposed borders, and ordered the park established. It became a reality on April 29, 1975, for the present a reality only on paper, yet it does exist. The difficulties of our Hunza trip were fully redeemed by this deferred pleasure.

Anyone who consciously observes the exponential destruction of wilderness becomes almost automatically an advocate for the natural world. To conserve a remnant of beauty becomes an ideal and this ideal possesses one until it becomes a faith: it takes a believer to understand sacrilege. I have devoted many years to this faith, but sometimes at night in the deep silence of my sleeping bag, when dark thoughts prowl the conscious, I wonder if I serve the cause only because I subscribe to Thoreau's dictum "In wildness is the preservation of the world" or also because I love the outdoor life I must lead.

I had ventured into the mountains naively, thinking that I would be penetrating one of the last great wildernesses. But seeing that here, too, man had become a destructive parasite upon the land, I became as much concerned with conservation as with studying wildlife, for protective measures are often needed more urgently than scientific studies. The supposed need for research has all too often become an excuse by officials to delay decisions. In many ways we remain ecological illiterates. Nevertheless there is enough knowledge to cure almost any ecological disease; it needs only to be applied. The first step is to make inventories and to define actual and potential problems. This was the logic behind my third visit to the Karakoram, to the K2 region, in April and May of 1975.

While Nepal became inundated with Japanese, Korean, French, Austrian, American, and other mountaineering expeditions, the Karakoram, for political reasons, remained largely closed to foreigners from 1961 to mid-1974. However, nineteen expeditions had permission to challenge various peaks there in 1975, and many of these were to center their activities around the Baltoro Glacier and K2. I feared that the onslaught of people might affect the flora and fauna, if, in fact, there was anything left. The Forest Department estimated 4,500 ibex and 2,500 Ladak urial in the area, but since no official had ever visited it, I placed less than wholehearted credence in these figures. Pervez and I therefore made plans to visit the Baltoro region early in the season before the various expeditions could disturb it. Of course the chance to see K2, geographically the least accessible of the earth's giants, was in itself a lure. So remote is K2 that it is not visible from any inhabited place and no local names exist for the peak. Captain T. G. Montgomerie first established it as the second highest peak in the world during a trigonometrical survey in 1856, and he designated it in his notebook simply with the symbol K2—Karakoram 2—a name it still retains.

A flight from Rawalpindi to Skardu, where a journey to K2 begins, is even more speculative than one into Chitral because planes must pass Nanga Parbat, which is notorious for its bad weather. Pervez and I waited for days in Rawalpindi, repeatedly going through the tedious process of checking baggage only to have the flight canceled at departure time. Also delayed by the bad weather was the American K2 expedition, under the leadership of Everest climber Jim Whittaker, which had rented a Pakistan Airforce C-130 to fly its eleven members and tons of equipment to Skardu. We were all staying at Flashman's Hotel, a rambling remnant of colonial days. The liaison officer of the expedition, Major Manzoor Hussain, was one of several officers who had helped us in Hunza the previous year, and he, Pervez, and I whiled away many days chatting and going to movies. I might never have met the other expedition members were it not for the fact that I received a telephone call from the United States for a Dr. Schaller —Dr. Robert Schaller, the expedition doctor. (Schallers seem to be partial to mountains. A Hermann Schaller fell to his death on Kangchenjunga in 1931.) While looking for my namesake, I also met Galen Rowell, who has excelled as an outdoor writer, photographer, and climber, all subjects in which I also have some interest. One midnight we received a note from Galen: "Our expedition is offering you a place on our flight to Skardu. If you wish to do this, contact Maj. Manzoor and meet him at 5:00 A.M. when he leaves for the airport . . ." We accepted the expedition's generous invitation with alacrity.

Our plane droned up the Kaghan Valley, past the stupendous western face of Nanga Parbat, toward white, storm-tossed peaks of the Karakoram ahead. Before landing at Skardu, the expedition had permission to reconnoiter K2 from the air. As we approached it, I identified various peaks to myself—Rakaposhi, Haramosh, Masherbrum—but restricted in view to a small porthole, I had trouble orienting myself and many ice giants passed by unnamed. However, K2 was unmistakable. Standing alone, it towered above the glaciers and surrounding peaks, a savage pyramid of rock so steep that even ice and snow found few holds. Nearby, the rugged mass of Broad Peak, at 26,400 feet the thirteenth highest mountain in the world, failed to detract from the solitary strength of K2. As the Italian climber Fosco Maraini accurately noted in his book *Karakoram: The Ascent of Gasherbrum IV*: "K2 is architecture. Broad Peak is simply geology."

The plane circled the mountain. Most expedition members had crowded into the cockpit for a better view of their proposed route and I did not see their reactions. Were they aghast, exhilarated, or merely intent on evaluating the technical difficulties? The west ridge, which they planned to ascend, filled me with trepidation even though I would never have to assault it. Steve Martz, movie photographer of the expedition, preserved the first spontanous responses of several climbers on tape:*

> You know, it doesn't look nearly as broken up as it did in those picture shots. It just goes up and up and up and up. It's incredible! On all sides! It's just steep.
> I think it's going to be extremely difficult. We've got our hands full, man!

* Quoted from Galen Rowell's *In the Throne Room of the Mountain Gods* (San Francisco: Sierra Club Books, 1977).

Did you notice the way you can slip by those gendarmes on the north side?

Incredibly difficult, we're going to be . . . I wouldn't be surprised if we get into trouble.

Words half wishful, half prophetic. But what spiritual terrors assailed these men in the dark recesses of their minds once they had viewed the awful route? All major peaks have known tragedy and K2 is no exception. In 1939, during an American attempt led by Fritz Wiessner, four climbers, including three Sherpas, vanished near 25,000 feet, their fate forever a mystery. In 1953 another American expedition, whose leader Charles Houston had also assaulted the peak unsuccessfully in 1938, returned, but a fierce storm, lasting five days, stopped the team at 25,500 feet. There one climber, Art Gilkey, collapsed with phlebitis, bloodclots in legs and lungs. Immediate evacuation was essential if his life was to be saved. Kenneth Mason in his book *Abode of Snow* laconically describes the struggle:

> They had just lowered Gilkey over a small vertical cliff, with Craig guarding the ropes and Schoening belayed, when Bell, who was hampered by frostbitten feet, slipped and dragged Streather with him. As they fell, their rope fouled that between Schoening and Gilkey, which checked their fall. The third rope with Houston and Bates became involved and they were thrown down the slope. Five of the climbers were falling—Houston, Bates, Molenaar, Streather, and Bell. By a miracle they were held by the firm belay of Schoening. "The nylon stretched like a rubber band," writes Houston, "but did not break." . . . Houston was unconscious with concussion, Bates hung on his rope upside down; Molenaar and Streather, bleeding and bruised, helped Bates who descended to Houston.

They anchored Gilkey firmly and erected a bivouac. When they returned less than an hour later an avalanche had carried him to his death. After a day's lull the storm continued, determined, it seemed, to sweep them off the mountain. Finally they struggled into base camp, having taken seven days to descend from 25,500 to 19,300 feet.

K2 was climbed for the first time in 1954 by an Italian expedition led by the geologist Ardito Desio.* Now this American expedition planned to climb the mountain again but by a new route, one even more terrible than that previous one which had defeated so many climbers. Why? Why seek a more difficult and dangerous route? While I have neither the passion nor technical ability to pit myself against a peak as grand as K2, I sensed what elemental longing attracted the climbers. Once in a while I also act on some wild dream to climb a summit, a minor one such as Orizaba, Kilimanjaro, or Ararat. The complexities of life vanish for a few days as my whole being focuses on an unsolved challenge; the objective is wholly clear, success or failure depending on myself alone, the limits of my strength and skill and especially my will. For once mind and muscle are perfectly integrated. It has been aptly said that climbing is a living metaphor for unifying one's existence. At its purest, climbing is done solely for its own sake, without anticipation of reward. But of course the rewards are there: moments of intense happiness, the satisfaction of extending the limit of experience, the feeling of having been a part of the natural world where death is meaningless and random. However, a human endeavor is not solely based on such pure motives; if it were, mountain climbers would not feel a need to justify themselves more than do any other kind of adventurers. There is something uniquely egotistical in scaling summits. Peaks are not climbed anonymously; success is not nurtured as a private joy. Few climbers follow Emerson's personal dictate: "My life is for itself and not for a spectacle." Years ago I made the first ascent of Mount Drum in Alaska with, among others, the Tibetan traveler and climber Heinrich Harrer. It is a small peak, a mere 12,000 feet high, but as long as it persists on the face of the earth our achievement cannot be surpassed; I treasure the heights I have won. And I suspect that others, too, seek

---

* In 1977, a team from Japan made a second ascent, using the same route as had the Italians. The Americans, again led by Jim Whittaker, returned in 1978 and this time were successful.

to accomplish some unique deed in which their heart can rest. But why reduce the complexity of climbing to a single meaning? Mountain-climbing is an intangible quest, and the reasons for it dwell, like all mysteries, within each worshipper.

Some climbers are Captain Ahabs in search of their Moby Dicks, tragic heroes, somehow flawed by the standards of our society, which with monomania pursue an icy summit as if it were the great white whale. But most climbers are Ishmaels. They partake in the quest but without the need to give their all to the sterile heights. Who were Ahabs, who were Ishmaels on this American team whose path had so accidentally crossed mine? I did not know until two years later when Galen Rowell published his remarkable *In the Throne Room of the Mountain Gods,* the account of this unsuccessful expedition. No other book so well describes the private demons which pursue the members of a climbing team over the mountain slopes.

At Skardu the Indus widens. Huge bars of silt line the river, gleaming like snow fields, and in the afternoon, when winds funnel down the valley, clouds of dust hang over the water. Several miles east of Skardu, near the airport, are large dunes which contrast strangely with the backdrop of snow peaks. Although little more than a large sprawling village, Skardu is the capital of Baltistan. Once a raja ruled the area but the dynasty ended in 1846 when the fort, perched on a knoll above the river, surrendered to the Maharaja of Kashmir. Like most other parts of the Gilgit Agency, Baltistan is bleak, as a few statistics illustrate: size—10,000 square miles; number of people —about 300,000; area under forest—36 square miles; area cultivated— 200 square miles.

On reaching Skardu, Pervez and I first made our round of official calls to explain the purpose of our visit, but were received with a wary cordiality that presaged little cooperation. Fortunately the development commissioner, Sher Ullah Beg, arrived the next day. A dynamic ex-brigadier, he was responsible for all development programs in northern Pakistan. He asked to meet me, and most Skardu officials were present when without preamble he greeted me: "Schaller, you have been causing me much trouble." But before I could become apprehensive, he clapped me on the shoulder and explained that the prime minister's office had repeatedly queried him about establishing Khunjerab National Park—and that this had now been legally accomplished. The commissioner's personal gesture sanctioned my presence. Divisional Forest Officer Muhammad Afzal was of particular help to us. He showed us forest plantations of spindly poplar and willow designed to ease a wood shortage so severe that villagers were burning their fruit trees for fuel. He took us trout fishing. (The British stocked brown trout in the Gilgit Agency as early as 1919.) And most importantly, he offered to transport us in his jeep up the Shigar Valley to a point where the foot trail to K2 begins. That Muhammad Afzal was just learning to drive, I had discovered the previous day when on a narrow mountain road he steered erratically, shifted at the wrong times, and otherwise made my stomach lurch until I insisted that it was a fine day for walking. I hesitated to accept his offer, fearing to expose myself to another such assault on my life; he, however, assured me that this time his official driver would be at the wheel.

The Shigar River joins the Indus near Skardu, the valley there being broad and heavily populated along its eastern bank. About forty miles north of its confluence with the Indus the Shigar forks, one branch becoming the Braldo River which drains the K2 area. From the mouth of this river to Ashkole, the last village in the Braldo Valley, is twenty-seven miles, and we hired four porters to carry our equipment and a one-month supply of food there. The Braldo Valley is narrow and with a path that alternates between following the silty riverbed and tracing contours of the naked slopes. Random rocks hurtle from the heights, reminding one of the transience of men and mountains. At intervals we passed through hamlets where stunted men with scraggly beards and wrinkled faces resembling desiccated turnips watched us pass, and women fled at the sight of us, their brown and black rags flapping like the wings of giant crows. Only a few impressions of those villages remain with me: Biano was the village of apricot blossoms where I walked over a carpet of fallen petals;

Chongo was the village of cretins where the deleterious inbreeding of isolated communities was even more obvious than usual; Ashkole was the village of fleas.

At Ashkole we hired new porters for the trek to Paiyu, a campsite twenty-three miles upriver near the Baltoro Glacier. Ashkole lies at 10,000 feet, and spring had not yet arrived; it snowed as the porters halted at the edge of the village to propitiate the forces of destiny with a chant. No one had been much beyond Ashkole since the previous autumn, so I hoped to see some wildlife. In the afternoon we crossed the rubble-covered terminus of the Biafo Glacier, and, just beyond, in the shadow of a huge boulder, we camped for the night. In the morning the porters were in no hurry to continue, because, they said, it was only five and a half miles to the next traditional campsite. Leaving Pervez with the porters, I ambled ahead to look for tracks on the river bars. Two wolves had loped along side by side, and further on, I found the faint pugmarks of a snow leopard; there were also dainty hoofprints, shaped like deflated hearts, of Ladak urial sheep. And later, upriver, I suddenly spotted many tawny bodies racing up a slope: a herd of twenty-three urial—nine ewes, six lambs, seven rams, and one individual whose sex I could not ascertain before the animals vanished over the crest of a ridge. Since it was the first time I had seen Ladak urial, I climbed a spur, hoping to observe them at leisure, but they fled once more, obviously very shy from being hunted. Ladak urial were once common in the valleys of the Indus and its tributaries wherever the terrain is rolling but not precipitous. In 1841 the zoologist Edward Blyth wrote: "Vast numbers of this species are driven down by the snow in winter to the branches of the Indus, near Astor . . ." Man and his livestock have now usurped most urial habitat, and although legally protected, the animals are still being shot. Fewer than one thousand survive in Pakistan. I had met a government engineer, Hussain Ali, who openly carried a rifle in his jeep around Skardu, and it was widely reported that he had shot eight urial and nine ibex illegally the previous year. When I asked an official why this man was not apprehended, he shrugged his shoulders and said: "What to do? He has important friends. And he shares the meat with them."

By midafternoon a fierce wind blew up the valley. Protected by boulders, the porters made a fire of twigs and baked *tok* for us. After heating a smooth fist-sized stone, they wrapped it in unleavened dough; baked in embers, the bread was soon smooth and hard like a fossil skull. A blow cracked open the crust, the rocky kernel rolled out, and we ate the bread shells, heavy and hot. Washed down with tea, they made a filling dinner.

With porters traveling so slowly, I had ample time to continue my search for wildlife and its spoor. The first sign I saw next morning was the fresh track of a brown bear heading determinedly downvalley, the animal having passed our bivouac sometime at night. All along the trail and on slabs of rock were the droppings of red fox; I collected a bagful of them, for each gray spindle of hair and feathers had some story to tell: half of the droppings contained the tiny curved incisors and miniature bones of careless rodents and pikas; there were also remains of hares, and those of snowcock, feathers as well as eggshells. Did foxes catch these wary birds on the nest? Some droppings had urial and ibex hairs in them. I could well imagine a fox discovering an avalanche victim and feasting with vulpine glee, or snuffling carefully around the abandoned kills of wolf and snow leopard. Once five urial rams trotted in single file up a sagebrush slope, their gray-brown pelage blending perfectly into the terrain. Last in line was a fine ram with heavily ribbed horns rising steeply from his head before arcing back. Although urial are basically low-country sheep, here in the Braldo Valley I saw them up to an altitude of 12,000 feet.

The trail crossed a boulder field deeply sliced by many ravines, and filling the valley ahead was the black snout of the Baltoro Glacier. Soon we reached the campsite of Paiyu where a rivulet trickled down a gully and a shepherd's hut provided shelter. Birches and willows crowded the water's edge, the first trees in many miles of valley. Three of the porters turned back to Ashkole while the fourth remained with us as cook. For two days we explored the valley around Paiyu, but found little to add to our knowledge of wildlife. The weather remained unsettled; rarely were peaks etched clearly against the sky and sometimes snow flurries blotted them out entirely. Every afternoon the winds began, lashing us with sand, and far into the night they battered our tents with resentful determination.

I needed to survey the mountains along the Baltoro Glacier for wildlife, but with the weather so awful, Pervez was not eager to accompany me. I went on alone. Beyond Paiyu the trail led to the northern edge of the glacier, but from old expedition accounts I knew that traditional campsites were along the southern margin where the slopes also looked more inviting than the sheer precipices and pinnacles and the many hanging glaciers that bordered the other side. It took four hours to angle across the Baltoro. Never before I had seen such a monstrously ugly glacier. As far as my eyes could follow the gentle curve of its flow, gray pebbles and boulders covered its surface; twisted and buckled, the ice presented a maze of ridges and defiles, and silty torrents rushed out of hidden tunnels to vanish again. The rocks seemed alive; tiny avalanches constantly rustled, and as it warmed up, stones released their hold on ice walls to clatter into the depths. Each step was an adventure as boulders tilted or debris slid from underfoot.

At last I reached Liliwa, a level, sandy spot crowded between glacier and mountain slope. Sometime during the winter an avalanche had suddenly descended, carrying with it two ibex males. Their bones and horns were still there, at the edge of the retreating snow, picked clean by scavengers and elements. High above, I spotted the survivors, a herd of nineteen ibex, including five large males. They were in the open among huge rocky slabs, making an approach difficult, but after ascending 1,000 feet while keeping upwind in the lee of a ridge, I could observe them well. On top of a flat boulder a male reclined, his curving horns silhouetted against the moody sky; another male was asleep, his head sinking slowly under the weight of his horns until his nose touched the snow, when it jerked up, only to descend again. A large youngster chewed cud beside its mother. The intimacy of the scene infused the mountains with special beauty. In the immensity of these ranges, at the limit of existence where man may visit but cannot dwell, life has a new importance. The winds shifted, bringing new snow. Sensing danger, the animals filed to the crest where, one at a time, they halted on the skyline and looked back.

An old trail followed the edge of the valley, sometimes along the glacier, at other times along the base of the mountain. And at all times it was a slow, tedious route full of sand, rocky debris, and rotten snow. The peaks were entombed by clouds, and winds attacked me. My pack felt heavy. At intervals I came across ibex horns, most of them avalanche victims, and these gave me an excuse to rest while I measured them. I crossed the mouth of a glacier-filled side valley. It was 4:30 P.M. Somewhere, not far ahead, was the campsite of Urdukas. From Paiyu to Urdukas is about fourteen miles but it seemed as if I had already gone twice that distance. To go on was not a decision, but an acceptance, for there was no reasonable alternative. I plodded on, body and mind now quite separated, the former concentrating on moving each leg, the latter focusing at the ground near my feet. I saw old brown-bear droppings of grass, roots, and ibex hair; I noted the color of glacier-worn pebbles, some mossy green with white flecks, some black with crimson marbling; I heard a snowcock cackling in a rising crescendo and the gurgling bell of a raven, but I was too tired to find them with my eyes. Another side valley with a glacier, and still no campsite. The toil of such hiking excludes romance. It was 6:00 P.M. when I reached Urdukas. A mountain had sagged here to form a bulge on which perched boulders each several times as large as a house. The sloping sides of these boulders formed natural shelters and wearily I erected my tent in one. In the warmth of my bag I chewed pieces of hard *tok* bread, then full of satisfaction from the hard day's walk, I stretched out to sleep.

Spring had not yet arrived at Urdukas. Here, at 13,400 feet, only the tops of grass tussocks poked above the snow. No ibex trails marred the white expanse; I suspected that most ibex along the upper Baltoro had moved downvalley for the winter and were now following the retreating snows back up. The only winter resident I saw at Urdukas was a Himalayan weasel with a foxy red coat. After briefly exploring the slope, I continued my hike up the glacier. Above me the sky was clear, a sunny highway of blue, but all peaks remained deep in clouds. Soon the ridge on my right came to an abrupt halt where the large Mundi Glacier joins the Baltoro. I continued on for another hour, walking over ice now, then stopped. Suddenly Masherbrum escaped from its prison of cloud to reveal a gigantic rock face with a white plume of snow blowing from its summit. Again and again the mountain repelled the continual attack of more dark clouds from the south, but inevitably it submitted to them. And then, at the head of the Baltoro, another peak, Gasherbrum IV, disentangled itself from the clouds and evolved into a vast pyramid of light, a celestial peak of symmetry and grace, over 26,000 feet high. As Keats once noted, there are moments big as years. But now, for the first time, I was uneasy. The nakedness of the peak revealed my terrible loneliness, my utter insignificance. Mountains are not chivalrous; one forgets their violence. Indifferently they lash those who venture among them with snow, rock, wind, cold.

One often gives names to things in order to establish a relationship with them, to achieve some degree of empathy. Most prominent peaks and glaciers here had been named long ago, but, in addition, an identity of another sort pervaded the area. Once only gods lived on mountains, but now mere mortals claimed the heights. Somehow I felt less alone when I remembered that off in the clouds to the north Francis Younghusband had in 1887 crossed the Muztagh Pass, that the great Italian climber Walter Bonatti had for the first time trod the summit of Gasherbrum IV in 1958, that the German Herman Buhl had claimed the glory of both Nanga Parbat and Broad Peak before Chogolisa had claimed him forever, that . . .

I had to decide whether to continue to the head of the valley, to a spot called Concordia, where the Godwin-Austen and Baltoro glaciers merge, or to return to Paiyu. It would take one long day to hike to Concordia, the only place from which I could obtain a full view of K2.

I wanted to meet this peak alone, yet an approaching snowstorm made my chances of seeing any mountains at all slim indeed. Prudence overruled passion and I turned back. And then, for a moment, I was no longer alone. Flying high above me were two cranes, their bodies white and black, colored like the crags and snows around them. A pair of rare Tibetan cranes? I was not certain. They had come from the clouds and soon vanished among them again, little more than vague visions that almost refused to become memories. All the way back to Urdukas and on down the glacier, my mind remained with the cranes, and they still fly on in my dreams.

I spent the next two days hiking leisurely along the glacier looking for ibex, and found forty-nine. Taking the whole upper drainage of the Braldo, an area of at least 500 square miles, there were perhaps no more than a hundred ibex at this season. I wondered why the animals were so scarce. Hunters no doubt shot a few, predators captured some, and avalanches took a heavy toll. But still, on the average, ibex lived an exceptionally long life in this valley: I found the horns of a dozen males that had died of natural causes and eight of these had survived for eight to ten years. The answer to the scarcity of ibex lies in the habitat. In this severe environment, this refuge of the ice age, the habitat is simple and fragmented, tiny meadows scattered among barren expanses. The mountains simply cannot support many ibex, nor, therefore, many snow leopard. Downstream of Paiyu there are more ibex, as well as some urial, but wildlife is obviously far less abundant than the thousands of animals postulated by the Forest Department.

Given these ecological conditions, I debated with myself how best to preserve the area. Scenically it is magnificent and will remain so for centuries to come. Biologically it is interesting but less so than several other areas I had visited. It would be easy to establish a national park around K2, for no one laid claim to the sterile uplands. But should the government expend its limited time and funds to establish a reserve mainly of stone and ice when other parts of the mountains required urgent attention? The trail to K2 is arduous and often monotonous, and a roundtrip requires some twenty days. Avaricious, argumentative, and unreliable, Balti porters are among the worst in northern Pakistan, and at the same time, the most highly paid, making the journey expensive and occasionally unpleasant. Of course, a road could be constructed to Ashkole, shortening the trip, or an airstrip be made near Paiyu. Even so, only a few hardy trekkers and mountaineers are likely to visit the area. Little would be gained, I thought, by establishing a park at this time. However, two problems required official attention. The ban on shooting needed to be enforced or one of the last populations of Ladak urial would surely vanish from Pakistan. The other problem affects all wilderness areas. Having spent an hour at Paiyu burying old cans and bottles of a few previous visitors, I could well imagine how the place would look after the American expedition with all its porters had camped there, and then the French, and Japanese, and Polish, and others. Within a very few years the last birches and willows will have been cut and the campsite turned into a garbage dump. No large expedition can pass through an area silently and without trace, and the fate of this fragile valley was obvious. Limit the number of expeditions, prevent tree-cutting, carry out cans and bottles, airdrop supplies at a base camp to eliminate armies of porters—I could think of various solutions, but I also knew that the government would not enforce stringent regulations.

It was time for me to return to Paiyu, but as I left Liliwa to cross the glacier a final time, I did so without elation. Here, all alone, I was free to be myself, free from the restrictions of society. There was anarchy in my emotions and actions; I was without limit. Yet I also knew that I could not transcend society, that this freedom was a mere refreshing interval in my usual existence. Culture triumphs over nature. What one feels fades quickly into faulty memory and self-deception, and in retrospect, I wonder just how long I could tolerate being free to be nothing but myself.

I returned to Paiyu. It was May 13 and spring had come during my absence. Willow catkins bloomed, tree sparrows scolded around the hut, and in the shallows of the river stood a gray heron. We left for Ashkole the following morning, heavy clouds still engulfing the peaks.

Within two hours after leaving Paiyu we saw an irregular line of porters wending its way up the valley. The American expedition had finally arrived after having been delayed for many days because of porter problems. I chatted briefly with Galen Rowell and Leif Patterson, and then, with Pervez and the porter, continued down the trail. I felt that the valley was not mine anymore; I wanted to leave. Toward evening it began to rain, and it still rained when we reached the mouth of the Braldo Valley four days later. I noted with regret that my earlier fears about the effect of expeditions on the valley had been fully justified. Campsites reeked and litter marked the route of the undisciplined hordes. Galen Rowell perceptively commented on this problem in an article in the *Sierra Club Bulletin:*

> Nineteen groups composed of up to 600 individuals far exceeded the meager resources of the lower valleys. Unlike other wildlife, these feral creatures had an apparent defect in their social mechanisms that lowered the carrying capacity of their habitat by concentrating them in some places, which became quickly denuded of vegetation. Traveling with the largest group, I once observed the result of a three-day layover in one locale. The earth, the water and the smell of the air were polluted by more than a thousand fresh piles of excrement! This barren, brown battlefield was but a wafting on the breeze of a human tornado yet to come. The Pakistani government forbids airdrops or airlifts, thus ensuring that mass human impact will continue to increase. For the journey to the base of K2, porters must carry their own food for ten days beyond the highest village. By government regulation, they are allotted two pounds of food per day and a maximum of a fifty-five pound load. In perfect weather, with no porter strikes, such as we experienced, and with only half rations for the return, more porters would have to be hired to carry food than to carry expedition loads.
>
> The problems of preservation in wildlands that have native residents are exceedingly complex. They cannot be solved within the normal concept of a national park. . . . One thing seems certain: remoteness alone will no longer do the job. What is at stake is not just another frontier, but one of our planet's final strongholds.

Mountains in the Desert

The hills of Sind still wear a veil of heat as I venture from the hut. In midafternoon the landscape is bitter, a desiccated world in which nothing moves under a sun so hot the sky is almost white. Nearby the hostile wall of sun-blistered cliffs rises nearly a thousand feet above the plains. With the thermometer registering 105° F. I wearily shoulder my rucksack, pick up my spotting scope, and approach the cliffs over a stony flat and up a dry wash. Soon I reach the angular shade of Kira, a gray slab of wind-sculpted rock, and then follow the switchback trail which ascends a ravine. The defile is oppressively still. Every boulder radiates heat; the rocks underfoot clatter aside with a dry rattle, and even the meager stands of acacia trees that had found refuge here seem dehydrated. My sweat is the only available moisture. But as I approach the hard-edged crest, a breeze funnels down a cleft, and with renewed vigor I scramble up the last few feet to the top of the Karchat Hills.

There, partially hidden behind an outcrop, I stand looking over the convex plateau and the deeply eroded ravines that dissect it; I peruse the rugged scarps that fall to the plains below, searching each shadowy nook for evidence of life. But there is no sign of the Persian wild goat I have come to observe. I wait. As cliff shadows on the plains lengthen, the land seems less cruel, less abandoned, becoming almost gentle and tranquil in the mellow light. Hills, plateaus, and plains extend to the horizon, not crowded as in the northern mountains but with long vistas between each range. A black eagle skims past Kira. When no wild goats appear I leave this observation post, my feet treading upon a world of great antiquity which was once far different from the barren mountaintops of today. Among scattered fragments of limestone on the surface I find fossils: stems of crinoid lilies resembling pieces of wood, fanlike ribs of scallop shells imprinted on stone, small snail shells huddled among pebbles, delicate and perfect as if only momentarily at rest, and very rarely a sea urchin, gleaming like marble. As I collect a handful of treasures, squalls begin to buffet me, and soon a desert wind howls among the crags and defiles, stinging my face with sand. It will now blow throughout the night and into the following morning.

In the lee of some boulders I clear away the rock rubble, unroll a thin foam rubber pad and on it spread a sheet, my bed for the night. After eating an orange and several crackers, I tuck my binoculars and scope into a rucksack to protect them from drifting sand, then recline facing the first evening stars. I listen intently, but there is only the wind. From far away it ripples over the rocks and reverberates in the defiles, subdued yet insistent, then swells in volume as it races howling over all obstacles until it hurls itself so wildly toward me that I brace my body against its impact. Although partly protected by boulders, the wind still shakes me and lashes me with sand. For support my hands clutch the ground, but they find only limestone pebbles—

and the fossils I had placed in a tidy mound by my side. I grip the fossils as the wind roars over me like waves of the sea, and for a moment I relive an ancient reality, floating among swaying stems of crinoids, water pressing me down, and sands from the ocean floor covering me slowly to form tomorrow's fossil. The earth's terrible power is palpably around me. Then silence until once again, far away, the wind begins another demented journey.

More than a hundred million years ago, during the early Cretaceous, that land which is now the Himalayan region was covered by the Tethys Sea, which separated Eurasia from the southern continent, Gondwanaland. At that time the Indian subcontinent was still attached to Gondwanaland, but then it broke away and began to drift northward. When the two land masses came into contact during the late Cretaceous, the earth saw the most spectacular period of mountain building in its history. India's northern edge buckled and slid beneath the Eurasian continent, thereby forming a huge depression which over the eons filled with sediments, the Indo-Gangetic Plain of today. Uplifts and horizontal thrusts slowly raised the floor of the Tethys Sea to create the Tibetan highlands. Restlessly the two land masses continued to grind against each other, crumpling and folding the rocks and sediments. The Himalaya rose in three major upheavals, during the Eocene, the mid-Miocene, and the late Pliocene and Pleistocene—and the mountains are still rising. Sediments of the Tethys Sea were folded not only into the great northern ranges, but also into peripheral ones, among them the Salt, Sulaiman, and Kirthar mountains in western Pakistan. The Karchat Hills on which I was lying had once been on the bottom of the Tethys Sea.

This creation of new mountain systems from the sea opened new habitats to the flora and fauna. Evolution proceeds most rapidly during periods of geological unrest, for at such times life is presented with new opportunities and necessities. The *Caprinae,* the subfamily to which sheep and goats belong, arose during the Miocene when mountains appeared and the Tethys Sea was in its final retreat. And today's sheep and goats made their appearance in the late Pliocence and Pleistocene when the earth once again buckled and climates cooled. Sheep and goats colonized many ranges of Eurasia together. They usually occupied simple habitats, such as deserts and terrain recently vacated by ice, where plant growth is sparse. It has become axiomatic in biology that when two related species of similar size inhabit the same area they tend to compete for the same resources and can persist together only if they are separated ecologically by habitat or food preferences or both. How then do sheep and goats divide their habitat? The goats—wild goat, markhor, ibex, depending on area—prefer cliffs and their immediate vicinity, whereas sheep occupy the plateaus above cliffs and the undulating terrain along their bases. American sheep are exceptions in that they usually are found on grassy slopes near cliffs, a habitat which in Eurasia is generally occupied by a goat. But true goats never reached North America to provide competition.

At first glance sheep and goats would seem to be rather dissimilar animals. However, their bones are notoriously difficult to place into the correct genus, and the animals are genetically similar enough to be able to produce living hybrids on occasion. Differences are rather minor. For example, sheep have preorbital glands at the inside corner of the eyes, inguinal glands in the groin, and pedal glands between the hooves, in contrast to goats which have pedal glands only on the forefeet, if at all. Goats also have anal glands, possess beards and a potent body odor, and have flat, fairly long tails, bare beneath, whereas sheep have round, ratlike tails.

For several years I had been intrigued by the possible similarities and differences in the ecology and behavior of Eurasian sheep and goats, wondering, for instance, how life on cliffs affected goat society and how it differed from that of sheep. As one step in gaining such an understanding, I was now in the Karchat Hills to study wild goat. The Karchat Hills consist of a small masif, about thirteen miles long and four wide, at the southern end of the Kirthar Range bordering the western edge of the Indus Plain. To reach these hills from Karachi, one drives forty-five miles north toward Hyderabad, then turns onto a track to the substantial village of Thano Bula Khan. The place has a derelict look, burned into submission by the sun. Forlorn camels drift down sandy streets between mud-walled homes, and the inhabitants scuttle like desert rodents across alleys from one burrow to the next as if fearful of the brilliant light. From there a tenuous trail heads across wastelands for thirty-five miles, alternately crossing stony and sandy expanses. One tends to accept the desolate scene as inevitable, the product of a desperate aridity, for rainfall is only seven inches a year. But then one begins to better understand the landscape. Here and there stunted acacias have been cut and left to dry, to be picked up later by trucks and sold for firewood in Karachi. Some sandy flats are abandoned fields where an itinerant settler coaxed a crop or two before giving the soil to the winds. Herds of black-haired goats, thin, bony creatures, scour the terrain, leaving only thorny and ill-tasting plants in their wake. Had man not misused this land for thousands of years, I would be driving through woodland, with wild asses standing in the broad-crowned shade of acacias and cheetah stalking unsuspecting Indian gazelle through swards of golden grass. Perhaps down by the river a pride of lions would be resting after the night's hunt. The forests are gone now, the rivers dry except after a downpour, and the lion, cheetah, and asses are dead. Only a few gazelle remain. No wonder the land seems lonely as one drives toward the distant hills, trailing a funnel of red dust made incandescent by the sun.

In the early part of this century the British made the Karchat Hills into a shooting reserve. Acccording to C. H. Stockley, there were about 400 to 500 wild goat and 80 to 100 urial there in 1929. But in 1931 the reserve was disbanded and the "local gentry swarmed in and slaughtered the animals," leaving fewer than 200 goats and 30 sheep. The Forest Department reestablished the reserve in 1956, and no legal shooting had been allowed in it since 1967.

Heavily hunted for meat and trophies, the wild goat had declined greatly in the hills of Sind in recent years, and the Karchat population was perhaps the largest one remaining in the province. Few people worked harder to decimate the wild goat than Dr. S. M. H. Rizvi, a renowned eye surgeon in Karachi. But in 1969 he was born again as a conservationist. Camera replaced rifle as with dedication he prodded the Wildlife and Forest Department to protect these animals, and with his personal funds he constructed water reservoirs for them. It was largely through his efforts, and those of the secretary of forests, W. A. Kermani, that the Karchat Hills were included in a national park in 1973. Rizvi first invited me to study wild goat in the Karchat Hills, where, near the base of Kira cliff, he had constructed three grass huts which were later replaced by permanent ones of mud and stone. A generous host, he permitted me to use these huts when some built by the Forest Department nearby were torn apart by wind. I first visited the area in September, 1972, with Andrew Laurie, then a student at Cambridge University, to study the rut of wild goat, and I returned there four more times in 1973 and 1974.

The bloody sun of morning finds me scanning the plateau for wild goat. The sky is yellow with sand, and sharp gusts of wind still hammer my body. Finally, far away I note a white spot moving up a cliff; and then, through the scope, a section of cliff moves as dozens of wild goat—large silver-colored males, gray-brown females, and youngsters—file out of a canyon to feed on the plateau. I count sixty-eight. Females resemble young males at a distance, and I am too far away to classify each animal according to age and sex. Shy from being hunted, the wild goat must be approached with care. I angle into a defile. The limestone along its bottom has been scoured smooth by rare torrents, and potholes have been carved into the rock. Brush grows here and stunted trees; a white-cheeked bulbul calls. I climb out of the canyon, and protected by a low ridge, follow the plateau until I judge the goats to be near. They are still ahead and below, about five hundred feet away. Lying with the scope propped on my rucksack, I watch them.

Most are foraging, cropping brittle tufts of grass that grow in cracks where soil has accumulated, and nibbling on the leafless twigs of *Leptodenia* and fleshy leaves of *Capparis*. Five adult males, sleek and glossy, have congregated in a bachelor club at the herd's edge where they walk around with stately steps as if to impress each other and the nearby females. It is now early September, and in preparation for the rut, they have molted from drab summer pelage to shining nuptial coats. Their necks and backs are a shining silver-gray, but their faces and chests are black, as are the collars encircling their shoulders and the dark crests of hair following along their spines. Sweeping up and back like scimitars, are thinly elegant horns over forty inches long. Seeing such magnificent beasts, it is difficult to remember that they are the probable ancestors of our domestic goats. Adorned with conspicuous horns and a striking pelage, wild goat males are designed by evolution to impress others, they are perambulatory status symbols. Any herd member knows at a glance that here is a prime animal, powerful, adult both physically and psychologically, a male which by his mere survival has shown himself to be of superior stock. Few dare challenge such an individual even in such minor matters as the right-of-way along a ledge. There is a dominance hierarchy among adult males based on size, especially the size of horns. Growing a bit more each year, horns reflect the age and by implication the strength of the bearer. Since any male usually defers to another with larger horns, wasteful interactions are avoided. Of course, wild goats do fight on occasion. Like markhor, they sometimes spar, pushing horn against horn, or one may rear up and then plunge down to bash the horns of his opponent. But not once this morning, in over an hour of observation, do I see a fight. Strife is most likely during the rut, which I suspect has not yet begun.

As the sun grows hot on my back and bleaches sky and hills, the goats become lethargic. Some recline, others drift toward a canyon. One by one they move out of sight to spend the day beneath trees, in shallow caves, or in other fragments of shade. Not until late afternoon will they reappear. I amble circuitously back toward camp, along the rims of canyons and the bottoms of ravines; I explore secret clefts known only to porcupines, and I search for traces of leopard. Probably no more than two leopards hunt this part of the Karchat Hills. Wild and domestic goats are their main food, supplemented with whatever else they can catch—porcupine, hare, gazelle, striped hyena. Although I occasionally find leopard scrapes and chalky white droppings on the

Hedgehog

stony trails, I never see the animals themselves. Life is sparse and cautious in these desert mountains. I peer into *Euphorbia* thickets; beneath the spiny arms of these plants many night creatures seek refuge, among them Indian mongoose and long-eared hedgehog. During their first fragile years acacia seedlings find shelter there too, but later repay this hospitality by killing their hosts with shade.

I seldom saw anyone during these rambles. Livestock grazing on the plateau had been prohibited in 1972, eliminating herdsmen, and poachers rarely ventured into the area while I was there. Occasionally a roving band of outlaws shot wild goat for food, sweeping through an area and stealing livestock like a pack of wolves. (Twice we abandoned camp for a day when villagers warned us that a band was heading toward us, but we never had direct contact.) Years ago wild goat were also the source of bezoar stones, small, smooth, greenish concretions, laminated like onions, which are found in the stomachs of some animals. Until the eighteenth century, such stones were so highly valued in England as antidotes to poisons and for other medicinal purposes that an ounce cost five pounds sterling. In 1694, India exported 1,960 ounces to England. Fortunately for the wild goat, the special qualities of its bezoar stone are no longer appreciated.

By noon I can feel heat from the rocks through the soles of my shoes. The defiles become furnaces. I am the sun's blazing focus, and slowly I am sucked dry. On a rock is a wingless grasshopper the color of limestone, perfectly adapted to this windy and gray stone desert. We two are the only ones to brave the sun; sensible creatures have long since found shady retreats. Now I also hurry home, half senseless, stone and sky vibrating around and in me. There is an earthen jar with brackish water in the hut, and I drink five, six, eight glasses without stopping before I feel partially replenished. Soon Mohidin brings a pot of tea, and it, too, my body absorbs. Mohidin is Dr. Rizvi's cook, kindly loaned to me during these sojourns; cadaverous in looks and laconic in expression, he accepts our solitary desert ventures without complaint, something few servants do. The heavy heat is so enervating that my mind has no goal except the evening coolness. I doze for an hour or two on my charpoy, then do trivial tasks. I press a few of the plants that wild goats eat, rubbery leaves of the *Salvadora* tree, feathery grass heads of *Eriochloa*. Sometimes I shift boxes of provisions checking to see if unwanted intruders once again share my room. Under one box a scorpion, greenish-yellow in color, raises its poison-tipped tail in defense. I hit it with a shoe. Once I killed a mouse; it resembled a North American deer mouse except that it was gray and on its rump had stiff hairs, almost like the spines of a hedgehog. I was angry with myself for having killed such a harmless boarder. Later it was identified as a Cairo spiny mouse and only the second recorded specimen from Pakistan. Still, I have something to expiate.

I liked having Andrew Laurie with me that first September. He is a good observer and a pleasant companion. While he monitors wild goat near camp, I sometimes survey other parts of the range. My favorite guide on trips to new areas is Bachhal, a short, bowlegged Sindhi from a nearby village. His face is pock-marked; he has a black beard, and an untidy plaid turban swathes his head. Dressed in a loose shirt, baggy trousers, and frayed sandals, he looks unprepossessing, with an ugliness that is somehow decorative. Not long after our arrival, I decided to check the cliffs on the other side of the plateau. Bachhal leads the way, and another local man, a game guard employed by the Forest Department, brings up the rear. I only remember his face, not his name. He is lean and taciturn, his eyes stare like loaded pistols, his golden earring flashes. As usual we cross the gravel plain toward the escarpment. In the shadows of Kira, beside some boulders, is a saw-scaled viper, pale like the desert rocks; it is often there before the first flares of sunrise penetrate the canyon and I always look for it—acquaintances are difficult to come by here. The guides and I walk to the crest of the plateau. As always the wind is with us, sometimes subdued, sometimes wildly panting as it comes across the maze of canyons and ridges. Bachhal borrows my binoculars and scans the terrain for wild goats, his crouched little body like a promontory of rock. Then I look, too. There is no sign of life except for the forlorn cooing of a collared dove in a nearby ravine. We walk on. The heat makes us indolent and we soon halt, retreating into a shallow cavern. I eat an orange; within a few minutes its peelings are shriveled and hard. Bachhal has a goatskin with water, smoky in taste and fetid in odor. Small bees are attracted by the moisture and swarm into our refuge, clustering on the goatskin and clinging to our faces and arms, but the sun is too hostile to tempt us back into the open. Instead we withdraw into ourselves, each of us lying in a quiet torpor, ignoring thirst, heat, bees.

At 4:00 P.M. we continue our exploration. In the depths of a ravine is a pool, the water slimy green with dead wasps floating in it. According to Bachhal there are only two such pools and a tiny spring in the whole southern half of the Karchat Hills at this season. The pools will soon be dry. Desert wildlife must be able to subsist without drinking, and indeed, wild goat live for months each year on whatever moisture they can obtain from their forage. Like many animals of arid lands they conserve body fluids. They concentrate their urine, and waste little water in defecation, eliminating dry, crumbly pellets. Like some antelopes they may also have a flexible temperature-regulating mechanism; instead of eliminating excess heat through perspiration, they permit the body temperature to rise several degrees, thereby conserving water until at night their temperature drops back to normal. It is almost dusk when we descend to the plains on the other side of the range. The two Sindhis make a fire and brew a kettle of strong, bitter tea, which with dry chappaties will be our dinner. Our repast is not exciting, and after days of such food I occasionally wish for something delectable. Yet once when several persons from the American consulate in Karachi visited my camp and served chilled Chablis, smoked oysters, and caviar, the ostentatious meal seemed terribly wrong in this continent desert. With the last light the two men kneel facing Mecca, intoning their words of obeisance. I unroll my sleeping pad. The desert is still, for once even the wind having exhausted itself; then far away a camel bell chimes, reminding me that solitude and silence are not vacancy.

In the morning we continue our search for wild goat, arcing northward over the plateau and then home. Based on this trip and others, I estimate a population of four to five hundred goats in the Karchat Hills. Most of them are in small herds with fewer than twenty individuals but occasionally as many as one hundred may briefly band together.

The 1972 rut began slowly as Andrew and I watched the goats from various vantage points in the mornings and evenings. As with markhor, the male goat often walks around with his tail folded up over his rump, presumably wafting enticing aromas from his tail glands, and occasionally one squirts urine on his face and chest. Restlessly he wanders, stopping to sniff or nuzzle the rump of a female, checking whether by chance she is approaching estrus. More often than not she trots aside, avoiding the crass overture. Persistently, the male may then tempt her with a display: holding neck low and muzzle forward, he approaches the females in a slight crouch, perhaps rotating his head while twisting his horns away from her when close. And sometimes he raises a foreleg as if to kick. All the while his tongue flicks and occasionally he grunts. Such displays probably arouse her interest or at least overcome her aversion. Sometimes she halts to urinate, but while he sniffs the urine, she hurries away. Indeed, she gives the impression of having urinated to divert his attention.

By recording how often males of various ages display, Andrew and I become aware that the rut's tempo increases dramatically on September 18 and 19. Instead of giving a cursory head twist or a casual kick, males now display again and again, insistently demanding attention. The adults are most active. Not that young males lack interest, but whenever one tarries near a female he is displaced, the mere approach of a powerful adult usually being enough to cause retreat. If not, a horn threat or lunge forces him to flee. Animals can assert themselves aggressively in two ways. In one they do so directly, threatening an opponent overtly or actually attacking him. In the other, they do so indirectly, attempting to achieve dominance not by a test of strength but by means of intimidation through the use of rank symbols. Wild goat, we note, waste little time on indirect methods: they usually attack. Although competition may seem intense, actual combat is rare because males do have a rank order to which they usually adhere. Competition follows certain rules. For example, once a medium-sized four-and-a-half-year-old male twisted his head and then kicked behind a female. Another male of the same age, but somewhat larger, hurried up, cut in front of the first, and appropriated the female without being challenged. An adult male then arrived and lunged at the second male so suddenly that the latter barely had time to turn around to catch the blow harmlessly with his horns. Another clash of horns convinced the smaller of the two to retreat. But the newcomer had barely claimed the female when a still larger adult appeared. With a self-assured jerk of his head he bid the rival leave and then followed the female. Thus, with a minimum of strife, the largest male appropriates the estrous female. If, as sometimes happens, two or three females are in heat simultaneously, the two or three largest males in the herd each claim one.

When a male finds a female in heat, he tends her closely. With his muzzle almost touching her rump, he follows her, moving and halting whenever she does. If she flees, he pursues, and the two then race in and out of ravines, along ledges, and down precipices. She may halt abruptly and butt her ardent suitor in the neck but he does not retaliate. Finally she accepts his overtures. As she walks slowly he kicks his foreleg behind her and twists his head sideways. Gently he licks her neck and just as gently he mounts. She may then rub her face against his. He mounts once more, and then again. Young males sometimes trail behind the courting pair, keeping a safe distance.

The wild goat rut reached its peak in early October. With a gestation period of about 165 days, most young would be born in March. And on March 1, the following spring, I was back at Karchat. It is somewhat cooler than in autumn and even drier. The grass is a hard stubble and most trees have shed their leaves. There is a Pashtu proverb that describes the desert seasons: spring is teeming, summer sweltering, autumn sickly, and winter needy. In this gaunt land every season looks needy to my undiscerning eye. Only after a rare summer rain are the hills briefly verdant. Yet a few trees select the harsh spring season in which to bloom; there are large orange blossoms of *Tecoma,* strangely flamboyant amidst all this restraint, and pink-flowering pendants of *Capparis* which attract iridescent purple sunbirds.

The wild goat are around the same cliffs as during the previous autumn, many males and females still together with some of the latter heavily pregnant. Some of the females are alone among inaccessible precipices, so reluctant to leave that it is obvious their newborns must be concealed in a nearby retreat. Finally, after several days of searching, I see a young goat following its mother. It is like a tiny gray hare, and I am amazed that its shaky legs can carry it safely over such jagged terrain. However, young travel little for the first three to four days after birth, remaining hidden until their gait has steadied. Judging by their slack abdomens and enlarged udders, most females have given birth by mid-March, but no more than a third of them are accompanied by young. I wait. Surely more females have young cached somewhere. But reluctantly I come to a grim conclusion: about half of the young died at or within a few days after birth. In the following months half of the survivors will die too. By autumn only one female out of five still has a young at heel. What is wrong?

Accidents, predation, disease, starvation, so many factors conspire
against a young between birth and weaning that one can only marvel
that any survive at all. However, nutrition of both mother and young
is the most critical factor determining success or failure of a breeding
season. Studies of domestic sheep show that poor nutrition decreases
ovulation rates and causes loss of ova. This may explain why some
wild goat females apparently failed to produce young, and why few
if any had twins. Their nutrition during the rut certainly had been
poor. The Karchat Hills had been gripped by drought for several
years, and the summer of 1972 was especially severe. Monsoon clouds
gathered, then dissipated, releasing only three brief sprinkles. By contrast, the summer of 1973 brought more rain, several heavy showers
greening the land, and the next spring twice as many young appeared, though still few if any twins. Another study of domestic sheep
shows that if ewes are put on a poor diet during the second half of
pregnancy, many young will die within the first four days after birth.
Poorly fed ewes not only lack interest in their lambs, but also give
less milk. However, if nutrition is ample, the fetus deposits fat, affect-
ing its subsequent chances of survival, and the ewes give more milk.
Valerius Geist has pointed out that the length of time a young
suckles is an indication of the mother's milk supply. Wild goat females
permitted young to drink for an average of only fourteen seconds before abruptly stepping aside; they apparently had little milk. It thus
seemed that not only were the young born weak, but also they were
deprived of milk afterward.

Not every year is one of hardship for the young. Conditions in
1975 were good, as stated in a letter to me from Tom Roberts:

> I hardly recognized the area because of the changed landscape
> following very good rains last summer and considerable rains this
> winter. There was green grass and vegetation everywhere and the
> place looked like savannah rather than desert. . . . We had nice
> views of 2 wild goats going to where they had concealed their babies
> and were pleased to note twins in both cases.

How tenuous is life in the desert. One good summer shower can determine whether a young will survive its birth the following spring.

Having observed one rut and one birth season, I thought that the annual reproductive cycle of wild goat at Karchat had been accurately delineated. Confidently I returned on March 20, 1974—a date on which in the previous year some females were still pregnant—and found the birth season well over. I came to watch the rut on October 9, 1974—a time when in 1972 mating was at its peak—and found it completely finished. Obviously the time of rut and subsequent birth season can vary from year to year. I should have suspected this for Tom Roberts had written a short report in which he noted that newborns are observed "from mid-January to early February." Therefore the rut may peak in mid-August in some years, at least one and a half months earlier than in 1972. Good food may advance estrus in domestic ewes by as much as twenty days. Wild goat live in an unpredictable environment where their forage supply depends on a few erratic showers. By keeping their mating season flexible, they can take advantage of a sudden rain and the subsequent nutritious forage. Being well fed, most females will conceive, and if conditions remain favorable, many will have twins and most young will survive. But during droughts most young will die. The two extremes result in a precarious balance. Conditions are different in the northern mountains where seasons of abundance and scarcity occur more or less predictably. Markhor and ibex rut during the same brief span each year. As Charles Darwin noted over a hundred years ago, when we view creatures as evolutionary products "how far more interesting . . . the study of natural history becomes."

Rising sharply for a thousand feet or more from the Indus Plain, the Baluchistan Plateau extends westward into Iran. It is a haggard land of huge plains and isolated ranges, lean and jagged. Some ranges, such as the Kirthar and Sulaiman, run north and south, and others spread sheaflike in a series of folded arcs toward Iran. It is a somber area, sienna and gray, with a sky that is often earthen from dust. The Karchat Hills present just a tiny fragment of this vast

Fossil shells

plateau. Wild goat exist on most Baluchistan hills, wherever remote cliffs provide favored haunts, and they range westward across Iran into Turkey and onto some islands along the Greek coast. Until the 1890s the species extended to Bulgaria, but it was exterminated on the mainland of Europe. The northern limit of wild goat distribution in Pakistan lies near the town of Quetta. Just north and east of Quetta, on such massifs as Takhatu and Zarghun, is the southern limit of straight-horned markhor distribution. From there this markhor ranges northward beyond the Khyber Pass and eastward through southern Swat to the Indus River. The general range of straight-horned markhor is known, but no one in recent years had checked on the status of the animal in Pakistan, where most occur and where it was suspected of now being rare. To find out the current status of this markhor, and if possible, to compare the behavior of markhor in Baluchistan with that in Chitral, Major Amanullah and I made several survey trips from one end of the range to the other. A large portion of the markhor's range lies in Pathan tribal territory, making surveys difficult. Pathans have resisted domination for centuries; the British, after innumerable skirmishes, were unable to subdue them, and even now the Pakistani government has only nominal control over large mountain areas. The main livelihood of many Pathans is smuggling goods in and out of Afghanistan, the major home industry is gun manufacture, and the prime form of entertainment is feuding over women and land. No self-respecting Pathan turns the other cheek. Villages cower behind high earth walls and defensive towers. The men, lean, tough, and black-bearded, consider rifle, pistol, and bandoleer a part of their apparel. Because most tribal areas are closed to foreigners, the Major and I could do little more than skirt or barely penetrate the districts in such places as Malakand, Parachinar, and Khyber, and make brief transects in the Suliaman, Tobar-Kakar, and other ranges. Much of our information was obtained during interviews with villagers. Usually we were told that markhor were now rare or entirely gone. Often only old horns decorating mosques and graves attested to the animal's former presence. Even forty years ago C. H. Stockley noted:

> Although the markhor of Kashmir has some sort of protection, his unfortunate relation of the Frontier hills is persecuted by all and sundry at all times of the year, while the local inhabitants are well-armed, and the peace which has latterly invested that country has only given the tribesmen more leisure to hunt. Small wonder that the markhor have decreased almost to the vanishing point and are likely to decrease still further unless measures are adopted for their protection. Such measures are difficult to enforce in a country where my last four trips have had to be carried out with an escort of forty rifles, but at least the authorities might make some effort in places immediately under their control.

In the town of Hindubagh I asked the extra assistant commissioner for permission to visit the Tobar-Kakar ranges, where, I had been told, herds of fifty markhor could be seen ten years previously. He asked if we had a rifle. "No, no!" I replied. "We just want to see some markhor." Then he added: "You are welcome to shoot. I can give you permission. Perhaps you want meat with your meals?" The next day Alif Khan, our guide, led us completely around Surghund, one of the many small massifs which was once noted for its number of markhor. It was a pleasant March day. Although from a distance the gray, serrated range had seemed forbidding, on closer acquaintance it had a gentle beauty with earthen folds of rust-red and yellow-blossomed *Sophoro* shrubs in the dry washes. We found only a solitary track of markhor.

The Major was invaluable on these surveys. Trim and tidy, with an affable personality and an ability to speak various languages, he allayed the suspicions with which villagers view all outsiders. His interest in, and knowledge of, hunting and firearms soon had him in animated discussion with local men, discussions which after many cups of tea always provided us with useful information and perhaps a few dusty trophies to measure. As a former army man, he had acquaintances everywhere. The commander of some forlorn outpost might well turn out to be an old friend. After several hearty hugs, it was time to inquire about mutual acquaintances: "Where is Babar now? Have you heard of Mahmood lately?" This led to hours of swapping stories, of past pranks and partridge shoots, the conversation in the mixture of English and Urdu that is so typical of the educated Pakistani.

Although our surveys were done mainly by car, they were tiring and often tedious. The hours of driving through heat and dust over bumpy tracks, the spare meals of *shami kabab,* a spiced hamburger, or something similar in seedy restaurants, the nights in gloomy rest houses, which had an abandoned look even when new, all tended to fray the nerves. Given these conditions, I was continually surprised that the Major and I traveled together for days and weeks without altercation, especially since our characters are so dissimilar. I am teutonically punctual, whereas he is generously mindless of time even by Asiatic standards; I leap out of bed at dawn and in ten minutes am washed, packed, and ready to go, whereas he, as befits a former officer, insists on a leisurely cup of tea in bed before indulging in a methodical and complete morning toilet; I find contentment in physical exertion and happily race over hills, whereas he prefers to contemplate a mountain from its base. If I displayed impatience the Major simply grinned in his fetching way and tense moments passed. We adapted well to each other's idiosyncrasies and greatly enjoyed our travels.

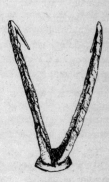

Wild goat

The results of our surveys showed that the straight-horned markhor was now threatened with extinction. Perhaps no more than two thousand survived in small, scattered populations.

It intrigued me that wild goat and straight-horned markhor each claim a part of the Baluchistan Plateau, that the two species remain discrete even though they are ecologically similar. How did speciation occur? I suspect that a population of the common ancestor of

Chiltan goat

the two species became isolated on some mountain massifs, perhaps because a dense growth of forest disrupted contacts, and there evolved a new identity. By the time the ecological barrier was finally removed, a reproductive barrier had appeared: members of the two goat populations seldom mated because they looked and smelled differently, and those that did hybridize possibly produced genetically inferior offspring. The logic of my speculation seemed good, except for one disturbing fact. Near the town of Quetta is a small area, the Chiltan Range, about one hundred square miles in size. In 1882 a local hunter gave a Colonel H. Appleton a set of horns from that range and it was ultimately donated to the British Museum. Richard Lydekker, a prominent zoologist of the time, looked at the simple spiral of the horns and in 1913 decided that the animal represented a new subspecies of markhor. However, some others felt that the goats on the Chiltan Range are hybrids between wild goat and markhor, a sensible conjecture because the Chiltan Range provides a bridge between the habitats of the two species. Here was a mystery requiring scientific detective work, a challenge to delve into the unknown and find something new.

Foreigners can travel freely in and around Quetta. Sprawled across a wide, dusty plain, the town gives the impression of an overgrown caravanserai. It retains a certain exoticism, especially in its ramshackle bazaar whose alleys are crowded with horse-drawn tongas, hawkers, bicycles, women shrouded in burqas, and tribesmen with features that bear traces of Persia, Arabia, Turkestan, and even Mongolia. South of town rises the Chiltan Range, naked and jagged, to a height of about 10,000 feet. I visited it first in November, 1970, with Zahid Beg Mirza. At the base of the range is a dismal cluster of mud huts, the village of Chiltan Anari, to which we came in search of a renowned hunter and guide named Khan Muhammad. The village had a deserted appearance as all livestock had been taken to the lowlands for winter where grazing is better and people can find work as road laborers. This village has no water. Every morning camels are led to a well several miles away to carry back goatskins full of water. Yet as recently as seventy-five years ago juniper forests covered the bare slopes, the wells were full, the fields lush. But with the trees felled for fuel and timber, rainwater ran off in torrents instead of percolating into the soil; then overgrazing by live-stock caused even further erosion. Everywhere the desert was en-croaching, not because of a change in climate, but because of human improvidence. As we sat in Khan Muhammad's guestroom with two of his friends, I tried to convey my ecological concern. The men listened silently, smoking cigarettes and spitting between their feet, and finally one said the desolate words, "Insha Allah." "It is the will of God."

Khan Muhammad showed me a set of horns of the so-called Chiltan markhor, and I examined it with interest. It certainly resembled that of wild goat, rather than of markhor, except that the terminal half of each horn was twisted inward in an incipient spiral. Each horn had a sharp keel in front, rather than in back as in markhor, and in cross section, too, it resembled wild goat. I was puzzled, and eager to see the living animals.

Tall and raw-boned, Khan Muhammad loped up the mountain with the ease of a goat to the base of a gigantic cliff where he waited for us. By the time we had labored up to him, he had already spotted several goats. Lying high on a ledge was a male, one foreleg dangling over the abyss, beard whipping in the wind. His back was silvery and he had a black shoulder band; he lacked a neck ruff. A wild goat, not a markhor, I said to myself. The animal had been wrongly classified. There is satisfaction in the solving of a biological prob-lem; however, at the time, I made no commitment to the idea that we were observing a wild goat with peculiar horns rather than a markhor. After four days of work we had tallied 107 goats, all males similar to that first one, and estimated a total population of two hundred on the range as a whole. But before deciding on the matter, I wanted to check several ranges south of the Chiltan. Over two years passed before I could return to the area, this time accompanied by Hussain Mehdi Kazmi, a relative of Dr. Rizvi. We visited several

Baluchi villages near the massifs of Koh-i-Maran, Koh-i-Siah, and Dilband-Moro where the local people told us that goats were now extremely scarce but that formerly males with scimitar-shaped horns and twisted horns occurred in the same herds. They showed me trophies with both types of horn to emphasize their veracity. And they even had a trophy with one horn of each type. Then we went on to Gishk, a massif with a sheer escarpment just south of Koh-i-Maran. Two Forest Department guards, both Baluchi tribesmen, lived there like nomads, their families in *gedans*, humpbacked and black-clothed tents. With one of them as guide, we clambered up a ravine to surmount the escarpment and soon reached a plateau. It was lovely up there in the hills; far below, dry river courses branched over the plains, dull-white like the skeletons of gigantic junipers. Leaning on his long-barreled *jezail*, a muzzle-loader with a strangely curving

stock, the guide talked to us of his life. His face was narrow and black-bearded; his eyes had the intent yet vulnerable look of quiet despair, the eyes of a man whose aspirations have been crushed by the world's indifference. He could not support his family, he told us, not on the one hundred rupees a month the government paid him. To survive he had to cut and sell the trees he was supposed to protect and he had to act as guide to illegal hunters. But who cared? No official had ever visited him in his isolated post. He was pleased by our interest and worked hard to show us several wild goats, all with typical horns, and a herd of Afghan urial. That evening in camp, the guide offered to kill one of his chickens for dinner. He owned only three. We declined this gracious hospitality, inviting him to share our own meager repast. He was a good guide and an honest man, his destiny made tragic by fate.

I was continually amazed at the ineptitude displayed by the government in handling its peoples. The character of tribes differs so much that little can function unless this is considered: if you want a Pathan to do something, every man has to be won or at least several of the ablest; Sindhis can traditionally be ordered or bullied; and Baluchis show implicit obedience only to their chiefs. Wildlife, for example, could readily be managed for meat and sport within Baluchi territory, if the chiefs were convinced that this would be in the tribe's interest.

After my visit to Gishk, I had enough evidence to support my surmise that the Chiltan goat is neither a markhor nor a hybrid but simply a wild goat. Probably the goats on the Chiltan Range had become isolated for a while and during that time developed a minor variation in horn shape, the genes of which spread southward after contact with the goats on Koh-i-Maran and other ranges was reestablished. Interestingly, there are two small ranges in Baluchistan, Murdar and Ghadebar Gar, on which both markhor and wild goat apparently lived without hybridization.

Urial sheep also occur throughout the range of wild goat and markhor, those west of the Indus generally known as Afghan urial, a different subspecies from the Ladak urial I had seen in the Karakoram. However, in many areas the Afghan urial has been so seriously decimated that I saw only an occasional individual or small group. For instance, one March day I followed a guide over the snow-streaked slopes of Koh-i-Maran. After peering over the rim of a gorge, the guide suddenly readied his rifle. Coming up behind him, I saw two pregnant Afghan urial below us and much to his disgust I prevented him from aiming by laying my hand on his arm. When I talked loudly the sheep bolted.

I never found a good study site for Afghan urial, but I did have one for another subspecies, the Punjab urial. This sheep differs from others in Pakistan mainly in having sickle-shaped horns with the tips pointing directly at the neck rather than twisted to point forward or backward. Confined to the small Kala Chitta and Salt ranges which transect the Indus Plain between the Jhelum and Indus rivers, the Punjab urial not only has a restricted distribution but also is so rare that perhaps no more than two thousand survive. About four to five hundred of these urial occur in the Kalabagh Wildlife Reserve at the western end of the Salt Range. This reserve belongs to the Nawab of Kalabagh whose family settled in the area several centuries ago. As most of the land is too dry and rocky for anything except livestock grazing, the nawab decided in the 1930s to establish a wildlife reserve to ensure himself and his friends good hunting. His son, the present nawab, Malik Muzaffar Khan, continues to conserve urial and gazelle with the result that more wildlife can be seen in a day's walk there than anywhere else in Pakistan.

Between 1970 and 1975 I spent about three months at Kalabagh. After weeks of futile searching for wildlife elsewhere, a visit to the reserve was always revitalizing. I reveled in the ease with which I could collect data after long, lean periods, and I liked the privacy of the reserve where no one lounged aimlessly around scrutinizing my every move. "*Selehmoo a laikum,*" "His peace be with you," the men said on meeting, and passed on. On every visit I was the

guest of Nawab Malik Muzaffar and his brother Asad. Their generous hospitality even included a guard whose duty was to protect me from the outlaws that make the Salt Range their base. I must admit that I found it distracting to observe urial while someone behind me played restlessly with the bolt of his rifle. Yet the nawab's fear for my safety was not idle; kidnappings for ransom are not uncommon. The nawab himself carried a pistol, and guards with automatic rifles always accompanied him on tours of his property.

The Punjab urial rut takes place between mid-October and mid-November, the peak varying somewhat from year to year. Temperatures at that season are moderate, seldom above 95° F., and the rams are at their handsomest: their neck ruffs glossy black, their bibs sparkling white, and their coats reddish like burnished copper. As always, my base was at Jabba village, in a thatched bungalow perched by the edge of a ravine. When long before dawn donkeys bray and camels groan, I know it is time to rise. A villager brings me tea and a *parata*, a fried chappati. It is still dark when I leave, the guard at my heels. As we travel along livestock trails, the hills grow distinct, revealing a rugged area of small plateaus and sharply tilted beds which culminate in a high limestone ridge. Many ravines dissect the hills and I ascend one of them to the crest of a sloping plateau where I have built a simple blind of lopped branches around a thorny acacia. I settle myself, becoming part of the landscape during the fleeting moments between dark and dawn when night still lingers in the hollows and a gray partridge gives its first grating calls. It is at this time that urial are most active: ewes and lambs seek tender grass blades among the scattered stubble and rams strive for high rank, the valleys resounding with the crack of their horns. Soon the sun emerges red and fierce beyond the hills. I remain in my blind—listening, watching, recording—until about noon, long after the sheep have retreated into shade to await the evening coolness.

For much of the year adult rams congregate into bachelor herds, indifferent to any nearby ewes. But in October they grow restless. The herds, which may contain as many as thirty members, break up as rams wander singly or in twos or threes over the hills. Their pace is determined, their bodies tense; often they halt motionless on a crest, their pointed ears cocked as they scan the slopes, and holding themselves erect, display their beauty. On spotting ewes, they first hurry, then saunter among them looking for one in estrus. The ram approaches a ewe with his head held low, and nuzzles her anal area. If, as often happens, the ewe ignores his overtures, he may become persistent, twisting and jerking his head sideways and flailing a foreleg stiffly at her or even thumping her in the side or thighs, the displays serving to attract her attention. If this still elicits no response, he often tries his luck with another ewe, and another. If no ewes are receptive, an adult ram seldom lingers long in a herd. He cannot afford to wait. With the rut so brief, he must quickly fulfill his biological imperative by mating with as many ewes as possible. Once again he roams, searching. Paradoxically, the adult rams, the ones that do most mating, spend the least amount of time with ewes. These rams, the largest and fittest in the population, are alone not because they are past breeding age or have been vanquished by stronger rivals—as claimed by trophy hunters and even some game biologists to justify the killing of such rams—but because they are looking for estrous ewes. Urial rams wander restlessly from herd to herd in contrast to wild goat and markhor which tend to remain with the females. This difference can be related to the social structure and, by extension, to the habitat. Herds of sheep tend to be widely and unpredictably scattered wherever there is forage, and rams must therefore search for ewes; goats live in relatively cohesive herds whose existence revolves around particular cliffs, and males have little need to wander.

If a ram finds a ewe in heat or nearly so, he remains with her, moving and halting as she does, staying close but not too close, careful not to frighten her away. She may suddenly flee and he races after her, twisting his head sideways and grunting until just as abruptly she may stop and casually feed. Sometimes the ram then mounts, but the abrupt contact often causes her to run away once more. However, rams are persistent and after repeated mountings one is successful. Then, his wanderlust asserts itself again. Among domestic sheep, a ram may inseminate thirty ewes in four days, showing well the transitory nature of their courtship.

Frequently other rams try to horn in on a courting pair. Young males, attracted by the chasing, cluster around until a lunge from the dominant ram drives them back. But at times an even larger ram arrives, and claiming the prerogative of his size, simply steps in front of the other, blocking access to the ewe. There is little actual fighting in such situations because most rams know and respect each other's status. All societies, beast or man, establish rules of conduct, rules which create predictability in interactions. While this reduces aggression it concomitantly increases the animals' fitness as they need not waste energy in unnecessary fighting.

Trying to unravel the intricacies of an animal society is exciting. I first noted only gross behavior in sheep, the fact that adult males tend to roam alone, that the white scrotum of a ram is exceptionally conspicuous, flashing from a distance like a heliograph, that ewes are placid, seldom interacting directly with others in the herd. Each observation raises questions which can only be answered by noting precisely who does what to whom, by recording every interaction, and it soon became obvious to me that the most pervasive aspect of sheep society was a subtle, and not so subtle, striving for dominance among rams. I thus concentrated on studying rams, not because of a chauvinistic choice, but because ewes are rather restrained in their social contacts.

The neck ruff, large body size, massive horns, and other physical attributes of a ram all serve as status symbols, just as similar structures do among goats. However, I soon noted a striking difference between the two genera. Goats usually threaten each other directly by lunging, and if the opponent cooperates, by bashing horns; they seldom try to intimidate each other indirectly. In contrast, urial often display to an opponent, kicking him or otherwise threatening him by indirect means. One might speculate that since goats live in fairly cohesive herds most individuals know each other and remember the outcome of any previous encounters; a male need not waste time in testing another whose fighting potential is known to him. But urial live in a highly fluid society where meetings between strangers are common. Rather than expose himself to possible injury by attacking an unknown opponent, a ram first tests his qualities, he tries to intimidate him without eliciting a retaliatory gesture. Whatever the explanation, urial rams spend an inordinate amount of time gently prodding, pushing, and displaying to each other, using gestures that range from broadside postures which show off an impressive profile, to twists of the head, kicks with a foreleg, and rather assertive mounts. Interestingly, sheep use such gestures as twisting and kicking during courtship as well as during aggressive encounters between males, whereas goats use them only in courtship. Rams tend to interact with others of similar size, a not surprising preference since it is a waste of energy for one ram to threaten a much smaller one, the two being well aware of each other's comparative strength. Besides, a youngster usually avoids any confrontation with an adult. Sometimes neither of the two displaying rams will accept a subordinate position and they may then harmlessly kick at each other with their forelegs, merely flailing the air without actual contact. However, some frays cannot be settled gently; they require a direct assertion of strength with a clash of horns. Their sweeping corrugated horns are what make sheep so unique. Several million years of evolution have perfected an animal which has become a self-starting battering ram designed to bash an opponent into submission. The whole head, not just the horns, is designed to give and receive blunt blows, as Valerius Geist has emphasized in his book *Mountain Sheep*. The brain is shielded from injury by sinuses sandwiched between two protective bony plates which may reach a thickness of two inches. Even the forehead hair is so dense and matted it is like a cushion. The skull is attached to the vertebrae in such a way that the whole neck helps to absorb the force of a blow. On impact the head tends to rotate downward but a bulge of fibrous tissue connecting head and vertebrae helps to counteract this. Thus designed for fighting, two rams will trot some thirty feet apart, wheel around, briefly exchange stares, and charge. They rush toward each other at full speed, then just before impact tuck in their chins, turn their heads slightly sideways, and to further increase the blow's force, give a slight leap before clashing head-on with a resounding crack. The impact may bounce each animal several feet back. Such fights are stunning in their power and also in the almost ritualized violence which enables each ram to catch his opponent's blow so adeptly between his horns. Precision is essential, for the speed of an attack is such that a miscalculation could cause injury. I once watched a ram rush down a slope toward another who was not prepared for the clash. Because their horns were improperly aligned, the glancing blow flipped the attacker over the other so that he landed stunned on the slope below. In this one violent moment rams use to the utmost those attributes for which evolution has designed them.

An urial ram uses more than a dozen gestures to express dominance and this enables him to convey his emotions with great subtlety. Each successful assertion of status by one ram also implies submission in the other. But in contrast to the many dominance displays, rams have only a few gestures of appeasement, such as averting the head or grazing with false concentration, both means of keeping a low profile. A low-ranking ram may also express submission, and at the same time friendliness, by rubbing his face on the head and horns of another. Subordinates often use this gesture to reaffirm their low rank, to help promote peace, after an aggressive encounter.

As if all this inveterate status-seeking needs an innocuous outlet, a release of tension, urial have also devised a gesture with which they can informally show aggression without risk of retaliation. Several males may stand in a circle facing inward, like players in a football huddle, and almost at random clash horns, kick, grunt, and rub faces in a veritable orgy of contact.

Occasionally urial showed a peculiar behavior whose function at first puzzled me. A tightly bunched herd would dash across a slope as if in panic, only to halt abruptly in a patch of tall grass. Some animals lowered their heads, others cowered, and still others raced off again as if pursued by a phantom enemy. I finally surmised that the commotion was caused by warble flies which buzzed the sheep in an attempt to lay eggs in their nostrils.

This unadorned enumeration of facts cannot convey the excitement with which I first observed urial in 1970, when, with Zahid Beg Mirza, I spent a month at Kalabagh. At that time urial behavior had not been described, in contrast to American mountain sheep which had received detailed study by Valerius Geist. With their bulky build and preference for the vicinity of cliffs, American mountain sheep resemble goats in many respects, and I was intrigued by how the two types of sheep differed in behavior. In brief, the basic behavioral repertoire of the two is similar except for some modifications; for example, urial run at each other on all fours before clashing horns, whereas mountain sheep often rear up and, while remaining unbalanced on their hindlegs, race at each other before falling into a clash.

As with most animal-watching, there is more tedium than excitement during a morning with urial. Huddles and clashes and other such energetic actions are only memorable climaxes to long periods when not even one animal is in sight. As the sun climbs higher, the morning glow vanishes and the stony slopes begin to quiver under a brilliant light; occasionally a breath of oppressive wind pants upward from the plains. The urial become lethargic and by 10:00 A.M. seek shade in dry washes and under trees. Soon afterward I leave my blind and turn toward home, retracing my steps of the morning. Pockets of cool air still linger in the ravines, and leaning trees form shady bowers. I walk silently in the sand, hoping to meet whatever wildlife has sought refuge here. Leopard have been exterminated in the reserve but on rare occasions I flush a jackal or desert fox. Urial often bolt away with a clatter of stones, halting at the rim of the ravine to look back, their black noses quivering. On leaving the shade, I am shattered by the white glare of the plains; in this flat light even the pale leaves of *Salvadora* and *Zizyphus* shrubs have a leached look. Off to one side, partially hidden by a bush, I note a slight movement: a gazelle buck is in there, watching me alertly, but when I stop he bolts, his lithe body colored like the wastelands that are his home. I often see him here, near this bush, where he awaits any females that may drift through his territory. A bit farther, on a gravel knoll, two red-wattled lapwings flush and circle me, breaking the silence of noon with their scolding.

Autumn heat is tolerable but that of spring is grim. Temperatures usually climb above 100° F. One June day in 1973 it was 122° in Mianwali near Kalabagh and 117° in Lahore. But such heat seldom persists and within a few days the Lahore newspaper headlined MERCURY DROPS TO 110.5 F. Yet spring is a time of renewal here, as in Karchat. At times winter rains green the land: yellowish blossoms crowd the acacia boughs like hordes of fuzzy caterpillars; the air reverberates with the coos of courting collared and little brown doves; the urial give birth.

It is April, and with Usman Khan as guard and assistant I scour the hills for newborn lambs. Typically a ewe separates from the herd and isolates herself one or more days before the birth, generally withdrawing into the upper reaches of a ravine where in some dusky cleft the lamb is born. During the first few days a newborn lies hidden and helpless in a retreat while its mother grazes nearby. We search for such young. Overhead the sun blazes while underfoot the shattered rocks burn. There are no vistas beyond the rust-colored walls of the ravines and these radiate a heat so intense that my lips crack. We find water in a few places but by its odor we know that it is tainted with sulfur. I soak my handkerchief and drape it over my head, but within five minutes the cloth is dry. In spite of the sun's leaden intensity, there is no perspiration on my face, only a crust of salt left from instant evaporation.

When we flush a lone ewe whose belly lacks the taut roundness of pregnancy, we search for her offspring. Usman is adept at spotting the cryptic gray forms huddled motionless with legs tucked under and head resting on the ground. How gaunt they are, just bundles of fragile bone and skin. Some youngsters remain quiet, watching silently with moist shiny eyes as I stroke them and pick them up; others struggle to their feet and stumble away on ungainly legs, bleating. Usman grabs them and cradles them. Tall and lean with a gray handlebar moustache, Usman has a fierce demeanor; but his features soften as he croons to his captives, "Shabash, shabash," "Well done, well done," before gently slipping them into a cloth bag for me to weigh. Most young seem healthy, averaging about five pounds in weight, but some scale only three-and-a-half pounds and one pathetic lamb only two pounds. After being released, the lamb usually crouches, although its drive to follow something, anything, is so strong in some cases that they try to remain with us. Only by suddenly running away can we deter them. A newborn only slowly learns to recognize its mother, whereas the reverse may occur within a few minutes, odor apparently being the most important basis of this social bond. A youngster follows its mother closely by the end of the first week of life, and it is then so agile and swift that it is difficult to catch. Mother and offspring then remain together, feeding and resting side by side, but as with most hoofed animals, there is little overt social contact except for nursing—they seem alone together. Yet the bond will persist until the following spring when once again the ewe gives birth.

Even though the urial as a species is known for its multiple births, twins are rare at Kalabagh, occurring in fewer than 10 percent of the births. About a third of the newborns die within a few weeks. Poor nutrition seems the most likely explanation, just as it does in the Karchat Hills. Yet, at first glance, there seems to be ample grass. Tall swards interrupt the rocky slopes and clumps have found footholds even on the most barren-looking bluffs. However, much of this grass consists of *Cymbopogon*, a species which urial and other hoofed stock do not like; the preferred species are eaten to the ground by urial and the nawab's livestock. In 1966 Guy Mountfort visited Kalabagh and in his book *The Vanishing Jungle* noted that the reserve held about five hundred urial. Ten years later the number of animals was about the same, indicating that under prevailing weather conditions, the population was more or less stable, and that animals were holding their own even if they did not approach their full reproductive potential. In 1973–74 the nawab cut most trees in the reserve to sell as firewood, razing the slopes and exposing ravines to the sun's full force, in general turning pleasant woodlands to wastes. However, within half a century new forests will have grown, and urial will still be there if they remain protected from the poachers that wait around the periphery of the reserve. Urial, as well as wild goat, are adaptable and continent, demanding only meager forage and a little water. Even on degraded land these species can survive, perhaps not at their most vigorous, but at least they can prevail until some day man has the wisdom to assure them a better future. To think that any can have a future may be ascribed to the pathology of human idealism, but in the final analysis there is little else for which to fight.

While studying urial, wild goat, and other populations, my mind dwelled more and more on developing possible means of preserving them—on improving habitat, raising birth rates, lowering death rates—and I collected knowledge that might serve this end. I often needed to remind myself of the basic and rather esoteric questions that my project was also expected to answer. Fortunately, all knowledge is a link in the development of ideas, of comprehending the subtlety with which animals have adapted to their environment. Facts that are useful in conservation also contribute to an understanding of animal societies. Whatever the purpose "the important thing is not to stop questioning," noted Albert Einstein. "Curiosity has its own reason for existing."

The differences between sheep and goats, between *Ovis* and *Capra*, are rather minor, as I explained in my book *Mountain Monarchs*:

> *Capra* prefer cliffs, a habitat choice which is reflected in the stocky build of the animals as well as in certain aspects of their behavior.

Confined as they often are to isolated cliffs, herds tend to be more cohesive than those of sheep. Males spend much time with females even outside of the mating season, and during it they wander little. Tending to be acquainted with each other, males have little need to test an opponent's strength by indirect means and instead threaten overtly when necessary. With food, rest sites, and other resources on cliffs localized, females may not tolerate intrusions into their individual space and they defend their young readily against conspecifics. Since a goat population tends to remain localized, a strong leader-follower relationship is not necessary. . . . In contrast, Eurasian *Ovis* are lithely built animals, adapted to flat or rolling terrain. With their habitat extensive and food resources often patchy, herds tend to be fluid. The animals are good followers. Rams spend little time with ewes outside of the rut and they rove much during it. Ewes are rather passive creatures. Combating rams tend to be strangers, making indirect forms of aggression adaptive even though differential horn size relegates individuals to a certain rank.

As to specific displays, clashing goats rear bolt upright, whereas sheep either rush at each other on all fours or unbalanced on their hindlegs, a method more suitable on slopes than on cliffs. The informal huddle occurs in sheep, though not in goats, as does the friendly gesture in which the subordinate individual rubs his face against that of the dominant one. A friendly gesture is probably not needed in goat society whose members lack finesse in their contacts: it is safer to stay out of the way. Goats spray themselves with urine and mouth their penises, behavior not typical of sheep. Courtship displays are similar in the two genera except that goats, by virtue of their anal glands, use odor more than do sheep.

Sheep and goats split from a common ancestor, perhaps in the early Pliocene, and then embarked on separate evolutionary paths. The former chose gentle terrain, while the latter specialized for a life on cliffs. Most differences in behavior that distinguish sheep from goats—social organization, fighting style, friendly contacts, and so forth—can be traced to the habitat. I had known that animal societies are malleable in evolution, readily adapting to the constraints of their environment, but not until I met the wild goats of Karchat and the urial of Kalabagh did I fully realize how a simple difference in habitat could impose such basic changes on a society.

Cloud Goats

Biologists like to have all species neatly classified and arranged into discrete categories based on the degree of relationship. Nature refuses to abide by such strictures, and to the chagrin of taxonomists there are many species which cannot be tidily stuffed into pigeonholes. The subfamily *Caprinae* contains several such aggravating animals, including the bharal and aoudad, which are so intermediate between sheep and goats that each has had to be placed into a genus of its own. There is also a peculiar kind of goat, called the tahr, which in several features, such as the small size of its horns, appears to be an evolutionary link between the primitive goat-antelopes and true goats. Not being true *Capra* goats, tahr have been given their own genus, *Hemitragus*. Although tahr ranged from Europe to India during the Pleistocene, they survive now in only three widely scattered areas. The Arabian tahr dwells in the desert mountains of Oman, the Himalayan tahr along the forested slopes of the Himalaya from Kashmir to Bhutan, and the Nilgiri tahr in the highlands at the tip of southern India. I wanted to study these animals, hoping to unravel the secrets of their past, but their behavior is difficult to understand unless viewed in the context of the evolutionary history of the subfamily as a whole.

During the Miocene period, some fifteen to twenty million years ago, there lived in the rain forests of Southeast Asia a small, plain goat-antelope, rather stocky in build and with stilettolike horns. It was the ancestor of today's sheep and goats. Like most forest dwellers it must have been rather solitary. There are good ecological reasons for its being essentially asocial: small ruminants have a higher metabolic rate and thus need a greater caloric intake per unit of body weight than do large ones. This great energy requirement can be satisfied only with a constant supply of highly digestible and nutritious forage such as is found in sprouting leaves, and in the depths of a forest such food tends to grow scattered—a bud here, an unfurling leaf there. Such a food supply disperses animals, tending to make them solitary.

It would be interesting to learn how this primitive creature, so different from today's sheep and goats, behaved. Fortunately rain forests, with their small seasonal changes in food and temperature, provide animals with a stable home in which they have little need to adapt to new circumstances, and over the millennia many forest species have remained conservative in appearance and behavior. So it is with the goat-antelopes. Two of these, the goral and serow of Southeast Asia, very likely resemble their Miocene ancestor in that they are rather drab, coarse-haired, and have short horns. A study of their habits could, in effect, provide a reconstruction of how their ancestors behaved.

Unfortunately, goral and serow have been little studied, and to learn about goat-antelope behavior, one must turn to two other rather specialized species, the American mountain goat and European chamois. The short, pointed horns of these and other goat-antelopes have a great effect on fighting styles. Head-to-head contact, so typical of sheep and goats, is too dangerous with such horns, and other forms of combat are therefore used. For example, according to Valerius Geist, a mountain goat may lower its head far down and hump its back when trying to intimidate its opponent. Or two animals stand side by side, facing head to tail, while jabbing vigorously with their horns at each other's legs and belly. Such combat methods can be considered primitive, and I wondered if tahr, with their short horns, also use them, or if they bash heads in the typical manner of goats.

The evolutionary transition from a solitary goat-antelope, such as goral, to a species like the herd-loving tahr also requires a speculative comment. The intense period of mountain building that gave rise to the Himalaya also created new habitats, and some goat-antelopes promptly took advantage of the ecological opportunities. But pioneers have problems: they are exposed to new selection pressures. Those that venture from the forest into the simple habitats of the open mountain slopes also leave behind their constant, high-energy food sources. Instead, they have grasses and other plants, which, though abundant, fluctate seasonally in their nutrient levels. Evolution in such a situation favors larger-bodied species whose energy requirements are lower, and in response, pioneer goat-antelopes grew larger. Being more in the open, where food is concentrated, animals had frequent contact and this ultimately led to a social existence. Food, however, is only one of several important factors that have an effect on the structure of societies. Animals can, of course, remain solitary feeders even in the open. However, each animal must not only eat, but also guard against being eaten. The best defense for a solitary creature in dense cover is to be cryptic, to crouch or sneak away, whereas herd life is of particular advantage when avoiding predators in the open. Many pairs of eyes and ears and many acute noses are more successful at detecting danger than just one. When actually attacked, herd members can crowd together, making it difficult for a predator to single out and pursue one individual. Having become social, some goat-antelope species in the mountains remained rather conservative in appearance and behavior and these were the ancestors of mountain goat and chamois. Other species evolved new forms of combat, such as head-to-head clashing and displaying various structures as status symbols, and in the process developed a great sexual dimorphism in body size and adornments. These animals ultimately became the sheep and goats and such close relatives as tahr.

I studied Nilgiri tahr in October and November, 1969. My journey to South India was more than just another short project in quest of abstruse facts, it was also a homecoming. Once again I was among chital deer, sambar, gaur, tiger—all species that I had studied and known intimately in Kanha National Park in central India from 1963 to 1965; once again the conservation problems of India became my concern. Although I went to find tahr, I also found echoes of my past.

The Nilgiri Hills rise abruptly from plains where the states of Karnataka, Tamil Nadu, and Kerala meet. High above a belt of evergreen forest tower granite cliffs which at 7,000 feet give way to a rolling plateau. Stunted forests covered these uplands until the pastoral Todas, a tribe of ancient Dravidian stock, settled in the hills; needing grazing lands for the buffalo around which their lives revolved, they set annual fires during the height of the dry season in January and February, gradually pushing back the forests until only patches remained when the first Englishmen penetrated this area. A surveyor named William Keys ascended the Nilgiris in 1812, and in 1818 sportsmen went there to hunt. News of the uplands' temperate climate soon spread through the European community on the hot, humid plains, and within a few years such Toda villages as Ootacamund had been transformed into summer resorts.

A main pastime of British expatriates was hunting, and such books as Fletcher's *Sport on the Nilgiris and in Wynaad* and Hamilton's *Records of Sport in Southern India* almost lend substance to the apocryphal Englishman who greets the morning with: "By Jove, what a beautiful day! Let us go out and kill something." Plants and animals in the Nilgiris and other isolated southern ranges are particularly vulnerable, for in effect they live on islands of habitat where they have evolved in isolation since reaching South India during the cooler and more humid conditions of the Pleistocene. Consequently many endemic species exist in the hills. Among these are the lion-tailed macaque, of which perhaps only five hundred survive in the wild, and the Nilgiri tahr. Tahr were once so heavily hunted for sport that in 1880 one writer could state that "the day is not far distant when they will have become extinct." When in 1877 the Nilgiri Wild Life Association was formed to regulate shooting, only a few tahr survived along the remote western edge of the Nilgiris. For over a hundred years this association has maintained an active interest in tahr. Certainly some of its members were more concerned with collecting a trophy than preserving a species, but the fact remains that under the aegis of the association tahr survived in the Nilgiris. Only a few males were legally shot each year—between 1912 and 1938 an average of 4.6, and between 1940 and 1966 an average of 2.3—and the loss of these few animals was more than compensated for by the protection given against poachers. I had read an article by E. R. C. Davidar in the *Journal* of the Bombay Natural History Society of 1963 in which he documented a tahr census. "The tahr actually seen and counted amounted to 292. . . ." With this and other background information I arrived one day at Reggie Davidar's door in Coonoor near Ootacamund.

Reggie is one of those unusual persons who openly displays his enthusiasms, and the fact that his enthusiasm is for wildlife makes him particularly unusual in a country where all too few show concern for their natural heritage. Slightly rotund, with sleekly combed hair, and a tidy moustache in a round face, Reggie has the appearance of an amiable lawyer, which he is. He has especially dedicated himself to the welfare of Nilgiri tahr, and generously he now helped me prepare for a visit to tahr habitat. First, he suggested, I should study the animals around Mukerti Peak, and then move some twenty miles south along the same cliff system to a place called Bangitappal.

A taxi took a guide and me thirty miles westward, along grass hills and numerous plantations of exotic eucalyptus and wattle, until we reached a water reservoir. After arranging with the taxi driver to pick us up in a week, the guide, Venkedachallam, and I shouldered our meager belongings to continue on foot under a drizzling sky. Venkedachallam was a thin, bandy-legged fellow with long hair restrained inside a shawl wrapped around his head, and a drooping moustache. At the head of the reservoir was a grass lean-to in which we sought shelter. Venkedachallam built a fire with sodden twigs; it sizzled and smoked but gave little heat. Dinner consisted of a bowl of glutinous rice. Venkedachallam had failed to bring a blanket, and that night, as we lay on our beds of grass with the temperature at about 45° F., he shivered and coughed until I shared my blanket and he his fleas.

At dawn we climbed up grassy slopes toward the rim of the escarpment. On the way we skirted a grove of stunted forest, or shola, huddled in a gully. It was my first opportunity to examine a shola, but the forest offered no gracious invitation to outsiders; crowded together and barricaded behind thickets of bamboo, the rhododendrons, myrtles, laurels, and other trees attempted to maintain their self-contained world, dusky, humid, with moss-covered trunks and leeches among moldering leaves. Surrounded by a biological desert, by denuded hills and plantations of exotic trees, the shola surely sensed that it was making a last stand against fire and ax: its future was already there. A Nilgiri laughing thrush, unique to this area, flitted among the gloomy leaves.

Half an hour later we reached the crest. At our feet a sheer cliff dropped to dark-forested slopes, and to our right the rock pyramid of Mukerti Peak, 8,380 feet high, punctured the clouds. To the Todas this peak was the gateway to heaven, the place at which they killed unwanted female babies. Far to my left, past rocky spires, I spotted nine tahr at the edge of the escarpment. Lying in the wet grass, I watched them for an hour as they grazed and then ambled to a cliff where safe from predators they rested on ledges. Traveling south along the rim, we encountered another herd, this one with six animals, and motioning Venkedachallam to wait, I approached it, moving first up a depression and then in the shadows of a shola until I was within three hundred feet. There, screened by a gnarled rhododendron, I could observe the herd which included two adult males, handsome, stocky creatures weighing about two hundred pounds; their silver-gray backs contrasted sharply with their dark brown pelage, readily identifying them in the hunter's vernacular as saddle-backs. With them were two young males, one and a half and two and a half years old and still gray-brown in color, and two females. For five hours I remained with the tahr as they slept and fed in desultory fashion, enjoying the sun which had at last pierced the mist. But soon the clouds returned, billowing up from the plains to crash like a monstrous tidal wave into the cliff. Bulging over the crest, they engulfed us in a mist so thick that it felt like water on my face, a mist that bore a scent of the forests below, of moss and humus, rich and damp; somewhere a waterfall splashed. Venkedachallam crawled up to me. He was tired and hungry, he said plaintively, and we had walked far; he wanted to go home. After a token protest, I followed him back to our shelter.

The following days I left my guide in camp and roamed the escarpment alone, checking and rechecking the same seven miles of cliff. Sometimes my searches were futile, at other times I found a herd or two. If the tahr spotted me first, they immediately bolted for the precipices, emitting piercing warning whistles. Those I observed undetected were disconcertingly placid. They had little reason to be otherwise, it being neither the rut nor the birth season. Published information on Nilgiri tahr had been so contradictory that I had to discover the salient facts of their breeding cycle myself. For example, some authors noted that young are born throughout the year, whereas others asserted that they appear in March or in June and July. Most young I saw were of about the same size, indicating a sharp birth peak; they were also quite large, and that, together with the fact that some females were visibly pregnant, suggested that births occurred in about December and January. The rut would therefore be from June to August, during the height of the southwest monsoon when much of the annual precipitation of three thundred inches falls. It must be an unpleasant season to observe tahr. Even now, in October, during the light northeast monsoon, the days were often dismal. Although there was generally sun in the early morning, it seemed that as soon as I found tahr the clouds moved between the animals and myself, obscuring everything, and by afternoon wind-lashed rain generally drove me back to camp. My census revealed a total of sixty-three tahr, a figure not much different from the seventy-nine recorded by Reggie in the same area. Three-fourths of the adult females had a young at heel, and yearlings were abundant too, showing good reproduction and survival. All was well with this population.

After finishing the tahr survey by Mukerti Peak, I moved to Bangitappal, a wild area of almost treeless rugged hills in the southwestern corner of the Nilgiris. On arrival I hurriedly set up a small tent which Reggie had lent me, and leaving Bokhan, my new guide, to construct a shelter of bamboo for himself, I set out to explore my surroundings before the lurking clouds could engulf them. I did not get far. Creeping over hilltops and up valleys the mists softly obliterated the landscape, but not before I had seen a brief vision of wilderness. The blossoms of *Strobilanthes*—a low-growing shrub that blooms at irregular intervals of from six to twelve years—suffused the slopes with a soft lavender glow. Growing alone on a slope in a shaft of sun was a small tree with a single yellow blossom which I recognized immediately as a *Hypericum;* ten years earlier, while studying gorillas in eastern Zaire, trees of the same genus had surrounded our mountain home, and as I returned to camp through the fog my mind was with the gentle apes on their mist-shrouded peaks.

The next morning, after walking for an hour along the edge of the escarpment, I saw ahead, barely visible in the fog, a saddleback standing motionless on a boulder. I waited, equally motionless,

Hypericum

while the moist chill seeped through my clothes and body; in the muffled silence a rock pipit twittered and Nilgiri langur monkeys whooped somewhere in the forest below. Finally the clouds parted. The male was still poised by the cliff, a dark bulky creature like an extension of the rock on which he stood. A slight movement drew my attention, and I saw other tahr, thirty-three females and sub-adults resting among the boulders, blending so well into the terrain that I had almost overlooked them. Like other goats, Nilgiri tahr are less alert to danger from above than from below, and the animals remained unaware of me until suddenly the wind shifted. Then a female whistled shrilly and all raced to the escarpment where their forms dissolved in the clouds.

The composition of several herds revealed fragments of the tahr's social life. For instance, there was a bachelor herd with seven males, indicating that the sexes may segregate when not in rut. Once, far inland, away from their usual cliff haunts, I met a yearling female accompanied by five young; it seems that at an early age tahr may desert their mothers at least temporarily in favor of their peers. Animals were generally sedentary, remaining for days around a particular cliff, although not all individuals in a herd remained together. One herd of forty-three split into two groups, one of sixteen and the other of twenty-seven; the following day a total of thirty-eight were together again, but of these a saddleback left alone, and eight others moved away as a separate group.

My tally showed 113 tahr in the twenty-square-mile area, as compared to Reggie's count of 114 some seven years earlier. With survival of young good, I wondered why the population did not increase. Poachers undoubtedly took a heavy toll in this remote and unguarded area, but predators were scarce, judging by how rarely I came across the spoor of leopard and tiger. And I saw no sign of wild dog or dhole.

The dhole interested me greatly for I had just finished studying their closest relative, the African hunting dog. Reggie knows more about dhole than any other person, and one day he took me to the Mudumalai Sanctuary, at the base of the Nilgiris, in search of them. We cruised in his jeep through a habitat very different from the cloud forests high above us. Here *Anogeissus, Albizzia,* and *Terminalia* form a dry, open woodland broken by occasional sluggish streams along whose banks grow clumps of tall, spreading bamboo. I am not a lister of birds, but so colorful and varied were birds along these streams that I automatically filled a page of my notebook with their names—golden oriole, paradise flycatcher, taylor bird, red-vented bulbul, white-bellied drongo, emerald dove, Jerdon's chloropsis . . .

But the most pervasive animals in and around the sanctuary were cattle, some twenty thousand of them, mostly lanky, feeble creatures with pelvis bones sharp against slack hides. A bullock needs about fifty pounds of grass a day. Even though the driest months were still ahead, most grass had already been cropped to a short stubble. A poor range such as this will degrade further if more than 25 percent of the annual grass production is eaten. Here, as in much of India, virtually all new growth is consumed by livestock, a condition that does not augur well for the future of most habitats. Whenever I see a situation such as this, I have a crisis of conscience. I know that the villagers need their livestock, yet I also feel that the forests and wild animals belong with mankind, that a country's survival depends on the health of its land. Conservation practices satisfactory to man, his livestock, and wildlife are needed to save the last from extermination and the subcontinent from degradation. (Yet here I sat in a jeep using gasoline, a scarce product, just in the hope of seeing dhole.)

It is often said that India has an excessively large cattle population. Indeed cattle permeate the landscape, there being one animal per two persons. In the United States there is one car for every two persons. Which has done more damage to the environment, cow or car? At first glance it might seem to be a relatively simple task to eliminate at least a few cattle, but the problem is exceedingly complex. Hindus worship cattle and it is a mortal sin for them to kill one. Not that cow veneration is a basic tenet of Hindu religion, for Hindus were once beefeaters and as late as the seventh century it was common to serve beef to honored guests. At one time Hindu Brahmans used the cow as a political instrument against the Muslims who were expanding their influence eastward; the fact that Muslims consume beef was used as an argument against Islam, further emphasizing the sacredness of the cow. But, as Jawaharlal Nehru noted: "In India, perhaps even more than in other countries, there is this difference between precept and practice. In no country is life valued in theory so much as in India, and many people would even hesitate to destroy the meanest or most harmful of animals. But in practice we ignore the animal world." Even worse, the mystical conviction of reverence for life is divorced from compassion. Not permitted to kill cattle, villagers cull them by neglect: an unwanted calf is simply tethered and allowed to starve to death.

Religion aside, the most important question is whether cattle are actually in excess. Two points must be considered. One is habitat. In large parts of India all wilderness has already been converted into fields and there the cow is merely an "exploited scavenger," as the anthropologist Marvin Harris phrased it. For example, one area of West Bengal has a density of four people and one cow per acre. The animals forage mainly along the edges of fields and are fed rice straw and other byproducts of crops which in this humid part of India grow all year. In return cows produce milk (although buffalo are more important as dairy animals) and dung. One cow eliminates about two tons of dung per year, providing not only fertilizer but also fuel, saving millions of tons of wood for other purposes. An Indian nursery poem lists some of the cow's uses:

> Living, I yield milk, butter and
>   curd, to sustain mankind;
> My dung is as fuel used,
> Also to wash floor and wall;
> Or burnt, becomes the sacred ash
>   on forehead.
> When dead, of my skin are
>   sandals made,
> Or the bellows at the blacksmith's
>   furnace;
> Of my bones are buttons made . . .
> But of what use are you, O Man?

However, in forests and other habitats, cattle can have an extremely deleterious effect, especially since more and more animals crowd into them to eat grass, tree seedlings, and even the leaves off low-hanging branches. Once there was much marginal land on which cattle could graze, but until the 1960s India increased agricultural production mainly by plowing up such land, and now little of it is left, putting ever more grazing pressure on the forests. In these situations cattle are obviously in excess.

But, in fact, India does not have enough cattle: it has a shortage of bullocks for draft, for pulling carts and plows. Frequently cows do not produce their first calf until four to six years old, as compared to two years in Europe and North America, and the calving interval may be as long as three years. Many calves die because people take the milk for themselves, and at any rate, cows often have too little milk to support an offspring. Cows simply do not get enough to eat to produce the needed number of calves. One solution would be to increase fodder supplies by eliminating the less efficient animals, yet fodder production itself cannot be raised when the available land is needed to grow crops for the fifteen million new people who crowd into India each year. It is no wonder that the cattle problem overwhelms Indians into inaction.

In spite of the many cattle in Mudumalai, the chital, or spotted deer, were common, probably because they can subsist on browse after all grass has been eaten. Some of the chital herds contained up to three hundred members, the most I had ever seen together. Unlike deer of northern climes, chital may rut and shed their antlers at any time of year, though with definite peaks. Driving along, I noted that about a quarter of the bucks had antlers in velvet, growing new antlers in preparation for the main rut in May and June; others still carried their old three-tined antlers, pale and smooth like weathered bone. Our chital watching was interrupted by a jeep that slid to a halt next to us. A dozen worried faces peered out and the driver told us breathlessly: "A pack of fifty wolves has killed a chital. Don't get out of the car." A few hundred yards along we found the "wolves." There were thirteen dhole, some taking last bites from their chital kill, others already drifting off through the trees. Their long-haired, brick-red coats and black tails contrasted strikingly with the sun-bleached surroundings. Several looked us over with shining eyes, then loped after the others. I had been absorbed by the unexpected beauty of the animals but now the scientist in me asserted itself. It was 3:30 P.M.; the kill was a doe, and the wear on her teeth showed that she was elderly; her last meal had consisted of grass, a few *Solanum* fruits, and some leaves.

By luck we met the dhole pack again the following morning. At 8:30 a boy leading a sheep down the road told us that he had heard a strange scream a short way back, and there we found four dhole in a clearing feeding on a yearling male chital. Seeing us on foot 150 feet away, the dhole trotted to the other side of a swale and lay down. I examined the chital, noting that the meat around his rump and thighs had been eaten. The dhole were restless, one calling repeatedly, a melodious resonant *oo-oo-oo*, remarkably like the contact call of the African hunting dog. Suddenly, nine other dhole bounded out of the forest and all milled around with wagging tails, exuberantly reunited. The pack trotted to within 120 feet of us, intent on reaching their kill, but one emitted a yip followed by a series of staccato grunts. All halted, and then in single file they disappeared into the forest.

With us that morning was Chief Forest Officer Thygarajan. The sight of dhole feeding on the chital was repugnant to him and now he declared vehemently: "We must shoot these dogs!" I pointed out to him that earlier he had suggested that Mudumalai contained too many chital, that they might have to be cropped. Why not let the dhole harvest the excess chital, for, after all, predators are the best wildlife managers? Many studies have shown that predators seldom if ever have a serious effect on large, healthy prey populations. I tried to seduce Thygarajan into seeing a new vision of life through my eyes, but without success. A deep-seated antipathy and fear of predators pervaded him, as they do so many people, and consequently even such harmless species as dhole are destroyed with irrational urgency. "It is most necessary to shoot wild dogs and so give sambar a better chance to increase," wrote a representative of an international conservation organization after visiting South India in the 1970s.

One day, when the clouds refused to budge from the cliffs and the chances of finding tahr were small, I headed inland toward some large sholas. Having no scientific goal, my pace was leisurely, and I noted a violet-like *Polygala* blooming in the grass and halted in a patch of white *Anaphalis* flowers to inhale their heavy fragrance. Somewhere below a gray jungle fowl crowed, stopping abruptly at the height of its call, as if he had forgotten his tune. Far ahead in the crown of a shola tree were three black creatures with gray caps —Nilgiri langur. When I approached they harshly called *ka-ka*, *kao-ka* before leaping off their perches to vanish with loud hoots in the dark canopy. Later that day a wild boar, also out for a stroll, wrinkled his long snout at me before bumbling off.

Ever since my year in Kanha Park I have had a special liking for sambar deer. Standing four or more feet high at the shoulder and weighing as much as seven hundred pounds, a sambar stag is an impressive creature, the largest deer in Southeast Asia. The massive antlers consist of a brow tine and a forked main beam. Both sexes have a coarse, dark-brown coat, except where rust-colored on the rump and inner sides of the legs, and the tail is black. Their unadorned functional look is relieved by an unkempt ruff of hair around the upper neck which gives them a comically scruffy appearance. Adept at hiding, they are generally difficult to observe. Instead of crashing noisily away in the manner of most deer, they either wait quietly, remaining invisible in the forest foliage, or they sneak off. However, in this secluded corner of the hills sambar had little fear of man. I counted twenty-five that day, singly and in small groups, feeding mostly along the edges of sholas. One group of four—an adult hind, a two-and-a-half-year-old stag, a yearling hind, and a young—watched me sit down 150 feet from them. Instead of retreating, they reclined and methodically chewed cud as if oblivious to my presence. Four generations of deer were in that group, and I suspected that they were one family, a mother with her offspring of the previous years. When I left, fifteen minutes later, the hind marked my departure with an alarm bark, a loud clear belling.

During the week in Bangitappal I tallied seventy-nine sambar, usually only a hind with her offspring and sometimes a stag or two. Although I saw no more than four together in this area, observers in other places have noted groups containing ten to fifteen individuals. I carefully scrutinized the lower neck of each sambar to see if it had what is commonly called a "sore spot," a raw area an inch or two in diameter which exudes a watery fluid. At Kanha this bloody spot was evident in November and December at the height of the rut. Here at Bangitappal the rut appeared to be only in its initial stages. Although most stags were in hard antler and some had dug muddy wallows, they still did not associate with the hinds; none had a sore spot. The function of this peculiar structure remains unknown, but it may be a seasonally active gland used to enhance the odor of courting sambar and perhaps it also marks vegetation as the animals walk through the forest. For the present it is one of many small mysteries that make fieldwork intriguing.

I recall one stag at Bangitappal trotting along a lavender slope on some private errand. With the hills behind him sloping up into a wall of cloud, he halted and sent his clarion call ringing through the wilderness. "They shall not hurt nor destroy in all my holy mountain," spake Isaiah the Prophet. Perhaps his vision will extend to this part of the Nilgiris, and the sambar and cloud goats and other creatures will remain safe in their peaceable kingdom.

South of the Nilgiris, across sixty miles of plains, rise the Anamalai and Palni hills and the High Range, a cluster of plateaus with deeply dissected valleys and massive peaks. D. Hamilton, one of the first visitors to the area in 1854, wrote that the area is "surpassingly grand, and incomparably beautiful." As my taxi wound into the High Range, flanked by crags and on more gentle ground by the velvety smooth expanses of tea estates, I agreed with his assessment. The High Range Game Preservation Association, whose members were primarily managers of tea estates, had protected tahr since 1895 on the Eravikulam Plateau. Too high and cold for growing tea or crops, this plateau was used as a private hunting reserve and now reputedly held the largest tahr population in existence. The man to see about visiting the plateau was Mr. J. C. Gouldsbury of the Vagavurrai Tea Estate.

After hearing that I wanted to census and observe tahr, he hospitably invited me to use his home as a base. Mr. Gouldsbury was one of the few British managers left here, and he felt that within a few years he and the others would also be retired, bringing to an end many lifetimes of commitment to the area. His father and grandfather had both been in tea here, starting in 1905. At the nearby hill station of Munnar is the Munnar Club, to which, like all such clubs I had seen, a generation or more of Indian independence had given the unloved look of an abandoned home. Dusty gaur, sambar, and tahr trophies stared from the walls; there were faded photographs of smiling men in tweeds holding trout, and tarnished silver cups commemorating forgotten sporting events. Ancient retainers served tea. The moist poignant mementos of faded hopes and dedication were hats—they covered a whole wall, dozens of them, felt hats and sun helmets, each placed there by its owner after completing thirty years of service as a tea planter in the district.

With my guides Rangasamy and Welaswamy in the lead, I ascended the steep trail to the Eravikulam Plateau. Both men were Muduwars, small, sinewy tribal people whose ancestors penetrated the highlands with their slash-and-burn agriculture sometime after the fourteenth century. They were also hunters; when Hamilton visited the hills in 1854 he found the wildlife much pursued, as he described in *Records of Sport in Southern India*. The tahr, or ibex as they are called locally,

> were extremely wild, which was accounted for from their having been lately harassed by hill men, the Moodowas, who had constructed across one of their runs, a barrier of stout bushes, forming a strong hedge, with weak places ten or twelve feet apart; across which a strong running noose was firmly secured. The ibex were then driven up to these barriers and were ruthlessly snared and shot.

The plateau consists of about thirty square miles of rolling, grassy hills with a few sholas tucked into the folds, and cliffs border it on three sides. After an hour's walk across the plateau we reached a hut nestled into a valley by a trout stream, and there we stayed for three weeks.

My first task was to census the tahr. Dividing the plateau into seven blocks, and accompanied by the Muduwars, I searched for tahr in one block each day, checking particularly the vicinity of each cliff. My seventh and last census included Anamudi Peak, at 8,841 feet the highest point in India south of the Himalaya. From its summit the whole green plateau stretched below me, and sitting on a boulder, I added up the number of tahr seen during my stay: 439. I had no doubt overlooked a few, and one herd vanished into the clouds before I could count it, so the total was about 500. My estimate for the Nilgiris was 300. Several other populations, all of them small, also survived in the Anamalai, Highwavy, Palni, Raja-palayam and other hills, for an estimated total world population of about 1,500. A few years later, after more surveys, Reggie placed the number at 2,000. Still, so tenuous is the existence of this species that one-fourth to one-third of all the Nilgiri tahr in existence were within my view from Anamudi Peak.

One morning, while searching for tahr, I spotted thirteen forms resembling Black Angus cattle resting on a slope. They were gaur, a type of wild cattle partial to forested highlands in southern and southeastern Asia. I had often seen gaur at Kanha, and now, as I watched these ponderous beasts, a sound from the past came to mind, a clear and resonant lowing, followed by another and another, each somewhat lower in pitch, like someone practicing musical scales. These calls had floated across the dark and silent meadows of a Kanha spring, the mating song of gaur. At that season the bulls roam from herd to herd in search of estrous cows. If two bulls meet, they try to intimidate each other to achieve dominance. Each displays to the other his striking profile—the six-foot shoulder height, shiny black coat and white stockings, swaying dewlap, and humped dorsal ridge. Slowly, stiff-legged, the two rivals circle each other, sometimes for as long as ten minutes, before one finally turns aside, accepting a subordinate position.

As if to heighten that day's nostalgic memories of Kanha, I also found the pugmarks of a tiger. It was a tigress judging by the size and shape of the tracks, and she had passed by the previous night. For four miles I followed, hoping for a glimpse of her striding across the green hills, seeking to see a tiger just once more. New impressions remain most clearly in the mind, and as I traced her tidy, round pugmarks I remembered my first meeting with a tiger.

One noon, not long after arriving at Kanha, a woodcutter came to our bungalow and told me that a tiger had killed a cow. He led me through the forest and along a streambed in which water remained only in shady pools until we reached the kill site. The cow was gone, a trail of rumpled leaves showing where the tiger had dragged the carcass up a ridge and into a clump of bamboo. As we followed the dragmark, a soft growl, like the purring of a distant motor, emanated from the thicket; a jungle crow cawed in a tree above. Heeding these ominous signals, I sent the guide home and sat down by the stream, waiting, listening, watching. There was the primal odor of leaf mold, faint yet insistent. A golden-backed woodpecker hammered, shattering the silence and somehow relieving the aura of tension that pervades the vicinity of a large predator. I waited through the hot stillness of the afternoon, and I still waited toward evening when the forest became resurgent with life, chattering flights of rose-ringed parakeets, whoops of gray langur. Finally, shortly after five o'clock, a tigress appeared and boldly strode to water. I remained motionless, wholly absorbed by this vision of her flaming, black-striped coat and barely contained power; her beauty was so great that my mind glowed while contemplating such evolutionary perfection. "Tyger, tyger burning bright / in the forest of the night." She crouched by a pool a hundred feet from me and lapped water, treating me with studied indifference. Once she fixed me with amber eyes and as a gentle warning bared her teeth. Then calmly she ambled back up the slope to her kill, and I hurried home through the dusk elated beyond measure.

For centuries man has viewed the tiger with fear, as the "embodiment of devilish cruelty, of hate and savagery incarnate," as one author put it. I had come to Kanha to remove some of the mystery that surrounds the habits of this nocturnal and solitary wanderer. Days sometimes passed without my meeting one of the elusive cats, but over the months I encountered the same individuals again and again, recognizing them by the distinctive stripe patterns on their faces, until slowly they revealed some of the secrets of their society. For instance, one day I found a tigress with four small cubs. She had killed a bull gaur, a remarkable feat considering she weighed about three hundred pounds and he two thousand. Five days the family camped in a ravine by the kill. During mornings the cubs sometimes played, stalking each other and wrestling and chasing, but during the heat of the day all rested, the tigress often cooling herself by reclining with her hindquarters submerged in a pool. As the forest grew dark the family resumed its meal, and I watched them from the branches of a nearby tree, fleeting shadows under a crescent moon. Early one morning, at 4:30, the tigress roared twice, and an answer came from far away. Since this tigress shared her range with three other residents, two tigresses and a male, and transients also wandered through the area, I wondered who the caller was. At 8:00 A.M. the male tiger suddenly appeared, a massive fellow with a short ruff of hair on his neck. From many previous encounters I knew that he claimed the whole center of the park as his own, although he shared it with several tigresses. Now he was visiting one of them, amicably checking on her and her cubs before resuming his solitary rounds. One night, at another kill, the same tigress and cubs, the male, and a second tigress, a total of seven, ate together, but by morning the group had split again. Similarly, two tigresses, each with cubs, fed together on a large kill several times.

From these and other observations, a new view of the tiger emerged. Far from being asocial, irascibly avoiding contact, tigers may meet, sometimes casually on a trail, at other times to share a kill. Solitary but not asocial, the tigers are part of a small community in which all resident members know each other and retain contact by roaring and leaving their scent on bushes and tree trunks. In India, where there are more tiger experts than tigers, my interpretation of the cat's society was coolly received, a few dismissing my observations and others accusing me of creating an abnormal situation, of luring in and concentrating tigers from far away by tying out an inordinate number of buffalo baits. In vain I pointed to my book *The Deer and the Tiger* which notes that only the same few resident tigers came to kills and that far from baiting profusely I used only sixteen small buffalo over a period of sixteen months, not enough to affect the habits of this tiger population. Then in 1973 and 1974 Charles McDougal, who has for years devoted himself to tigers in the Chitawan National Park of Nepal, also observed adults together at kills, with, for example, an adult male, a young male, and two tigresses sharing meat on occasion. His well-documented book, *The Face of the Tiger*, presents the best available account of the tiger's social life.

I also gained other insights into tiger behavior, learning, for instance, that a mother provides her cubs with experience in the art of killing. On one occasion, a tigress pulled down a buffalo without killing it, then stepped back while three of her four large cubs attempted to subdue it. But they were so inept that the buffalo shook them off. Once again the tigress felled the animal and with much effort the cubs finally managed to dispatch it. I learned also that although a tiger has a seemingly unbeatable array of weapons, such as acute senses and formidable claws and teeth, it must still work hard for its meals. Nearly three-fourths of the tiger's food consisted of deer—chital, sambar, swamp deer—animals that are difficult to catch. One morning a tigress hid in tall grass near some swamp deer, which, unaware of her dangerous presence, slowly drifted closer. When only forty feet separated deer and tiger, the lead hind gave a shrill bark and the herd wheeled and scattered. The tigress rushed from concealment, swiping the air with a forepaw in a futile attempt to hook an animal. She then strode off while the deer followed contemptuously some seventy feet behind her, knowing that deprived of the element of surprise the tiger could do them no harm. Since most hunts end in failure, the tigress with four cubs had great difficulties in securing enough food to satisfy her ever more ravenous brood, and when her cubs reached the age of one year she had to resort to desperate measures. Repeatedly she invaded the cattle enclosure at a nearby village and only the fact that the area is a national park prevented her from being shot. One night she clawed a hole into our bamboo shed and extracted a lamb that Kay and I were fattening for Christmas dinner. Unable to obtain enough food at home, the sole male cub in the litter went on hunts of his own; inexperienced but determined, he went to the village where he appropriated a pig, and another time he demolished our chicken house, eating all five occupants. When the cubs were one and a half years old, the social bond between mother and offspring had grown so tenuous that she visited them only on occasion, at times providing them with a kill, just enough to tide them over from partial to complete independence.

Scientific considerations aside, I was pleased to find that tigers are even-tempered, gentle beasts which assiduously avoid any confrontation with a person on foot, an exception, of course, being the rare man-eater. The tiger's reputation for savagery is mainly a myth perpetuated by hunters. Shot, poisoned, and its habitat destroyed, probably no more than two thousand tigers survive in all of India today. "My total bag of Tigers is 1150 (one thousand one hundred and fifty only)," wrote the Maharaja of Surguja to me in 1965. One afternoon I found a kill in a ravine where the tiger had covered the remains with grass to protect it from vultures and then departed. I waited nearby, sitting with my back against a large boulder. When hours later I heard a leaf rustle behind me, I slowly raised myself and peering over the rock looked straight into the eyes of a tigress who calmly surveyed me from a distance of ten feet. Casually, she turned and walked away, forgiving my intrusion.

Belatedly, India has become aware that the tiger is more than just one more vanishing forest creature, that it is, in fact, a symbol of her intention to make future generations inheritors, not just survivors. It is admittedly difficult for man and tiger to coexist: a villager cannot condone a tiger killing his precious livestock unless he receives compensation for his loss. To provide the tiger with space and protection, India has established nine tiger reserves, including an enlarged Kanha Park, in collaboration with World Wildlife Fund.

One day in the Ootacamund cemetery I found a weathered tombstone with the inscription:

CAPTAIN THE HONOURABLE
HENRY HANDCOCK

KILLED BY A TIGER
16TH DECEMBER 1858

In the context of today's perspective, the inscription evoked in me not only thoughts of tragedy but also served as a reminder that tigers were once numerous in the hills of South India.

I did not meet the tigress in the High Range that day, nor on subsequent ones, but her pugmarks were there and the feeling that somewhere in the shadows of a shola a tiger might be watching added new dimensions to each journey.

A large canyon bisects the Eravikulam Plateau. Although the cliffs and hilltops are frequently in cloud, as in the Nilgiris, the canyon sometimes remains clear except for tendrils of fog along the precipices. Many tahr lived along the canyon, where I often observed them. One morning, through a thinning mist, I saw a herd at the canyon's edge. Hurriedly I sought concealment in a tiny, weedy hollow. Moments later, the clouds lifted, and I found the hillside around me alive with feeding tahr. There were 104, only three of them saddlebacks. Now, in early November, most adult males had separated from the females and either roamed alone or congregated in one corner of the plateau. As I scribbled notes I tried to ignore crawly sensations on various parts of my body. Then I saw a leech humping up my pantleg, stopping occasionally to wave its small terminal sucker back and forth like radar scanning the sky. Looking farther, I discovered leeches on my legs, groin, back, neck; my socks were spongy with blood and my underpants had turned from white to scarlet. This grassy nook was filled with ravenous land leeches all hurrying to partake of an unexpected bounty. I devoted the next five hours to alternately plucking leeches off my body, flicking attacking ones out of the hollow, and taking notes on tahr, a combination of vigorous yet necessarily restrained exercise amid the unsuspecting herd.

I hoped that the aggressive interactions of tahr would help clarify the evolutionary position of this genus. Usually two animals sparred with horns, either facing each other or standing side by side. Since such clashing is typical of most horned animals it was of only passing interest. But once a male reared bolt upright in front of another as if to clash with him. A previous visitor had described how "two animals almost simultaneously reared up on their hindlegs and seemed to 'dance' in front of each other, while keeping their distance and circling. Suddenly they would close in and bring their heads together with a resounding crack" in the style of fighting so typical of true goats such as markhor and wild goat. On several occasions I saw head-to-tail combat with two animals standing in a reverse parallel position and pushing with the shoulders as they circled and hooked their horns into each other's side, flank, and belly. This was a particularly exciting observation, for although goat-antelopes may fight in this manner, to my knowledge true goats do not. In yet another aggressive stance, a tahr hunches its back and arches its neck so far down that its nose almost touches the ground. Males, and on occasion also females, use this display to intimidate an opponent. Mountain goats have an almost identical posture. Tahr seem to have straddled an evolutionary fence in that they not only retain several kinds of behavior which point to their goat-antelope past, but also display fighting styles, such as the upright stance before clashing, which are typical of true goats. I concluded that tahr appear to be behavioral as well as physical links between the goat-antelopes and true goats, but the idea needed confirmation with a study of other tahr species.

Over ten years have passed since I censused tahr in the Nilgiris and High Range. Reggie Davidar is still there, keeping a possessive eye on the tahr cliffs. In 1975 he censused tahr in the Nilgiris and found 334, as compared to 292 in 1963. And the High Range Game Preservation Association still maintains its interest in Eravikulam Plateau even though the government has turned that area into a state reserve. For the present the tahr's future looks secure.

Kang Chu

Up the canyon wall we labored, following the threadlike trail along precipices and through thickets of bamboo and rhododendron until after three hours the slope leveled. Sherpa Phu-Tsering wearily dropped his heavy pack in a clearing among patches of snow, and the two Tamang porters and I did so too. Over 1,500 feet below, too far to hear its roar, the Bhote Kosi River rushed through the gorge whose walls crowded around us. In Nepal the name "Bhote" or "Bhota" is added to a river's name to indicate that it arises in Tibet. I looked northward; ahead the canyon branched, and beyond, through a chasm of rock, I could see snow peaks repeating themselves to the horizon. Somewhere just past this chaotic maze of ridges and gorges should be the Tibetan border. The Himalaya was upthrust after the

Tibetan Plateau. Existing rivers such as the Bhote Kosi, being older than the Himalaya, tried somehow to retain their channels during the uplift, and in the process carved the gigantic canyons that now slice through these mountains. A map told us that we were at Hum, the site as boldly marked as if it were a thriving village, but there was nothing here except for two tiny fields clinging to the hillside. However, we had been told that farther on there was a village called Lamnang, along the Kang Chu, a western fork of the Bhote Kosi. It was mid-February, too cold to tarry long, and we soon shouldered our loads and continued, down again into the canyon and across a torrent on three swaying logs.

In the Kang Chu gorge it was gloomy, the sheer bulk of its cliffs oppressive. Passing first through a jungle of bamboo, alder, and other shrubs, we were soon among stands of gnarled *Buxus* trees whose moss-encumbered branches screened out the sky to suffuse us with an eerie green glow. The darkly silent trees and dusky boulders gave the forest an aura of desolation that seemed to threaten travelers, and we hurried on. Finally, two and a half hours after crossing the river, the forest retreated. Here was a field, a pasture where several yak grazed, and barely visible on a knoll upvalley, a stone hut. Lamnang was just ahead. According to a Tibetan saying, monasteries should be neither too close nor too far from a village, and the same applies to campsites. The pasture seemed a perfect place to pitch our tents; we were at 8,500 feet and from here could range up or down the valley in search of wildlife. As my pack slipped to the ground, I was relieving myself of a mental as well as physical burden: we had finally arrived.

In the early 1970s the large mountain mammals of Nepal were still unstudied and because of the unique political history of the country even their precise status and distribution remained largely unknown. In 1766 the Gurkhas, a small tribe in the hilly midlands of Nepal, began a campaign of conquest. At the peak of their power they held all of what is now Nepal, as well as Sikkim and parts of Tibet and northern India. This brought the Gurkhas into conflict with the British, and after a series of inconclusive battles, the treaty of

1816 defined the present borders of Nepal. In 1820 a Mr. Brian Hodgson was appointed assistant to the resident. His diplomatic coups, if any, have long since been forgotten, but his name lives on as a naturalist. Not permitted to leave Kathmandu Valley, he sent native collectors into the hills, and among a number of new species brought back by them are some which now bear Hodgson's name—including a redstart, a tree pipit, and a hawk cuckoo. In 1833 Hodgson first described the peculiar blue sheep, a species whose behavior I was to study a hundred and forty years later. Not content with describing new animals, Hodgson also did basic ecological work, being the first to divide the Himalaya into three altitudinal zones, each with distinct faunal elements. He left Nepal in 1843. Three years later, Jung Bahadur Rana took over the government, establishing a line of ruling hereditary prime ministers with the king a mere figurehead. Rana rule lasted until King Tribhuvan assumed control after a revolution in 1951. During the century of Rana power, Nepal remained essentially closed to outsiders, and the first road linking Kathmandu to India was not completed until 1956.

The wildlife of the terai, the forested lowlands bordering India, was known because the ruler sometimes invited important visitors to Nepal to participate in massive hunts there for tiger, great Indian rhinoceros, and water buffalo. For example, King George V and his party once shot 39 tigers in eleven days during the winter of 1911–12, and between 1933 and 1940 the rulers and their guests shot 433 tigers and 53 rhinoceros. (The total tiger population in Nepal is now estimated to number no more than 150.) However, the literature was almost silent about mammals of the high altitudes. I wanted to study Himalayan tahr and blue sheep, and to delineate the distribution of large mammals. For advice about research possibilities, I wrote to John Blower, at that time a United Nations wildlife adviser to the Nepalese government. I first knew John in 1959 when he was with the Uganda Game Department in East Africa. Now he was concerned with establishing national parks in Nepal, and with typical initiative roamed over much of the high country in search of possible reserves. Along the upper Bhote Kosi he had seen tahr and been told of blue sheep. The area might suit my study purposes, he wrote, and a wildlife survey was also needed there.

I arrived in Kathmandu on January 24, 1972. Through Mountain Travel, a local expedition outfitter, I obtained tents and other camping equipment, and hired three Sherpas to interpret, guide, and cook. Nepal sensibly requires every trekker to obtain a permit for the area he or she wants to visit. The Kang Chu—*chu* meaning water in Tibetan—drains a finger of land that projects into Tibet; in fact, the valley was part of Tibet until in 1961 it was ceded to Nepal in exchange for other land. One ministry said that the Kang Chu was open to foreigners, another that it was closed. For a week I trotted back and forth between the Home Ministry, Foreign Ministry, Immigration Department, Forest Department, and Remote Areas Development Board in search of a permit. Then, King Mahendra died suddenly and all offices closed in mourning for five days. Finally I received the necessary permit, and on February 9 flew in a rented Pilatus Porter to Jiri, a small airstrip among the hills. There we hired a dozen porters to carry our flour, sugar, rice, and other food, enough for two months, as well as our equipment.

For four days we walked northward, mostly along the contours of hills bordering the Bhote Kosi. Chaletlike houses dotted the slopes and terraced fields rippled down from the crests. It was a scene of bucolic splendor, if one overlooked the ecological problems those hillsides implied. Although Nepal's midlands were once covered with forests, over half of the land has been cleared in the past twenty-five years to provide more space to grow food and to produce lumber as a "significant contribution to the national economy," in the words of a United States AID program which encouraged such stripping. With monsoon rains heavy, much topsoil is carried off by flood waters. In some areas, productivity of the fields has waned so much that a third of the land has been abandoned. The biggest export of Nepal is soil, some sixty billion tons being carried by its rivers down into India each year. The philosopher Santayana once noted that "those who cannot learn from the past are doomed to repeat it"; unfortunately, even those who are aware of the past repeat it. Once man has destroyed what the mountains have offered, the forest and the soil, there is no reprieve. I wanted to hurry through the midlands; so many people darken my spirit. Ahead, cutting the horizon was the 23,000-foot peak of Gauri Sankar, its summit deeply notched as if bitten by a disgruntled giant, and there lay the Great Himalaya I strove to visit.

Finally, at an altitude of 8,000 feet, we reached Lambagar, a Sherpa village scattered among the rubble of an ancient rock slide. The Hindu tribes of the lowlands were behind us and we were now in Buddhist Nepal; we had crossed a cultural barrier into another human world, into a caste-free society whose spiritual ties lie to the north and east in Tibet. Indeed, the word *Shar-pa* means People from the East. Although constituting only a small tribe mainly in the Solo-Khumbu region, which also includes Mount Everest, Sherpas have achieved world fame not just as mountaineers but also as self-confident, amiable, and loyal people.

The next day, only two hours north of Lambagar, where the Bhote Kosi narrows to a gorge, all except two porters laid down their loads and quit. The trail ahead was too difficult and dangerous, they said, and not even more money would induce them to continue. However, the Sherpas told me the actual reason for the defection: the Nepalese New Year was in two days and the porters did not want to miss the festivities. I sent Kancha, the head Sherpa, back to Lambagar to find porters, told our cook, Mingma, to guard the equipment, and taking the others with me, left for the Kang Chu to find a suitable campsite.

The following morning after we had established base camp, Phu-Tsering and I climbed up a trail to the village. The houses were new, built solidly of gray stone and roofed with wooden slats; rocks weighed down the shingles, protecting them from storms, and firewood was piled high against walls. Stone corrals held goats, sheep, cows, and shaggy cow-yak hybrids. Black mastiffs lunged on their chains as we passed. The place resembled a Swiss hamlet except that over each house towered a slim pole from which fluttered prayer flags, or wind pictures as the Tibetans call them. The printed religious texts on prayer flags are intended as talismans, invoking good luck from the mountain deities. An elderly man leaned against a corral gate, a disheveled, wrinkled fellow, his hair twisted untidily into a braid and his body wrapped in a sheepskin coat; he wore high cloth boots resembling Eskimo mukluks. Obviously curious, he invited us into his home where we sat cross-legged on rugs by an open hearth, a pale shaft of light from a tiny, paneless window barely squeezing into the gloom. Leather saddlebags, for use on yaks, lined the walls, as did bedrolls which would be laid by the fire at night. Our host's wife wore a black sacklike dress, a *chuba*, held together by a striped apron. She busied herself in the dark recesses of the hut and finally emerged with a porcelain cup, black with sooty grease. A grimy rag failed to clean it, as did her thumb, which was even dirtier than the rag; at last she spit into the cup, and vigorously smearing the sputum around with her index finger, washed it to her satisfaction. First filling it with *chang,* a sour yellowish beer made of barley, she next placed a small wad of rancid butter on the rim, then handed it to me. I drank. Retrieving the cup, she deftly wiped off the butter and rubbed it into her hair to deter lice.

Several villagers joined us and children crowded into the doorway. Tibetans do not wash unnecessarily, and the children in particular are filthy, their necks and hands crusted with dirt, their faces inflamed and scabby from constantly seeping noses and raw elements. Because the Sherpa language resembles Tibetan, Phu-Tsering could communicate quite well with the villagers. We learned that Lamnang consists of twenty-seven households with about six hundred head of livestock; once all lived in Tibet, but seven years ago they moved here to escape the compulsory road labor of the Chinese. Lamnang is their winter village, summer quarters being located at Lapche on the Tibetan border, a walk of several hours up the Kang Chu. Like many mountain people, each family here has at least two homes at different altitudes, for with fertile land scarce, they must practice seasonally alternating cultivation. The villagers were not very informative about wildlife. Yes, there were a few tahr around; yes, there were blue sheep at Lapche; no, they could not help us find animals. They seemed reticent, held back by an obscure suspiciousness of our persistent questioning. Our attempts to explain the purpose of our visit were probably unsuccessful. Being Tibetans, Bhotiyas, nature to them is not an object of man's investigation; man is one with nature in Buddhist religion, not a privileged being who examines and analyzes everything. My omnivorous probing for fact was alien to them.

A subtle personal incident the following day illustrated this difference in attitude between the Occidental and Eastern minds, although at the time I did not consciously think of my actions. I had surmounted the cliff behind camp to explore the conifer forest there. It was lovely among the straight-stemmed firs and hemlocks, and the understory of gnarled rhododendrons with their reddish bark added a unique distinction to the scene. This east-facing slope, deprived of the sun, was still in winter's grip with snow two feet deep and the rhododendron leaves curled tightly against the cold. As I descended, there suddenly came to me the scent of spring, insistent as if I had strayed into a bed of hyacinths. Nearby, in an opening, a sapling reached above the snow, a *Daphne*, its leafless twigs full of purplish-white blossoms. While admiring its solitary defiance of winter, I also wondered what selective advantage the flowers derived by blooming this early, when temperatures still dropped to 20°. I plucked a petal, crushing it between my fingers to see if this would accentuate its aroma.

A scientist recently expressed a creed when he wrote: "And it is deep in our own natures to seek enlightenment about the world and our place in it, and to be exhilarated by its magnificent and challenging answers." But this sentiment expresses mainly a Western attitude toward nature. Daisetsu Suzuki in his book *Mysticism, Christian and Buddhist* gives an illuminating example of a different world view when he quotes Alfred Tennyson's "Flower in the Crannied Wall":

Flower in the crannied wall,
I pluck you out of the crannies;—
Hold you here, root and all, in my hand,
Little flower—but if I could understand
What you are, root and all, and all in all,
I should know what God and man is.

Then, by way of contrast, he cites a Haiku by the eighteenth-century poet Bashō:

When closely inspected,
One notices a nazuna in bloom
Under the hedge.

Suzuki then writes:

When Tennyson noticed the flower in a crannied wall he "plucked" it and held it in his hand and went on reflecting about it, pursuing his abstract thought about God and man, about the totality of things and the unfathomability of life. This is characteristic of Western man. His mind works analytically. The direction of his thinking is toward the externality or objectivity of things. . . . If he were scientifically minded he would surely bring it to the laboratory, dissect it, and look at it under the microscope. . . . When the scientist finishes his examination, experimentation, and observation, he will indulge in all forms of abstract thinking; evolution, heredity, genetics, cosmogeny.

Compare all this with Bashō and we see how differently the Oriental poet handles his experience. Above all, he does not "pluck" the flower, he does not mutilate it, he leaves it where he has found it. He does not detach it from the totality of its surroundings. . . . Bashō simply refers first to his "close inspection" which is not necessarily aroused by a purposeful direction of his intention to find something among the bushes; he simply looks casually around and is greeted unexpectedly by the modestly blooming plant which ordinarily escapes one's detection. He bends down and "closely" inspects it to

be assured that it is a nazuna. He is deeply touched by its unadorned simplicity, yet partaking in the glory of its unknown source.
He does not say a word about his inner feeling. . . . He makes no
allusions whatever to "God and man," nor does he express his desire
to understand.

I doubt if I could adapt wholly to the Eastern point of view: the
quest for knowledge is too much a part of me, and besides I enjoy my
studies. Perhaps being an ecologist is the best compromise, for one
attempts to understand nature as unity, as the harmony of living
things.

We had various difficulties during our first week in Kang Chu. One
problem was that we could not find tahr, and I was not even certain
of where to search. The literature contained conflicting opinions about
the habitat preferences of this species, although all agreed that the
animal "revels in the steepest precipices," to quote one source. Some
accounts claimed that tahr remain in dense forests, and one was
emphatic that they live in the subalpine zone above 12,500 feet. There
was no sign of tahr in the snowbound forests on the east-facing slopes
near Lamnang, but on those facing west winter had already begun its
rapid retreat. For three days I clambered there alone among the
crags, carrying tent and food with me so as not to be bound to my
valley camp. The search for tahr took me from bamboo and rhododendron thickets upward into the zone of stunted junipers, and finally
onto alpine meadows, where, above 13,500 feet, the snow was still deep
in many places. There I found only a few old tahr droppings. The
beauty of the scene was some consolation, the wisps of cloud wandering along the crestlines, and in the solitude of night, the slopes gleaming silver in starlight. I delighted in the birds: once a golden eagle
made a futile stoop at a covey of blood pheasants, its pinions clatter-
ing against a shrub beneath which the frantically screeching birds
sought shelter; monal pheasant cocks sailed from cliff to cliff against
a backdrop of low-flying clouds, their iridescent blue and green

Monal

feathers shining in the alpine light as they gave ploverlike calls; flocks of starling-sized grandala wheeled over the snow fields. But no tahr. We were told that itinerant Hindu hunters scoured the hills in summer. Had they shot them all?

The villagers were a second problem. Both adults and children liked to visit our camp to chat and scavenge for empty cans, or anything unguarded and portable. An early explorer found Tibetans "scrupulously honest," but this reputation has not penetrated to Lamnang where the people pilfer with marvelous deftness. Soap, matches, towels, plates, anything and everything vanished into the depths of their gownlike *chubas*. One night, when I was away in the hills and the sherpas slept soundly, someone slit open the back of our cook tent and stole an armload of food. Two sherpas were needed to guard camp at all times. In fact, after a month we established a new base near Lambagar, not only to be near tahr herds but also to escape the facile fingers of these Tibetans.

Finally, after a week of searching, I spotted two dark forms travers-.

ing a cliff face high above the valley near the confluence of the Kang Chu and Bhote Kosi. Two tahr males cropped mouthfuls of dead grass and leaves of evergreen oak. Dark brown and shaggy, like bears, male Himalayan tahr are powerful, robust creatures weighing perhaps two hundred pounds. Their most conspicuous feature, one that easily distinguishes them from their relatives the Nilgiri tahr, is the coppery brown ruff and mantle of flowing hair that drapes from their necks, shoulders, and chests down to their knees, and from their backs and rumps to their flanks and thighs.

Following this first encounter, I continued my daily search for more tahr, at first with little success until I climbed up to Hum from where I had a sweeping view of the cliffs on the western bank of the Bhote Kosi. There, on precipices which no hunter could reach, several tahr herds had found refuge. Yet I almost overlooked these animals. As I later discovered, tahr do not like cold mornings; when night temperatures hover around the freezing point, they seek shelter in thickets, and not until sunlight has descended the cliffs, usually after 8:30 A.M., do they venture into the open to feed. No wonder my dawn searches had been futile.

Opposite Hum was a cliff, a huge pyramid-shaped rock face about a mile long at the base and 3,000 feet high, on which lived at least forty-five tahr, including twenty-two females, ten young, and thirteen males. They were divided into two distinct herds, separated by a vertical strip of forest. Each herd member seemed to remain on its own half of the cliff. Males were exceptions to this in that they wandered off in small groups as well as alone. With my scope steadied on a tripod, I watched the animals from across the gorge; sometimes only two or three were in sight, at other times a large herd. Well aware of my feeble facility on cliffs, I could only marvel at the virtuosity with which tahr traversed rock faces. They balanced readily along ledges only a few inches wide, and at times would leap with precision onto small tussocks growing on a sheer cliff a few feet below. Tahr are well adapted to such rocky realms. Their hoof pads are soft and surrounded by a horny rim, providing good traction. When confronted with a sloping cliff, a tahr may rock back and forth, then suddenly propel itself upward with a series of leaps, using its broad, furry chest pad and the callus on each knee instead of hooves to fleetingly grip the surface. These animals also have one other advantage over man —they lack fear. Since fear is a subjective sensation, an anticipation of future feelings based on past events, tahr can walk a tightrope between earth and sky without imagining the consequences of a misstep. And the rare beast that has survived a major mishap has no direct means of communicating the terrors of its experience.

The herds were placid assemblages at this season, somewhat dull to watch as they were mainly concerned with feeding, replenishing their bodies after the long winter and the rigors of an early-winter rut. However, one female came into heat late. In some ways the courtship was quite different from that of other goats, and I was fortunate to witness it.

On March 25, shortly after 8 A.M., a large male hovered near the female, while somewhat farther back, were two smaller males. When one of the latter approached, the big male arched his back, lowered his neck, and with legs bunched stiffly beneath him, advanced threateningly toward his rival. Seeing this bristling apparition, the aspiring swain retreated. The dominant animal then faced the female, his neck lowered and muzzle straining ahead. Slowly he raised his muzzle until it pointed almost straight up, displaying his white chin, while, by retracting his neck, he transformed his shoulders into a hump and his ruff into a disheveled haystack. Though only half his size and lacking a ruff, she ignored the impressive display. An hour later he tried again, this time with lips curled back, creating a striking contrast between his white teeth and black face. For fifteen minutes they stood there, he with muzzle raised, she with head averted in submission. Then they rested side by side for two hours. Once more the male displayed, this time more urgently, now shaking his head rapidly from side to side and at the same time nodding it vigorously. His tongue flicked in and out, and he raised a foreleg limply as if to kick. Again and again he shook himself and, tipping up his muzzle as before, raised it ever higher as his passion increased. If her attention wandered, he nudged her with his nose, and when she looked at him, he intensified the display. Finally, at noon, after his antics had habituated her to his close presence, he casually stepped behind her and mounted, leaning against her so gently that she did not respond at all. The young males waited nearby all morning for an opportunity that never came.

The raised muzzle while facing a female and the violent head-shaking were courtship displays seemingly unique to Himalayan tahr, though it is possible that studies on other tahr species will reveal similar behavior. As noted earlier, a true goat male may mouth his penis and spray urine over his face, chest, and forelegs, as if to enhance his presence with the potent odor. I wondered if tahr behaved similarly, but during my weeks in the Kang Chu I never saw such behavior. However, the question was resolved two years later when I visited New Zealand. Himalayan tahr were introduced into the mountains of that country in 1904 and thrived so well that probably more occur there now than in the Himalaya. In New Zealand I observed not only penis-mouthing during the rut, but also examined carcasses of tahr that had been shot commercially for meat—a total of 19,000 animals were harvested in 1973 and 1974—and found that adult males, four and a half years old and older, had soft belly hairs heavily soaked with urine. Himalayan tahr thus resemble true goats in their courtship displays and have also evolved idiosyncrasies of their own.*

Earlier, in the chapter on Nilgiri tahr, I mentioned that tahr appear to be evolutionary links between goat-antelopes and true goats, both in physical characteristics and aggressive displays. For instance, the Nilgiri tahr has a head-down display during which it hunches its back, and two combatants may stand head to tail as they jab each

* In May–June, 1978, Clifford Rice observed that courting Nilgiri tahr males twist heads and kick when displaying to females and that they mouth penises and soak themselves with urine, resembling in these respects the Himalayan tahr.

other in the belly with their short horns. Both of these aggressive patterns are primitive in that they are generally found in those hoofed animals that lack such striking display structures as large horns. The mountain goat, a goat-antelope, uses both of these displays according to Valerius Geist and, as I was interested to learn, the Himalayan tahr does also. In addition, Himalayan tahr may also use another display when vying for dominance: two males stand broadside, sometimes for several minutes, showing off their ruffs, until one defers to the other. Once, for example, two young males stood side by side, the smaller of the two on a ledge just above the other. The smaller refused to budge. Suddenly the larger jerked up his head and stared at his opponent who promptly turned his muzzle aside. Among tahr, as among people, an unwavering stare is a threat. Subtlety having no effect, the larger male then leaped onto the same ledge as his opponent. Finally, the smaller male responded, first by taking a few bites of grass to show his lack of aggressive intent, and then fleeing uphill.

My days in the field were long, five hours of hiking to and from the tahr cliffs plus indeterminable hours of chilly waiting for tahr to appear or do something besides eat and sleep. However, during these silent travels over forest trails, I occasionally met some rare and elusive creature. Once a rust-gold Temmincks cat bolted into a bamboo thicket. Another time a goral—a plain grayish animal belonging to the goat-antelopes—stood by a rocky niche snorting in alarm as it peered intently into the shrubbery below. I had seen this goral in the area before and wondered why it was now so excited. Suddenly it fled. Thirty feet away a leopard rose and vanished smoothly into the undergrowth, its hunt a failure. Although serow, the other species of goat-antelope inhabiting these canyons, seldom leave the dusky ravines in which they spend their solitary lives, I occasionally saw one crossing a grassy slope. The serow is a large ungainly creature with black pelage, white lower legs, and a stiff mane, resembling, according to one author, a cross between "a cow, donkey, pig, and goat."

In the early afternoon a group of Assamese macaques sometimes descended to the river to drink. One group near camp contained twenty-four members: a husky male who revealed his high status by his swagger, three young males, seven females (none of whom carried infants), five large youngsters now almost two years old, and seven youngsters born the previous year. And tagging behind the group, careful to keep his distance, was a scruffy, dejected male, who, though an outcast, strove to retain contact with the community of which he had probably once been a part.

But birds, not mammals, provided the greatest delight. At first there were only a few resident species or early arrivals—Simla black tit, white-winged grosbeak, Nepal rosefinch, yellow-billed blue magpie, large hawk cuckoo, Himalayan tree creeper—and I did no more than record them casually. Then, in late February, when night temperatures climbed above the freezing point and daytime ones rose to 60° F. or more, spring suddenly invaded the Bhote Kosi, and with it came so many birds that I could only take note of the most dazzling species. Long-tailed minivet, black-capped sibia, beautiful niltava, Nepal sunbird . . . the ones I could identify were far exceeded by those that passed by unnamed; *Birds of Nepal*, an excellent field guide by the Flemings, had not yet been published. On March 4, the first rhododendron bloomed, a scarlet cluster of blossoms leaning over the abyss of a gorge, and soon many other plants joined the birds in adding brilliance to the slopes. Perhaps most memorable was a blustery morning when winds whipped in great rhythmic gusts up the canyon. Yet near the mouth of the Kang Chu it was quiet, the bend of the valley apparently deflecting the blasts to create a vacuum into which thousands upon thousands of white butterflies funneled; for hours they whirled about, drawn ever upward from the depths, until they vanished into the sky, a living snowstorm defying the laws of gravity.

Sometimes I took Phu-Tsering with me. Like all Sherpas he was small and sturdy with straight black hair and light coppery skin. I liked his broad, kind face, his gold-toothed laughter. After a hard search for animals he would report back to me: "Jharal, sah," using the local name for tahr, and point delightedly in their direction. He would wait for hours as I watched tahr, neither asking why I did so nor showing any interest in what I recorded in my notebooks, yet there was a feeling of companionship. As he was in his late twenties, he had already been on several major climbing expeditions. However, like many Sherpas, he found trekking much easier and less dangerous. Because high-altitude climbing has involved such frequent mishaps, some Sherpa wives have forbidden their husbands to accompany expeditions, many of which misuse Sherpas by exposing them to climbing situations for which they lack proficiency. Sherpas generally climb for money, not enjoyment, and a small tribe cannot afford to lose so many of its best young men to the mountains: that April, ten Sherpas died with a South Korean expedition to Mount Manaslu, the previous year five had died on another expedition, the year before that, six on Mount Everest, and so on, each year taking a frightful toll. Let foreign climbers carry their own loads to the high camps. Why decimate a valuable tribe to satisfy someone's hobby?

At camp Phu-Tsering was in charge of cooking, with Mingma to help him. His speciality was stew, and he frequently went to Lamnang to trade for potatoes, meat, and other ingredients. One afternoon I arrived home earlier than usual and noted an army of maggots emigrating from the cook tent. Searching for their source, I found the greenish shoulder of a yak. "Some bad," said Phu-Tsering with a disarming smile. "Much bad," I replied. Now I could place the unique tang of some of his stews.

The villagers invited us to a wedding. I went with Kancha, who of the three Sherpas spoke the best English, leaving the others to guard camp until our return. Having arrived somewhat early, we visited the small monastery which housed five monks, all of them *trapas* or students, none with the superior rank of lama. It was gloomy in the squat stone building and suffused with the fragrance of incense. We entered a small room and sat on the floor against a wall, opposite two golden Buddhas gleaming in the light of several butter lamps. A shaft of sun fell through a hole in the roof on two *trapas* wrapped in wine-red *chubas* sitting cross-legged behind a wooden chest. Hunched over, each read aloud from the loose pages of a religious book; at intervals one interrupted his recitation to beat a drum with a curved stick while the other clashed cymbals. Orthodox Buddhism forbids religious rites; spiritual enlightenment can only come through personal effort. However, monks can help heal the sick, avert calamities, conquer malevolent beings, and guide spirits of the dead through the other world. In the subdued light and heavy air the smooth monotone of the reciting *trapas* flowed without emphasis, punctuated by the booming of drum and cymbals; it gave the room a disquieting atmosphere, and I could well imagine that occult forces were here manipulated. On leaving I placed an offering of ten rupees at Buddha's feet. Outside I breathed deeply, drawing in the freshness of the mountains.

Below us, along a stone-walled corral, we saw members of the marriage party converging on a house. From one side came five men, walking slowly, one carrying a large bowl of *chang* and a second one clashing cymbals. From the other side approached a chanting line of men and women, relatives of the bridal pair. The man first in line carried a yak-tail whisk. It was a gaily dressed crowd; men and women wore short-sleeved wool *chubas*, red or black and made on their own looms. The rather somber color of the *chubas* was brightened by blouses with billowing sleeves of white or purple. Both men and women wore necklaces of orange coraline stones and silver pendants inlaid with turquoise. Turquoise is greatly favored by Tibetans as having special virtues, bringing good luck and protection against demons. On their heads the villagers wore embroidered fezlike caps trimmed with red panda and marten fur. Married women had aprons, blue, red, yellow, and green in color, a short one in front and a longer one behind, as is typical in Tibetan dress. The two parties met at a gate, where the man with the yak-tail whisk dipped the tip of it into the *chang* bowl, then flicked his wrist outward, spraying droplets over the ground. He then drank *chang* and placed a thin white scarf of welcome around the neck of the bowl bearer. Called *katas*, such scarves are customarily given to honor a guest or distinguished person. A second man followed the same ritual; then others drank, one at a time, each first immersing his or her little finger instead of a yak tail, and still chanting, all entered the house.

It was crowded inside and noisy with everyone milling around drinking *chang*. Six feet tall, I towered over most Tibetans, and in this low-ceilinged room the aroma of unwashed bodies, sour *chang*, and rancid-butter coiffures rose upward until I was almost overpowered. The bride and groom were upstairs, they and the guests sitting behind long, low tables, chanting. One at a time each guest rose, bowed over a wooden bowl of *chang*, then sipped some through a tube, whereupon cymbals clanged and the host placed a ceremonial *kata* around the guest's neck. Kancha presented the bridal couple with a large can of biscuits and some toilet soap. Several women then began to harangue Kancha in a demanding manner, and puzzled, I asked why. Sherpas are so polite that they avoid saying anything unpleasant. Kancha hesitated and finally mumbled: "All women want presents. It is not the custom." We withdrew and returned to camp to relieve Phu-Tsering and Mingma, both dedicated *chang* drinkers. I wanted to pack; tomorrow Kancha and I would make a four-day trip to the Tibetan border to look for blue sheep.

With a local man as porter and guide, Kancha and I headed north along a trail that followed the slope above the river. Soon after Lamnang we entered a dense fir forest still deep in snow, but then the trees thinned and the valley widened. An avalanche had swept across the trail, carrying with it an Assamese macaque; I could see its stiff body among the river boulders below. Junipers now grew among the firs, and, as the hills retreated still more, our path went across valley flats, past snowbound huts abandoned for the winter, and into a birch forest draped with pale green lichens. Although our goal, Lapche monastery, was no more than eight miles from Lamnang as the jungle crow flies, our progress in the soft snow was terribly slow and tiring. Several times we came upon musk deer tracks. With its broad hooves this thirty-pound creature can almost skim over the snow surface, whereas I struggled along knee-deep and continually

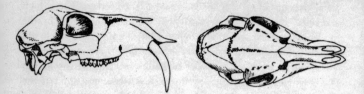

slipped on hidden boulders and logs. Somewhat later, I spotted one of these gray-brown deer skulking from one birch thicket to the next. I never saw another.

With hindlegs longer than its forelegs and with tusklike upper canines rather than antlers, the musk deer would merely be a zoo-logical oddity were it not for the fact that each male has a musk gland beneath the skin of his belly, the musk probably being used to scent-mark the boundaries of his territory. Unfortunately man has also found uses for these secretions, mainly in perfumes and patent medi-cines. Musk is sold locally by the *tola*, one *tola* equaling about 0.4 ounces, and each gland containing three to four *tolas*. In 1972 a hunter received 400 rupees, or about $40 per *tola*, and by the time various middlemen had made their profits, a *tola* in Kathmandu was worth 1,200 rupees, or $360 to $480 per musk gland: an ounce of musk was several times more valuable than an ounce of gold. No wonder musk deer are relentlessly persecuted. In a recent year the Japanese imported 11,000 pounds of musk, which, at an ounce per pod, represents 176,000 musk deer. Since hunters shoot and snare muskless females and young as readily as males, at least 400,000 musk deer in Asia died to supply just one small country. The biggest illegal exporter of musk from Nepal was rumored to be the Toyota agent in Kathmandu. Fortunately the Chinese have recently devel-oped a technique for raising musk deer in captivity and of withdraw-ing the musk twice a year without killing the animals.

The river expanded to a braided channel, then forked. There, high on a bank, was the monastery, crouching square and squat by the river as if guarding the approaches to Tibet. Juniper and birch still straggled along the slopes, but at 13,000 feet we were at timberline. Wearily we passed through a gate into the courtyard, the trip having taken eight long hours. Filling the center of the courtyard was the temple, a whitewashed building with a band of ochre along the top of its walls. Two elderly monks sat by the door in the afternoon sun. One wore sheepskin pants and a six-inch-square piece of cloth on his head; his clothing and skin were blackened and crusted with years of dirt and smoky juniper fires. While Kancha explained to him the reason for our visit, he continually twirled his prayer wheel. This ingenious instrument had attached to its handle a hollow metal cylinder, some three inches high and two wide, inside of which were rolls of printed prayers that revolved with the spinning cylinder. Since every revolution is the equivalent of reciting a prayer, and since prayers represent credit in future life, the monk could converse with us while pursuing his spiritual aims. His name was Kusang and this was his mother, ninety-eight years old, said the monk, motioning with his prayer wheel. I had not even noticed her, huddled in the corner like a discarded mound of rags, motionless except for a mummified hand counting the rosary of 108 prayer beads in her lap. The other monk, Pa-Tenzing by name, watched us with twinkling eyes. His nose was bulbous and the wisp of hair on his chin quivered when he spoke; slight and bowed, he resembled a gnome whose home might be among the lichen-draped birches nearby. He had a Thermos—an incongruous object in this ancient world—from which he offered us tea. Though it was strong and salty, I drank it gratefully. Since Tibetans lack sugar, they flavor their tea with salt, and, if it is available, also add milk or butter, making it nutritious. Few foreigners come to Lapche, Pa-Tenzing informed us. Three years ago an old man arrived, but stayed only a few hours, and before that he could not remember, it was so long ago, over

Prayer wheel

twenty-five years. Aligned along the inside walls of the monastery were several huts and stables. One hut was empty and into it we were permitted to move. On the way to our quarters stood a solitary tall fir; at the base of the tree, carved into a flat stone, sat Buddha, his left hand in his lap holding an alms dish, his serene posture having a special affinity with these quiet surroundings.

On the slope behind the monastery we collected firewood. Here the mountains were more remote than downvalley, the views wider; there was a breath of Central Asia. By the time we had enough wood, the sun had slipped behind the hill. Below, the monastery was in shadow, terribly lonesome, and as if impervious to the weather, Kusang slowly circled it, as he did for hours each day, always in a clockwise direction, spinning his prayer wheel while intoning over and over the sacred incantation *Om mani padme hum* (Hail the jewel in the lotus).

At dusk we crouched around the fire, indifferent to its smoke, drawn into ourselves, as we silently absorbed the heat. The porter had brought with him the partial head of a yak, its flesh already boiled, and for dinner we pried off slivers of meat to eat with our

rice. Then, tucked into my sleeping bag, I wrote the day's notes by candlelight.

At dawn Kancha and I ascended a steep trail behind the monastery, following the most easterly of the two river forks, until we crested a rise. Even though a furious wind edged with ice tore at us, we stood there, looking at the long valley ahead. Its west-facing slopes were still deep in winter, whereas the others, exposed to spring sun, were now largely clear of snow, revealing alpine meadows and dark precipices and fields of jagged boulders; and beyond, rising like an ice adze into the Tibetan sky was Tingri Himal. The shaggy forms of several domestic yaks made the scene complete. Adapted to high altitudes, yaks are uncomfortable in warm weather, and even such places as Lamnang are unsuitable for them in summer. There villagers use a yak-cattle hybrid, or zhom as the female is called, which can tolerate heat better and also gives more milk than either yak or cow. Hybrid males are infertile and used mainly for plowing and carrying loads. At still lower altitudes, below 8,000 feet, cattle are raised. Following the slope northward, we came upon ground black and bare where villagers had burned off the mat of procumbent juniper and rhododendron the previous year to open up more grazing land for their livestock. Eventually we reached the Tibetan border, marked only by a small cement block with the inscription NEPAL, 1962.

Suddenly I saw several gray forms moving on the stone waste at the base of a cliff. Nine blue sheep: an adult male, a yearling male, four females, and three young. Excitedly, I began observing the animals. When Brian Hodgson first described the blue sheep in 1833, he gave it the scientific name *Ovis nayaur* on the assumption that it was a sheep, not a goat. Now, observing one of the males, I could easily see the basis for his reasoning. With its powerful body and stocky legs, the animal greatly resembled a bighorn sheep, though not the lithe urial of desert hills. Sheeplike, his stout horns swept out, then back; and he lacked a goat's beard. Females had puny horns, as do sheep, in contrast to goats which have sharp, functional weapons. Yet in other traits, such as the broad, flat tail and the striking black and white marking on the forelegs, the male was goatlike. Sheep have eye glands and pedal glands between all their hooves, whereas goats have no eye glands at all, and have pedal glands, if any, only on the forefeet. Blue sheep, I had read, are confusing in that some individuals have rudimentary eye and pedal glands and some lack them. Sheep also have inguinal glands in their groin, but blue sheep and goats do not. No wonder Hodgson was puzzled, and thirteen years after he first named the animal he placed it into a separate genus, *Pseudois*. Thereafter the blue sheep was considered to be a goat with sheeplike affinities, and the name "blue sheep" obviously is inappropriate. The Tibetans call the animal *na* or *nao*, and the Hindus and some British hunters call it *bharal*. I like the term *bharal* and prefer to use it.

Behavioral information can sometimes supplement other data in solving taxonomic problems. Although the German zoologist Ernst Schäfer had written an informative article on bharal in the 1930s, no attempt had ever been made to study the species' behavior. This is not surprising, for bharal live in one of the most remote regions on earth, the Tibetan highlands and some of the ranges bordering them.

Their haunts are above timberline, usually from 13,000 feet upward to the limit of vegetation at 18,000 feet. Thus I eagerly watched the bharal. At first I was so intent on the scientific problem of placing bharal behavior either into the sheep or goat category that I forgot to enjoy myself. But as I watched the grazing animals, I began to unwind, satisfied to observe the animals just for themselves. Admiring the handsome male with his dark neck and black-striped side, I perceived how the coat color seemed to change from gray-brown to slate-blue depending on the angle of the sun; I noted what food they liked, mainly grasses but also a leguminous forb, the leaves of *Cotoneaster*, and the green twigs of shrubby *Ephedra*. After five hours the animals moved from sight into a ravine.

Kancha had returned to the monastery hours ago, and now I too retraced my steps. While I ate a lunch of tea and boiled potatoes, Kancha told me that several villagers had passed through from Tibet on their way to Lamnang and that they had seen a bharal herd near Lapche village. I walked the half mile to the village. Abandoned by man during winter, snow had drifted around and even over its stone huts; now bharal laid claim to the village—their tracks were on stone walls, inside sheds, on roofs. On a slope nearby was a herd of twelve, among them several youngsters. One of these reared threateningly on its hindlegs bolt upright, with forelegs drawn close to its body in front of a second young, an erect stance typical of goats, not sheep; it was an important clue to the evolutionary affinities of bharal. When dusk sent me home, it was with the feeling of satisfaction.

Not only had I found bharal and observed them for seven and a half hours, but found also an ideal study site here, with the serene monastery as base. The following day brought more hours with bharal, and the next day we descended to Lamnang with plans to return as soon as possible.

At Lambagar the police checkpost had been monitoring my activities by interrogating villagers, and within three days of our return from Lapche a constable, Hem Bahadur Shresta, arrived to say that he would accompany us on our next visit to the monastery. Meanwhile I sent Mingma and two porters with a two-week supply of food to Lapche with instructions to guard it until my arrival with Phu-Tsering in about three days, after I had checked the tahr at Hum. But during the night of March 5 it snowed, large, heavy flakes which within hours deprived the valley of spring. Our cook tent collapsed under a foot of snow, and instead of departing for Lapche we dug out our camp with frying pans and pot lids. That night Mingma arrived, exhausted after traveling many hours in deep snow. Crossly I asked him why he was here instead of guarding our belongings, and he replied that some Lamnang men had moved into the monastery. They would not sell him firewood and the snow was too deep to collect any. Being little more than a teenager, he probably had been afraid to remain among the Tibetans.

On March 9, Phu-Tsering, Hem Bahadur, and I reached the monastery. A hard-eyed villager met us at the gate, saying that we could not stay here. Phu-Tsering translated, then added, "He bad man," and pushed past him with a laugh. Kusang, the monk, had guarded our equipment and we thanked him with a present of sugar and crackers. The attitude of the villager bothered me: I had no idea why we were unwelcome. Were the people afraid that we would stop their illegal musk deer hunting? The first Buddhist precept states that "I undertake the rule of training to refrain from injury to living things." Tibetans believe in reincarnation: if one leads a pure life, if one does not kill, one passes on to a higher form. But greed readily overcomes religious sentiment, and many Buddhists in Nepal now kill wildlife, even around such monasteries as Lapche. Perhaps the Lamnang villagers smuggled temple images and other valuables out of Tibet for sale in the illegal art market of Kathmandu. Or did they suspect me of wanting to rob their monastery which contained a number of painted religious scrolls or *tankas*?

A cup of tea helped dispel my worries. With two hours of daylight left, I ambled toward Lapche village and almost immediately came across a snow leopard track, made since that night of the big snow. The cat had walked steadily toward the village and on into Tibet. Just before the village the tracks of a second snow leopard crossed those of the first—and it had dragged something uphill. I followed the dragmark slowly, glassing the slope every few steps. By a large boulder were several depressions in the snow where the cat had been resting: it had seen my approach and fled. Fresh pugmarks showed where it had bounded away under the cover of a rise and vanished in a broken cliff. Nearby were the remains of a bharal, a male almost four years old. From spoor in the snow I reconstructed the course of events leading to his death. He had wandered alone around the village, then, angling into a shallow valley, had gone to a rivulet to drink, his descent no doubt observed by the snow leopard. Its advance hidden by a boulder, the cat had stalked closer, and as the bharal stood by the water, it attacked, pulling its victim down at the point of impact. After disemboweling the animal and eating parts of the viscera and the rib cage, the snow leopard dragged the carcass some 500 feet uphill to where I found it.

I checked the kill again at dawn. The last meat had been eaten during the night, and once again the cat had vanished unseen. It did not return. Five village men moved into the eastern valley, occupying a crude hut of stone walls roofed with old skins. They were there to cut grass on the snow-free slopes for livestock fodder. They also tried to accustom the yaks to being handled again after a feral existence all winter; they talked to them gently and fed them salt by hand until the shy beasts tolerated being touched. One of the men mentioned to Phu-Tsering that he had heard a snow leopard calling in the valley at dusk. The next day I stopped alone by their hut to inquire about this. They sat cross-legged around a furiously boiling pot, and one motioned me to join them. They had slipped out of their sheepskin jackets, and matted hair hung to their bare shoulders. With long knives they fished in the foul-smelling pot for chunks of meat from a yak that had died a week ago. The *plat du jour* was decayed liver of which I ate a polite portion. Although I have a strong stomach, it forcefully rejected this meal an hour later.

The men showed little interest in providing me with information about snow leopard. Vaguely and indifferently they indicated that it was somewhere, anywhere. Knowing that cats, like people, prefer to travel along easy routes, I seated myself above a well-worn yak trail and waited. Clouds descended the slopes, obscuring the lofty peaks as it grew dusky. In shadowy solitude I waited, huddled among dark boulders; it began to snow. Then out of the dark came a wailing miaow, a wild, longing sound from a creature doomed forever to wander these wastes searching for someone to share its fate. Minutes later, another miaow. And after that, silence.

I observed bharal daily for as many hours as possible. The animals were scattered in small herds, ranging in size from two or three to as many as twenty-two. In the mornings they were on the lower slopes but as the villagers became active they slowly retreated uphill. Generally, they were quite tolerant of a person moving casually around, sometimes permitting me to approach to within 200 feet. This was especially true after I scattered salt on one of the knolls. Obviously partial to salt, the same animals returned to the site for three consecutive days, where, crowded together and competing for a scarce resource, they became more than usually aggressive. Powerful males threatened one another by presenting their impressive profiles; with slow, measured steps they walked broadside, chins tucked in and horns tipped toward each other. At times a bharal reared up, hopped forward on its hindlegs, then lunged at a rival who caught the blow on its horns. Or two bharal faced, and after rearing bolt upright, heads cocked sideways, fell forward in unison to meet horns with a crash. There were other forms of aggression as well, such as butting and thrashing shrubs with horns, and I recorded them all with an uneasy sense of urgency.

The villagers harassed us openly in small but annoying ways. Men shouted to drive away whatever bharal I was watching. When a yak died, they suspended bloody chunks of meat all over the room we occupied. And one day Kancha came from Lamnang trailing dejectedly behind four government officials who asked to see my permit. I showed it, pointing out that it was in order and that we had a constable with us as a liaison officer. I asked one official, Ragonath Upadya, why they had come, but he evaded my question with irrational shiftiness and unhelpful smiles; I never learned the purpose of the trip. The following morning, as usual, I went to watch bharal, but, after I left, the officials told Kancha that I was expected to leave Lapche immediately. By the time I returned to the monastery, they were gone. Knowing it was a futile gesture, I sent Kancha and Hem Bahadur to Lambagar to argue the case—at least it would buy three days of time. No longer exhilarated, I continued my work; something had gone wrong, some mysterious force had turned the spirits of the Kang Chu against us.

Three days later Mingma came with a porter to fetch us. We returned to Lamnang, and, a day later, moved camp to the banks of the Bhote Kosi near Lambagar where, until early April, I continued my tahr studies. Now, after having us ordered out of Lapche, that odious official, Upadya, instructed local police that I must not be allowed to leave Lambagar. I sent Kancha to Kathmandu to find out just what was happening. Many days later he brought back word: of course I might leave. But inexperienced in dealing with officials, he had failed to obtain this statement in writing, and even worse, he had forgotten to bring back my trekking permit and other papers. The policemen at Lambagar rightly pointed out that we could not travel without a trekking permit even if we had permission to leave.

Kancha also brought a letter to Phu-Tsering from his wife in which she informed him that she was leaving him for another man. With tears streaming down his face, Phu-Tsering mounted a rock cairn in the courtyard of the police station and to an assembled crowd publicly read his wife's letter. Then the others cried too, the constables, shopkeepers, housewives, children, all formed a circle around Phu-Tsering, sobbing loudly in sympathy.

Hem Bahadur resolved the impasse about our permits by escorting us back to the lowlands.

On this trip, as on all trips, there had been problems and annoyances, but I had accomplished my purpose. I had made the wildlife survey, studied the behavior of Himalayan tahr, complementing the population research done by Graeme Caughley in New Zealand, and observed bharal. The precise evolutionary position of bharal remained unresolved, but two of their behavior patterns provided clues: bharal mouth penises and rear bolt upright before clashing, resembling in these respects goats, not sheep. However, numerous other aspects of bharal behavior remained unknown. Do adult males tend to attach themselves to a particular group of females during the rut as do some goats, or do they roam from herd to herd in search of estrous females as is characteristic of sheep? To answer this question and others I would need to observe the bharals' rut.

The past is prologue. As we left the great white mountains behind and once again passed through terraced fields and villages, I was planning to return, to take Phu-Tsering with me, and somewhere continue my study of bharal.

Journey to
Crystal Mountain

We assembled beneath the spreading boughs of a pipal tree at the edge of Pokhara, a small town west of Kathmandu. The fifteen porters readied their loads, baskets with enough food for two and a half months, camping equipment, various personal items, and whatever might be needed to conduct a study of bharal. As each porter balanced his sixty-pound load and adjusted his tump line, the four Sherpas busied themselves with final preparations: Jang-bu, our head Sherpa, went from load to load, hefting some to test their weight and tightening ropes, while Phu-Tsering, who had been with me in the Kang Chu the previous year, moved among the men, urging them to hurry; Gyaltsen, as combination courier and porter, arranged his pack; and Ang Dawa, the kitchen assistant, organized a few pots, some food, and any other item we might want for lunch or in the evening at camp before lagging porters arrived. Throughout these preparations Peter Matthiessen and I stood at the edge of the throng, our packs ready, eager to begin our journey to Shey Gompa, the Crystal Monastery that lies in the shadow of sacred Crystal Mountain.

These final preparations seemed somehow illusive; the barefoot porters dressed only in shorts and shirts, the sun's humid warmth, the ochre-colored houses surrounded by an intense green lushness of bamboo, banana, and rice, all had an aura of softness, of a casual life-style in no way indicating what was ahead. Only to the north where the summit of Machhapuchhare, the Fish Tail, pierced a bank of clouds was there a reminder that our journey would include harsh high altitudes and winter snows. The previous year, John Blower had shown me photographs of bharal taken by him at a place called Shey Gompa, a monastery where the animals are tame because the local lama prohibits hunting. John suggested that Shey would not only be an excellent place to study bharal, but that it would also help the Nepal government if I were to make a wildlife survey and assess the potential of that area as a reserve. However, Shey lies in the Dolpo district at the edge of the Tibetan Plateau where few foreigners have been because the region is not only remote, but also politically closed to casual trekkers. To reach Shey we would have to cross the Himalaya from south to north over several high passes. This presents few problems in summer when travelers usually go to Dolpo, but in winter, when I wanted to study bharal, the uplands are deep in snow and porters are reluctant to travel. I read the few published accounts concerning visits to Dolpo, such as J. D. A. Stainton's *Forests of Nepal* and David Snellgrove's *Himalayan Pilgrimage*, but learning nothing about winter conditions, I finally decided it would be best to go there in October before the snows are deep, do my work, and then worry about returning. The trek from Pokhara to Shey would probably require no more than three weeks, first following a route along the lower slopes of the Annapurna and Dhaulagiri massifs westward to the village of Dhorpatan, then heading northward over passes and through gorges of the Himalaya.

As I watched the porters straggling away from the pipal tree, muscular legs taut under the strain of their loads, I did not dwell on possible problems that might deny me Shey; I knew too well that a mountain journey is never a triumphant progression toward a shining goal, but rather a limited quest, a daily struggle to reach the village or campsite just ahead.

Pokhara to Dhorpatan, September 28–October 9

The village path is wide and long, flanked by clumps of bamboo and an occasional banyan in whose shade the porters halt to rest their loads by setting them onto high stone benches. Banana trees surround each home, the primitive elegance of their arching leaves offset by yellow-blossomed pumpkin vines growing in careless intimacy over the thatch. Calmly purposeful, village life is not affected by our passing intrusion; women continue to spread millet and pulses on mats to dry, black pigs snuffle along ditches, and a Gurung woman shuffles by, bent under a load of wood, the large brass disks in her ears flashing in the sun. Children splash in a sluggish stream around several submerged buffalo, and only they pause as we draw near. Their almond-shaped eyes sparkle as they call "Hello" in English and the older ones recite school lessons: "How are you? What time is it? Where are you going?"

At the end of the village is a tea shop similar to the many others along each well-traveled route. Only an open-fronted shed, a bench, fireplace, two kettles, and half a dozen glasses are needed to establish such a business. Not daring to drink unboiled water in these heavily populated parts of Nepal, I stop gratefully for a glass or two of milky tea. It is lunchtime, and Peter and I share a cucumber large as a melon and some bread.

We enter the Ghabung Valley not far beyond the village, first following a braided stream channel, then angling up a slope into a patch of forest. Its cool wildness startles me. We have walked for

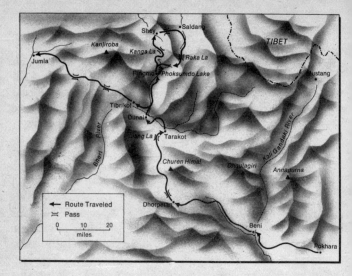

hours in sun, through villages and fields and along terraced slopes
where forests once grew, unconsciously accepting the man-made
landscape. By the trail blooms a bright-pink *Osbeckia*, resembling
a wild rose, and shading me are trees of the edible chestnut, *Casta-
nopsis,* their boughs laden with spiny-shelled fruit. The forest canopy
is closed, the undergrowth lush, with an abundance of evergreen
leaves which will ultimately decompose into a rich water-absorbing
humus. Villages high on the ridges depend on humus like this for
their perennial water supply. When all trees are removed, the humus
washes away and the streams begin to dry up quickly after the monsoon; soil nutrients disappear with the humus and the productivity
of the land declines. Nepal will soon be derelict unless it protects
its watersheds. Although ecological crises are usually gradual and
insidious rather than rapid and dramatic, in Nepal the reverse is
true. Interestingly, early this year several villages in the Gharwal

area of the Indian Himalaya have shown how private initiative can protect forests. Having finally realized the misery which total deforestation ultimately brings to the lives of hill people, villagers began a Gandhian movement to save their trees. Called *Chipko Andolan,* literally "movement to embrace," the villagers determinedly hug those trees which contractors and forest officials have come to fell. After several successful confrontations, demonstrations on behalf of forests increased until the local governments had to accede to various demands such as that felling of oak be prohibited. True, in Nepal the villager himself is often an important agent in his own destruction, for he circumvents laws that prohibit the cutting of live trees by ringbarking them. A tree thus slashed soon dies and may then be legally felled. Perhaps some day the hill people of Nepal will also develop an ecological conscience.

Leaving the forest behind, the trail climbs steadily to the top of a ridge where, in a small bazaar, porters traditionally eat and sleep the first night after leaving Pokhara. On a grassy spot near the bazaar, Peter and I each erect a small tent, and the Sherpas set up a tent for themselves. Phu-Tsering brings me a pan of water for washing and shaving. At dusk we eat at the bazaar to conserve our supplies, a simple meal of chappaties and *dal,* a type of lentil dish.

As we pass through the village at 7 A.M., from an obscure doorway someone calls "Checkpost" and we stop to show our trekking permits to a constable who duly records our presence in his ledger. Checkposts make me tense. Although our permits are in order I know that the farther an official is from the constraints of Kathmandu, the more he may become a local despot with the arbitrary power to turn us back. At midmorning we reach the crest of a ridge, the Bhadauri Deorali Pass, 5,500 feet high. Our porters prefer to eat their first meal at this time and they now stop to prepare rice while Peter and I walk ahead. A path paved with slabs of slate endlessly follows along terraced fields, brilliantly green, with squadrons of sienna-colored dragonflies hovering above. Finally, we descend a spur into the valley of the Modi, a tributary of the Kali Gandaki. Durga Puja or Dasain, a national festival of Nepal, is about to begin. Hindu religion celebrates the victory of the goddess Durga over the demon Mahisasoor, a victory of goodness over evil, and in preparation for the ten-day festival women everywhere are cleaning their homes and painting them with a mixture of brick-red earth and water. We travel through a stand of *Pinus roxburghii*, a denatured remnant consisting solely of tall trees, the undergrowth and seedlings having been grazed and burned off. Yesterday we passed briefly through evergreen forest in which the chestnut was a distinctive tree; today we come upon arid conifer forest. The change is an important one along the foothills of the Himalaya, for in this part of Nepal, near the slopes of Mount Dhaulagiri, is the vegetation transition from moist east to drier west. At dusk we camp at the village of Gijon.

With morning comes news that we have one too many loads: a porter sneaked away after working only two days against his three-day advance in pay. However, Jang-bu finds a local man to take his place. We have now established a pattern of travel: Peter and I generally walk ahead with Phu-Tsering and perhaps a fast porter or two, while the others trail behind, each moving at his own speed, Jang-bu being last in a procession that may extend over several miles. Though near each other, Peter and I often hike alone, content to assimilate our impressions independently. We are both private persons, still uncertain about sharing our feelings, and when we meet our conversations are casual. "There's a tree back there with lavender, orchidlike blossoms," Peter notes. "Do you know its name?" "A *Bauhinia*, I think. I saw an orange-bellied squirrel a while ago. The only wild mammal on this trip so far." We had first met in 1969 in the Serengeti National Park of Tanzania where I was studying lions. There we watched a pack of hunting dogs chase zebra, searched for cheetah on the plains, and made other daylong excursions, his easy charm making him a pleasant companion. Peter is the best of today's nature writers, and I enjoyed exposing him to the Serengeti and its wildlife, knowing he would transform his experiences into an informative, honest, and sensitive account. Later, when I began research in the Himalaya, Peter expressed an interest in accompanying me on a journey, for as a Zen Buddhist, he sought to become familiar with Tibetan Buddhism. A week earlier we had met in Kathmandu, he coming from the United States and I from my studies in Pakistan.

The trail winds down to the Modi River which drains the flanks of Annapurna and Machhapuchhare. At a small bazaar we halt for tea and bananas, then continue, crossing the river on a narrow suspension bridge. Surmounting a ridge, we see the silty waters of the Kali Gandaki along whose banks an important trade route once passed between Nepal and Tibet. Flanked by bluffs and deforested slopes we ascend the valley. In one village, in the shade of a banyan tree, is a small peaked temple dedicated to the goddess Shiva. Beautifully carved lizards and gargoyles adorn its wooden supports, and in a shaft of sun before the temple kneel two stone cows, massively simple in the manner of an Eskimo soapstone carving, a red hibiscus blossom adorning the back of each. We reach our campsite just before a downpour lashes the valley.

The next day we must leap from stone to stone to avoid the puddles and mud from yesterday's rain. A bridge spans the river at the large bazaar of Beni, and from here we head westward again, following the Mayangdi Valley. Sheer cliffs broken by grassy alps laced with waterfalls crowd in, leaving only the lower slopes for cultivation. "Hey, didi! Hey, sister! Cucumbers? Bananas?" calls Phu-Tsering to women working by their homes, trying to buy something for our lunch, but today he is not successful. Late in the afternoon we halt at the bazaar of Tatopani. Human feces litter every possible campsite—there are no pigs here to clean up as near Pokhara—but we finally locate a spot for our tents half a mile beyond the village.

Around midnight it begins to rain, steady perpendicular shafts which still continue when at dawn I peer out of my tent. White clouds huddle in the valleys, leaving the crests of hills black against a sullen sky. When the rain eases at 9 A.M., we follow the porters into the sodden hills. Here the houses are of stone with slate roofs, two or three stories high and as solid and permanent as the cliffs beyond. In midafternoon we reach Dabang, another police checkpost, the fourth in five days. The weather is dampening our enjoyment of the trek and we decide to remain for the night, Jang-bu obtaining permission for us to sleep in the schoolhouse. Peter and I select the best room, CLASS IV, a dingy place with uneven stone floor and rough-hewn benches six inches high. When it begins to rain again and continues through the night, we are pleased to have shelter, even this leaky one.

It still pours in the morning, but to my surprise, only one porter quits. The others continue, plastic sheets drawn over their heads and loads. The trail has been transformed into a stream, muddy cascades tumbling over cliffs, and small avalanches of earth and rock slithering past our feet. Ragged edges of cloud creep low along the valley. We ascend a precipitous slope, covered partly with pine, until the terrain once more becomes gradual and cultivation is possible. At one village we see a group of people standing around a tethered buffalo; a man swings his two-foot kukri once and the animal drops, its head nearly severed. Several villagers collect the flowing blood in woven trays, generally used for winnowing grain, and drink it fresh and warm. Then, as men shout and dogs hover excitedly, the buffalo is butchered, and somewhere downslope a drum beats. The Durga festival has begun. We buy several pounds of meat, planning a feast for the Sherpas and ourselves after days of mainly rice and *dal*.

Nearby is an unused cowshed, an adequate home for the night. Scraping aside some of the wall-to-wall carpet of dung, each of us locates a dry spot for his bed between drips from the leaking roof. We are at 6,000 feet, 3,000 feet higher than the Kali Gandaki, and the air is chilly. As I lie in the warmth of my sleeping bag, listening to the murmur and splashing of rain in the blind night, I worry about the days ahead. The monsoon should be over by now, but obviously it is not, and at this season rain at low altitudes means snow in the uplands. Will we be able to cross the passes? Rain slants down in sheets all the next day, making travel impossible. We remain in bed, reading and dozing, while the Sherpas and porters participate in the Durga festivities, especially the *rakshi*, an alcohol brew made from millet. We try some: it tastes like vinegar and dirty dishrag.

By morning the downpour has changed to a drizzle, and once more we move upvalley. With increased altitude the fields become smaller and stonier, and solitary houses replace villages, drab like the earth, only clusters of yellow maize cobs hung to dry on the verandas adding a touch of color. Fields soon give way to thickets and expanses of bracken fern; fringes of oak curve stiffly along the crests like the bristles of a mane, the branches of each tree lopped for live-stock fodder. The bitter weather has halted all movement of birds from these heights and the brush is alive with long-tailed minivets, Himalayan goldfinches, and other migrants. At an altitude of 8,500 feet the trail enters a forest of oak and cedar with an understory of rhododendron and ilex, a brooding place, strangely solemn, all sounds muted by a quilt of moss on ground and trees. The air is tangibly lighter at this altitude, and no longer resenting the toil, I hurry uphill until sweat drips into my eyes in spite of the chill. I halt at 9,500 feet; it is 1:30 P.M. and the others are somewhere behind. Gathering a few sodden twigs and using bits of toilet paper, I try to start a fire. When after an hour of nursing smoldering stems and timid flames, I finally have a warming fire, Peter arrives and then two Sherpas. Only a few porters trickle in after dark, the others having remained at the last habitation. We crowd around the fire, our bodies giving off a heavy odor compounded of damp clothes, manure, wood smoke, and sweat. As I enter my tent for the night two leeches hump in with me.

With the first gray tones of daybreak I question the sky. There are clouds, but before long the sun sends a few pallid rays into the forest gloom, burnishing ferns and mossy trunks with gold. Soon after leaving our campsite, we enter a new vegetation zone, this one with maples, a few ash, and fir; lichens festoon the branches; a flock of white-throated laughing thrushes chatters in the virburnum. At 11,000 feet the first birches and junipers appear and the forest opens onto meadows. Waiting there for the porters we delight in the late-blooming alpine flowers: gentians and primulas and yellow composites. To the north, beyond several forested ridges, the lower slopes of the Dhaulagiri massif are dusted with new snow and the upper ones are solidly white, extending into the clouds. A forested valley descends westward toward Dhorpatan. At first we travel through reaches empty of man but soon pass homesteads hacked into the wilderness—a shack, raw stumps, half-burned trees, and a patch of turned sod—the first of many as we near Dhorpatan. After five hours of wading down a miserable trail deep in mud and water, the valley broadens and we reach the first village. It is occupied by Tibetans, over sixty thousand of whom fled into Nepal and India after the Chinese forcefully annexed their country in 1959 and 1960. Dhorpatan, also a Tibetan village, still lies an hour ahead. A snarling Tibetan mastiff, black and shaggy like a miniature bear, greets us there and retreats only when Peter shakes his walking stick and shouts at it and I hurl a chunk of wood. In a small hotel we settle ourselves by a glowing clay oven where we sip tea and eat boiled potatoes sprinkled with salt, a satisfying meal after the long day. The first portion of our trip is over, the easy part to be sure, but I feel content, deferring possible problems until tomorrow.

Our main concern now will be porters. Five Tamang tribesmen have come with us from Kathmandu, lean, hard, professional porters who intend to accompany us as close to Shey as possible. A Sherpa named Tukten signed on in Pokhara as a porter, and with smiling persistence and ever-willing helpfulness has become a peripheral member of our group in spite of the somewhat distant attitude of our Sherpas. Finally there is Bimbahadur, a stocky, bowlegged Mangar who joined us en route; he salutes us smartly each morning, a memento of his mercenary service in the British army. This core of seven will strike north with us, but we need another seven men. As we spread our sodden tents to dry in the patchy morning sun, Jang-bu informs us that it may be difficult to find porters here because all available hands are needed now for the potato harvest, and afterward for carrying it to market in the south. Jang-bu is gone most of the day, visiting house after house in search of porters. I write letters and give Peter a haircut, "short like a pelt," according to instruction. No Tibetan wants to carry, reports Jang-bu later, but several men of the Kami Mangar tribe agree to come, accepting an advance in pay as a form of agreement. By afternoon the weather deteriorates, dark clouds first smashing through a gap in the hills to the south, then carrying the surrounding ridges with a rush. Later, as I lie on a wooden pallet in the hotel's damp storeroom, I listen once again to rain on the roof.

It rains all the following day and most of the one after that, and we remain in our sleeping bags much of the time. Peter has brought several books on Buddhism, Blofeld's *The Tantric Mysticism of Tibet*, David-Neel's *Magic and Mystery in Tibet*, and others, and I peruse these, gaining knowledge of a religion which has much to teach the Western mind. Peter also encourages me to compose haiku. To evoke an image with simplicity and clarity appeals to me, and several hours pass easily as I try to distill the past few days; however, my results seem forced, they miss the essence of the moments. But no matter how we occupy ourselves, the weather pervades our existence: when the rain eases briefly we comment on it; when the milky plastic that covers our window shines somewhat more brightly, I peer hopefully through a crack at the sky. We talk of alternate routes, knowing there are none; we plan for the morrow but hedge each statement with "if it's nice." An American student, Robert Cartier, who has been studying Tibetan religion at Dhorpatan, visits us briefly. In passing he mentions that we may have trouble with the checkpost in Tarakot, a six-day march to the north; a few months earlier he had not been allowed to proceed to Tarap in Dolpo in spite of the fact that his Kathmandu permit was valid.

Certain regions along the Tibetan border, such as Mustang and Dolpo, are considered politically sensitive. Not long after the Chinese invaded Tibet in 1950, the Khampas, the people of Kham in the eastern part of the country, revolted against them. Long known as warriors and bandits who continually harassed the Tibetan governments, the Khampas now began a guerrilla war against the Chinese which continued even after the Dalai Lama fled from Tibet to India in 1959. Finally, the Chinese crushed the rebels—except for those who had sought refuge in northern Nepal. From there the Khampas not only continued their raids against the Chinese, but also, in a regression to their robber past, stole from and bullied their reluctant Nepalese hosts. Careful not to irritate its powerful neighbor, the Nepal government denied the presence of Khampas in Nepal, and to avoid incidents, it banned most visits by foreigners to the border regions.*

Thinking about bad weather, snowed-in passes, lack of porters, and unsympathetic officials, I end our third day in Dhorpatan in a dejected mood. But "in worrying about the future, I despoil the present . . . ," as Peter aptly phrased it in a different context, and I derive some solace by remembering that, after all, we are now in the mountains.

Dhorpatan to Tarakot, October 10–18

The storm has exhausted itself. I am anxious to move on, but of the Kami porters there is no sign. Sending the others ahead, I wait while Jang-bu tries to find the tardy men. At 11 A.M. he returns, bringing the recalcitrant porters after a big row during which the men not only declined to go because of the fresh snow on the ridges but also refused to refund the advance in pay. However, everything seems settled now, although the glum cluster of men does not inspire

* The Khampas caused so many problems in Dolpo that the Nepalese government finally sent troops there in 1974, the spring after our visit. I was told that many Khampas were killed in a battle, and for over three years after that the Doplo area, including Shey, was closed to outsiders.

confidence. I wonder how Jang-bu convinced the porters to come. Jang-bu's slender build, soft, almost womanly features, and somewhat diffident manner conceal, I am learning, a great loyalty to us and a strong determination to make the trip a success.

Obviously a mountain expedition does not march along, all porters in lockstep spaced evenly like a flock of migrating geese; rather each man travels at his own speed, the rate of progress unfortunately determined by the slowest porter. Impatient with such strolling, I hurry ahead of Jang-bu and the Kami. I climb up through a forest of fir and pine to the alpine meadows, first dappled with snow, then wholly white, the tendril of trail finally vanishing into cold gray clouds. I continue upward to the crest at 13,400 feet, tracing the porter's bare footprints in the snow, then down until I overtake Peter and the others near the first birches, and together we reach a shoulder of the mountain where there is wood and water, a good place to camp. Phu-Tsering quickly starts a fire and makes a kettle of tea; we crowd around, our hands enfolding the cups' warmth as we gratefully slurp the hot liquid. Jang-bu does not come, having no doubt camped on the other side of the pass. An easterly wind pushes the clouds aside and beyond a series of shadowy ranges the Dhaulagiri massif reveals itself to us for the first time, an enormous jagged wall of ice, flat and hard, devoid of detail. Putha Hiunchuli, Churen Himal, and several other pinnacles, all over 23,000 feet, tower over the lesser ones. "Just as the dew is dried by the morning sun, so man's cares disappear at the sight of the Himalaya," as so rightly expressed by an Indian saying.

Dawn is intensely clear, so much so that the sky over Dhaulagiri is black as in outer space; only a rosy band high above reveals that order has not become chaos, that the earth will still lean toward the sun. While Peter and I have porridge for breakfast, the porters mix for themselves a crumbly dough of coarsely ground maize flour. Then we leisurely break camp, intending to wait for Jang-bu and the Kami at a lower altitude. We descend through woods suffused with the gray-green glow of bearded lichens, and misty against the morning

sun are the enormous snow peaks. "This is the first time I really feel that I am in the Himalaya," comments Peter, as he tarries on a spur to record his observations and impressions.

Jang-bu rejoins us toward noon, and after lunching on boiled potatoes we move downvalley, through a forest of oak and fir, with the Ghusting River foaming white below. Because the Kamis still seem morose and shifty we remain close to them, like a police escort. The trail crosses a ridge and angles down so gradually that the full moon lights our final descent to several huts clinging to a slope, the hamlet of Yamarkhar. The Kami plan to return to Dhorpatan tomorrow, and no porters are to be had here. Finally one man agrees to transport our baggage to Tarakot on his horses.

In the morning our path lunges down to a stream where in the gloom of a bamboo forest is a bridge, its approach guarded from evil spirits by a roughly hewn wood-woman, nude, vagina open. Above is the Mangar village of Jagir. Crowded pueblolike against the slope in several tiers, the front porch of one family serves as the roof of the one below. Villagers stand on the roofs watching our approach, and some continue their morning tasks, the crowded scene arranged, as Peter notes, like the stage set of a play. One woman combs her hair, then ties it in a bun at the side of her head in the manner typical of her tribe; she wears a golden disk in each ear and a necklace of silver coins and two musk deer tusks. Another woman rhythmically sifts maize flour, while a third empties a basket of beans to dry on the flat roof of her house. A shriveled old woman absorbs the morning sun, sitting beneath a bouquet of scarlet peppers drying under the eaves. Each family uses its roof for storing its harvest, walnuts, maize, pumpkins, buckwheat fodder, and messy piles of cannabis, which, when dried and ground, is smoked in small wooden tubes. The ground floors house livestock, the men now driving their goats and sheep out to the hills for the day's foraging.

All day we march north, up and down and along the contours, the hills here grass- or brush-covered, most forests having been slashed and burned. Barberry is common, and I walk along browsing like a bear on the sour berries, occasionally varying my diet with a rosehip. The sky clouds over by late morning and drizzles as we stop for the night in a hollow among oak trees at 11,000 feet. As usual the Sherpas set up camp with efficient speed: while Phu-Tsering arranges rocks on which to set cooking pots, several of us including Dawa collect firewood; Phu-Tsering then makes a fire as Dawa fetches water; by the time tea is ready, the tents are up. The five Tamang have their own fire. And so usually does Bimbahadur, the Mangar; at dusk, with the drizzle now an icy downpour, I see his earth-colored figure hunched alone by his solitary flame. Jang-bu arrives just after dark saying the pack horses have found shelter in a nearby cave. Throughout the night, whenever I wake from a restless sleep, I hear the wildness of the storm, rain pelting on the tent, wind warring with the oak branches. And the rain continues heavily all the next day. When Jang-bu reports that the villager is taking his horses home, leaving us stranded, I heap invective on the weather and the fickleness of men. Then we have good luck: several travelers arrive on their way home to Tarakot and they agree to carry our loads. When toward evening the rain ceases, I walk up a nearby ridge. Smoke rises from our hollow and the tents there look cozy beneath the dark trees.

We are traveling again after the loss of yet another day, ascending to timberline. A flock of six monal pheasants flushes, and wildly cackling, the birds skim downslope. Here the path balances along a narrow ridge, its flanks golden with grass and moss, and a wren flits among a tumble of boulders. We descend into the Seng Khola, its grassy slopes receding to the northeast until valley and cloud merge; except for a frizz of birch along the stream there are no trees. I see an animal bound off near the foot of a cliff. A goral perhaps. However, a closer look reveals it to be a bharal young, all alone and apparently lost. Delighted with this sighting, I carefully scan the slopes and soon spot two more bharal high above within the skirts of the clouds. Toiling up to them, among the damp crags, I am rewarded with a close look at four males, their pelage richly gray-blue in preparation for the rut. Then rejoining the expedition, I follow it to this night's campsite, a soggy meadow at the snow's fringe. After quickly erecting my tent, I hurry back over the trail in search of more bharal, and soon find three herds, the animals having descended from the heights to feed. I watch voraciously, elated over every new observation, overcompensating for the many lost days. Since I hope to reach Shey before the onset of the rut, I note with satisfaction that as yet the males show no interest in the females.

A sharp, clear dawn. With frost sheathing every grass blade, the ground crackles under my boots. The barefoot Tarakot men wish to wait for the sun to warm the snow before starting, so Peter and I move upvalley ahead of the others. A red fox breaks cover, then sits and watches us inquisitively. Wending its way toward us is a gnomelike figure wrapped in a burlap bag. It stops and salutes. Bimbahadur has slept alone on some damp shelf of rock. We ask him for directions to the pass and he points directly up the mountainside, left into a couloir, and right along the crest. There being no path visible, we begin a slow but steady climb, first over patches of frost-hardened ground, then through fresh snow, away from the somber confines of the valley toward the dazzling light at this planet's icy extremity. With snow reflecting the sun's white heat we shed parkas, sweaters, and gloves as we gain altitude. The silence is intense, an enormous stillness, quite unlike the animate hush of a forest glade.

I see a bharal herd resting on snow slightly below and beyond a bulge in the slope. Carefully sliding closer, I count and classify the animals before they flee: three males, four females, and three young. This herd raises my tally for the Seng Khola to fifty-two bharal. Between 1974 and 1977 the Nepalese government sponsored a bharal census on the western slopes of the Dhaulagiri massif, including the Seng Khola, because it was interested in establishing a hunting reserve where for a fee both local and foreign sportsmen could shoot tahr, bharal, and other trophies. According to biologists Per Wegge and Paul Wilson, approximately 100 bharal inhabit the Seng Khola, and about 800 to 850 exist on the west side of the massif within an area of some 370 square miles. Of these an annual quota of 20 to 30 large-horned males may now be legally shot.

After climbing for two and a half hours we reach the crest at 15,300 feet. Around us is a wild scene of rough snow peaks, and no possible route or pass to the north, at least not at this season. However, in a basin a thousand feet below we see the Sherpas and porters like a line of black insects crawling through the lonely whiteness; down we go, with giant steps, the soft snow breaking our momentum. Then we track our caravan, sometimes sinking to our thighs in the sun-warmed snow; a barefoot porter has left a trail of pink blood spots. The sun blazes and I can feel the skin of my face tightening and lips cracking. Peter and I have worn goggles all day to protect our eyes from glare. When we finally overtake the others, I am distressed to see only Phu-Tsering with goggles. I give my extra pair to Jang-bu and suggest that everyone else protect himself, like Tukten and a Tarakot man, by tying a strip of cloth around his head, leaving only two slits for the eyes, but no one heeds me. We cross a pass and descend a wide valley into the Saure Khola where at 13,400 feet we camp on a snow-free knoll near the ruins of a shepherd's hut. There is no wood here, only a dry forb whose stems give off an intensely acrid smoke before flaring into brief flame. The Tarakot men make no attempt to be comfortable, no fire, no lean-to against the wildness of the night wind; they merely pull their brown cloaks around themselves and lie on the ground, huddling together for warmth like sociable beasts.

Dawn reveals a scene of utter desolation. Some porters kneel on the frozen ground, moaning and holding their hands over their faces, while others stumble about, their red eyes draining fluids and swollen almost shut. Six Tarakot men, three Tamang, Bimbahadur, Dawa, and Gyaltsen are snow-blind in varying degrees, the tender surface of their eyeballs burned by yesterday's sun. Only time can cure the gritty pain and restore keenness of sight. The Tarakot men leave for home in a pitiful procession, the blind clutching the cloaks of the others for guidance. I decide to send the rest to Tarakot with light loads, keeping only Bimbahadur, who is too ill to travel, and Phu-Tsering here. Jang-bu will, we hope, find new porters in Tarakot and be able to return within three days. Peter and I are content to remain at this camp for at least a day to search for wildlife.

First because of bad weather and now because of sunshine, we have already lost a week of travel time, a period during which the porters must be paid whether they work or not. I now add worry about the cash supply to my collection of other possible misfortunes. Shey begins to represent more than just a place where I can study bharal; it becomes an existential quest, a search for something intangible that may remain forever elusive.

I saw bharal grazing high above camp yesterday evening, and we now go in search of them. But instead of bharal we meet a red fox, debonair in black stockings and fluffy white-tipped tail. He meanders in search of breakfast, investigating tussocks, nosing rocky retreats. Occasionally he halts to wait tensely a second or two, his hindquarters lowered in preparation to leap, takes a careful step, then pounces with his forepaws. Once he captures a vole which after a few swift bites he swallows whole; once he grabs something wiggly, probably a lizard; two times he snacks on grasshoppers or similar small items. And twice he misses. Eight hours later I see him hunting again: one vole in two tries. An unusually successful hunter.

The following morning Peter and I decide each to carry a load toward Tarakot where we can camp at a more hospitable site. Without firewood even Phu-Tsering has been unable to give his customary dawn greeting of "Tea ready, sah." I soothe Bimbahadur's swollen eyes with a poultice of tea leaves; he will be able to travel tomorrow, and we leave him in Phu-Tsering's care. We cross a ridge into a shallow valley, then climb a slope deep in snow, and descend again, plodding bent under the heavy packs, almost dizzy with the sun's glare. I also feel intensely, vibrantly alive, filled with a wild, inner joy at being almost free for one brief day among these peaks. With tent and bed and food on my back, I am dependent on no one. A final climb takes us to the top of Jang Bhanjyang Pass, 14,800 feet high.

From here we look into a new world of remote peaks crowned by remoter snows, a Buddhist world in the heart of the Himalaya. For five hours we descend, reversing seasons as we abandon snow for the birches and oaks of autumn. I can see Tarakot below, prayer flags winking above many homes, and still farther down, the silvery thread of the Bheri River. We meet Jang-bu, Tukten, Gyaltsen, and a porter on their way to retrieve our baggage; by tomorrow evening our expedition should be together again. Since the outer Himalayan ranges catch most of the monsoon rains, the Bheri Valley is quite dry. Only after receiving directions from some passing villagers do we find water, a clear spring in a dusky grove of conifers, and there we camp.

It being only an hour to Tarakot, we spend an idle morning writing in our journals, dozing in the sun, and listening to the raucous *kraa-a-a* of a nutcracker. Peter seems content, much more relaxed now than at the beginning of our journey, but I cannot yet submerge myself in the beauty of our surroundings. I have a specific and clearly defined goal, to study bharal at Shey and to make a wildlife survey there; success or failure depends on reaching the destination, no matter how high the passes, how deep the snow, how reluctant the porters.

With logistic problems pervading our daily existence, I am unable to establish a personal relationship with the mountains. But for Peter, each new perception, from the pain of a blistered foot to the animation of a snow slope in the sun, adds to his private quest; he does not need Shey to complete his experience.

We descend to Tarakot in midafternoon; it consists of several dozen stone houses with flat roofs of logs and earth. Most people here are Mangars, but, unlike those to the south, they are Buddhists. Jang-bu has arranged for us to stay on the roof of the headman's house, and there among mounds of beans drying on the vine, stacks of firewood, and hens with clutches of fluffy chicks, we wait for his return. A woman removes drying millet and barley from mats and stores them in baskets for the night; another arrives from a spring, carrying a water-filled brass urn. A herd of goats and sheep has returned home from the hills, and as the animals enter their stable, the owner counts them carefully. With dusk the Tamang porters and Dawa emerge from the house shadows, squinting like moles, their burned eyes still sensitive to light. Nevertheless, we must continue tomorrow, and Jang-bu, after his arrival, arranges for porters. Bimbahadur decides to return home, but the Tamang agree to continue.

The porters are ready at 7:30 A.M., but before proceeding down the Bheri River to Dunai we must show our permits at the checkpost. I follow Jang-bu up a ladder made of a notched tree trunk to the roof of the police station. The official, whose reputation for being difficult is already known to us, sits there behind a table on a metal folding chair, a symbol of status in these parts, and scans our permits, very tight-lipped, as Jang-bu explains the purpose of our journey.

Peter turns to me and says, "I bet he hasn't cracked a smile since he was weaned."

I reply evenly: "Some officials speak English." This one does not, and a tense moment passes.

Suddenly a shot explodes just behind our backs. A constable climbing up the ladder has accidentally discharged his rifle.

The official nods to Jang-bu. We may go. The official's morose visage does not change as we heartily shake his hand, more in relief than thanks.

Tarakot to Ringmo, October 19–24

Moving once more, our caravan slants through fields of millet, buckwheat, and beans toward the Bheri River. In a millet field a group of gray langur feeds and cavorts, forty-one animals breaking stalks and tearing at the rich seed heads; a woman hurries over to pelt them with rocks, but they retreat with such casual reluctance that it is obvious they will return as soon as the woman turns to other tasks. Silver-gray animals with inquisitive black faces and elegantly long tails, the monkeys withdraw to a nearby bluff; a large male, weighing some forty pounds, brings up the rear. In Hindu religion, Hanuman the monkey-god is a langur, the loyal servant to King Rama whose exploits are related in the epic *Ramayana*, dating from about the fifth century B.C. Given the Hindu's veneration of langur and the Buddhist's general aversion to killing, the langur remains perhaps the most abundant and certainly the most widespread monkey in South Asia, its range extending from sea level to above timberline at 14,000 feet. Field studies have provided fascinating insights into langur society—and that of man. As related by Sarah Hardy in her engrossing book *The Langurs of Abu*, the dominant male presides over the group, but at intervals of two to three years a roving band of bachelor males may enter the group, and after a battle, oust the resident male. Then one of the new males usurps power, evicts the other invaders, and with grim determination kills one by one all small infants in the group. Such infanticide confers great evolutionary advantage on the male. By eliminating the offspring of his predecessor and impregnating the females, which come into estrus soon after the death of their infants, a male perpetuates his own genes, thus increasing his reproductive success. According to conventional wisdom, man alone in the animal world murders his own kind, and as the descendant of a race of killer apes, he lacks the inhibitions of other species. Yet nature teaches otherwise. As zoologist E. O. Wilson notes: "Murder is far more common and hence 'normal' in many vertebrate species than in man." For too long man has burdened other animals with the aspirations and idealizations of his own society; only by discarding all myths can he hope to understand himself.

All day we follow the Bheri's course downstream, flanked by sere mountainsides covered with grass and remnants of pine, and high above where the slopes become less precipitous, by terraced fields. After days in thin, cold air, the heat of this valley at 7,500 feet is oppressive, and we seek the shade of rocky niches along the trail. Late in the afternoon we reach Dunai, the last and most important checkpost on the way to Shey. With brave smiles and timorous hearts we enter the government office the following morning. There a gentleman introduces himself in elegant English as Ashok Kumar Halal, the local *panchayat* officer, head of the democratic village council. Both the district officer and head constable are away, he says, but he can help us. We explain the purpose of our journey. The local doctor, who has joined us, notes that according to the radio, H.R.H. Prince Gyanendra, brother of Nepal's king, has just left for Germany to attend a conference on wildlife conservation, and that if the royal family has such interests, our mission is obviously important to the country. Permission for us to continue is readily granted.

As we leave Dunai, now heading north up the valley of the Suli, I feel elated, as if freed from a great dark beast that has pursued me persistently over the mountains. The trail follows mostly gaunt slopes covered with spear grass and sagebrush. In midafternoon we arrive at a miserable clutter of huts built into the hillside, the Thakur village of Rohagaon. Animistic wood effigies with outstretched arms, called *dok-pa,* perch on the houses, invoking the good will of the spirits. Squat women, darkly clothed, scurry in and out of hovels and screech to each other across rooftops; old men hawk, and children, spindly legged and indescribably filthy, play among refuse heaps and bleating sheep and goats. The whole scene is enshrouded with veils of dust and swarms of flies. Later, after dark, dogs bark their discontent. Seldom have I been in a place so lonely yet so full of sounds, in an atmosphere so stygian.

I am glad to move on in the morning. A flock of over a hundred snow pigeons banks past me to settle in a nearby field. Soon Peter and I follow the river, turquoise in its more peaceful moments, frothing white in others. We are in forest now, among tall pines, cedar, and spruce, and near the water's edge, among red-leafed sumac and wild grape. In a grove of walnut trees we search among rattling leaves for fallen nuts. Many of those we find have a hole drilled neatly into each side, the work of flying squirrels; a few are still in one piece, and we pound them open to extract the meager contents. All day we continue with barely a rise in altitude, up along the slope and back toward the river, through bracken and forest, yet in spite of the sameness there is a feeling that we are entering a world within a world. Standing at one point in the river is a curiously shaped rock carved by the waters into a massive figure of a man, his stomach hollowed like a starving Buddha, beckoning with his left arm.

Not long after leaving our night's campsite the character of the land changes: sandstone and limestone cliffs crowd us and the forest becomes sparse; there is much sign of human activity, fields of buckwheat on old river terraces, plaits of hay draped over branches to dry, and after we ascend a steep slope, the village of Murwa. We wander through the village, past its dozen widely spaced houses, and looking back, see a waterfall some five hundred feet high. According to our map its waters come from Phoksumdo Lake, which lies just beyond the gigantic earthen wall that here blocks our access to the upper part of the valley. A switchback trail surmounts this wall, and at the crest we leave behind its desiccated slope for a stunted conifer forest. Soon, on reaching a rise, the land slopes gently away, and in the distance I see the southern tip of Phoksumdo Lake. As Peter and I hurry along, the forest thins, then abruptly gives way to fields and, near the lake, the village of Ringmo. Three pagoda-shaped stupas mark the entrance to this village, the sacred towers shining white and ochre in the westering sun. Flat-roofed houses stand in a cluster, their high stone walls and narrow window slits giving them the appearance of fortresses ready to defend themselves against the elements. With a backdrop of lead-colored cliffs rising into everlasting snows, the village seems terribly vulnerable, a medieval vision that might vanish with the shrug of a mountain.

As we erect our tents in a stone corral, a noisy throng of villagers crowds around or watches from roofs and windows. We inquire about Shey. Apparently no one has either gone or come from there in a month, not since the first winter storms, and to indicate the height of the snow, one man, dressed in a wine-red *chuba*, places his hand flat against his neck. Between us and Shey is Kanga La, the Snow Pass, which according to a U.S. army map is nearly 20,000 feet high.* The five Tamang porters are not dressed for high-altitude climbing and plan to return home; Gyaltsen and Tukten will travel south and west to the town of Jumla to pick up the mail that we hope awaits us there and to replenish our depleted supply of sugar and other items. Shey is still a three-day trek to the north, and to reach it we obviously need help from the people of Ringmo. The men argue loud and long with each other about carrying our loads, finally agreeing reluctantly, but with the strange proviso that we give them two whole days to repair their cloth boots. Being in no position to bargain, we agree to this excessively long time for a minor task.

I buy a goat to provide all of us with a big meal and the Tamang with a farewell feast. While bits of goat sizzle over the fire and a pot of intestines bubbles, Peter and I write letters to send out with the couriers. Afterward I check over our food supply and equipment. There is a large tear in the cook tent. Made aware of it, Jang-bu shrugs, "It is old tent, sir," and ignores the matter. "Have Dawa sew it up," I order, and continue my daily inspection. Providence is not the Sherpas's forte, and I must keep an eye on all such minor aspects of the expedition.

In the afternoon, with Peter as teacher and companion, I explore the religious shrines around Ringmo. People here adhere to the B'on religion, a pre-Buddhist faith of many spirits reminiscent of shamanism. When Buddhism was brought to Tibet in the seventh century, the B'on priests incorporated the new religion into their own to such an extent that the two became outwardly almost indistinguishable. For instance, the B'on Po, the followers of this faith, walk around the walls of prayer stones in a counterclockwise direction to show respect rather than a clockwise direction in the manner of Buddhists. The stupa, too, is now a part of the B'on religion even though it is basically a universal shrine symbolizing the one Buddha. Different parts of the

* However, I discover later that this map is highly inaccurate. Many listed altitudes are 2,000 feet too high and trails are in the wrong places.

stupa are identified with the five elements—spirit, air, fire, water, earth —and other such aspects of man's total existence as the sun and moon and his four stages of spiritual progress. We enter the largest stupa. Frescoes of Buddha, large and small, in blue, ochre, and white, cover the walls of the single room, and nine mystic circles or mandalas are on the ceiling. However, the fine paintings are beginning to peel with age and neglect. Leaving the stupa, we cross potato fields to wander along the lake, edged with silvery birch and pine, toward a monastery tucked against the side of a cliff. Passing here seventeen years earlier, David Snellgrove felt that he "had come at last to the paradise of the Buddha 'Boundless Light.'" Two lamas and a dozen other men lived at the monastery at that time, but one lama has since died and the rest have moved away. The buildings are shuttered now, and grasses and wild gooseberries grow around eleven stupas where once the faith- ful trod, placing as tributes tiny stupas of clay and ash and voicing their sacred incantation. We leave the dilapidated sadness of the monastery and return to our tents.

With a guide I climb a slope behind Ringmo shortly after dawn to look for bharal; women are already high on the mountain, cutting dry grass for livestock fodder. We continue upward until the whole lake lies visible within its prison of rock, stubby arms stretching northward into two valleys. From the heights it is easy to see how the lake came into being. Previously there had been a peaceful valley down which flowed a river with forests along its banks, but one day the earth trembled and the mountains shook; a mountain on the east side of the valley, and one on the west side too, released millions of tons of rock and earth, their landslides forming a dam. Slowly the river filled the valley, rising a thousand feet before it could flow over the dam to continue its journey.

My guide locates a herd of bharal, twenty-nine animals of all ages and both sexes. Overhead two ravens circle, a good omen, for from Alaska to the highlands of Africa my most treasured wilderness mem- ories include these birds.

Ringmo to Shey, October 25–November 1

The porters assemble in our corral and as if on prearranged signal begin to complain loudly about the size of the loads and their meager pay. For two hours they quarrel with Jang-bu and each other, urged on by spectators on the rooftops, yet knowing that the loads are light and their pay generous. Reluctantly we accede to their demands, but another argument starts about who is to carry which load. To solve that problem, Jang-bu collects a boot thong from each porter and places one at random on each load. Every man recognizes his distinctively embroidered thong, and finally the burdens are hefted without further protest. At first the path is little more than a ledge clinging to the vertical face of a cliff, at places made passable only by wooden pegs driven into crevices and covered with flat rocks between which the blue waters of the lake are visible far below. However, the way soon becomes less hazardous, winding up a steep spur of the mountain. I walk ahead of the others to look for tracks on the dusty trail and am rewarded by the pugmarks of a snow leopard and a set of droppings containing bharal hair. Having descended into the valley at the northern end of the lake, the porters insist on camping, although we have traveled only four hours.

In the morning the men prepare for the day with deliberate inertia. A goiterous fellow once again complains loudly about his load, trying to goad the others into revolt. I tell him to shut up or get the hell out of here, the tone of my voice transcending any language barrier, and he sullenly subsides. Our caravan moves with unbearable slowness, the porters halting every ten minutes for a lengthy rest: they obviously have no intention of ever reaching Shey. As we wend our way up the valley, Peter and I find several dead redstarts. The valley is remarkably silent, almost devoid of birds, and we surmise that an early winter storm killed these birds before they could depart for lower altitudes. The discovery of the fragile bodies dead among the autumn bushes of barberry and wild rose does nothing to lighten my dark mood. Leaving the main valley, we enter a dismally narrow gorge down which cascades a stream around dark boulders glazed with ice. We walk up one bank until the cliffs dictate that we wade through numbing cold water to the other. The porters are reluctant to continue, and when at 13,600 feet, we reach the last clump of birch, they lay down their loads. It is only 2:30 P.M. The Sherpas occupy a shallow cave while Peter and I squeeze our tents into small level spots between boulders; the porters descend the gorge to sleep somewhere at a lower altitude.

Peter, too, has felt depressed today, as he relates in his journal:

> This evening I feel much better—why? I disliked the gray Phok-sumdo Khola and hate this black ravine; thick clouds are moving north, with threat of snow, and already porters are pointing toward the pass, shaking their heads. Yet I feel calm, and ready to accept whatever comes, and therefore happy. The turn in my mood occurred this morning, when the brave Dawa, attempting to catch Jang-bu's pack, hurled across a stream, dropped it ineptly into the water. Wonderfully, Jang-bu laughed aloud, as did Dawa and Phu-Tsering, although it meant wet clothes and a wet sleeping bag for the head sherpa. That happy-go-lucky spirit, that acceptance which is not fatalism but a deep trust in life, made me ashamed.

Peter and I depart before the porters arrive, moving rapidly up the gorge to keep warm. Two hours later, where the valley forks, we meet the sun. Sitting on a snow-free patch of grass, we absorb the warmth of the sun and study our map. The trail to Shey is clearly marked up the left fork. Leaving Peter to wait for the porters, I scout ahead, climbing over a cliff into a huge snow bowl surrounded by serrated peaks. On the skyline is a rent in the wall, the pass. The snow is hard and I travel fast, determinedly escaping from the terrible solitude of people crowded together, alone for the first time on this month-long journey, away from the pressure of the constant demands, decisions, and worries imposed by others, free to abandon myself to time and place. I hurry on. To reach the pass, to force my will against the gods and devils that seem to make the mountains retreat before me, becomes my supreme purpose. In the shattering light of the snow my mind shuttles between illusion and reality, and though I now feel that this may not be our route, the blue notch of the pass remains a shining beacon, beckoning me on until the world vanishes at my feet. I am at 17,600 feet. Barely glancing at the pathless chaos of peaks beyond, I hurry back to where I abandoned Peter.

Tracks in the snow lead up the other fork and I follow until I meet everyone coming back. Peter relates that the porters have balked all morning and that they refused to continue, saying that the snow is too deep, the route impassable. Most of our things have been cached at 16,500 feet. Back at the previous night's campsite, we discuss what to do next. The Sherpas are dejected, certain that we cannot cross the Kanga La, but I know they will follow my lead. Peter wonders if it would not be better to study bharal at Ringmo; however, this is his first journey into high mountains and he has no basis for judging the limits of the possible here. These Ringmo porters are wholly undependable and cannot be retained; other matters aside, the constant delays have depleted our funds beyond the point where we can afford to pay porters on the mere chance that they might work. I suggest that Jang-bu, Phu-Tsering, and I go to Shey tomorrow, using a Ringmo porter as guide. Perhaps we can find porters at Shey; if not, at least we will know what problems lie ahead.

We leave shortly after dawn, accompanied by two Ringmo men, and within three hours reach the cache. The supposedly impossible route to the pass is not difficult, a stiff climb with snow at most knee-deep, and at noon we stand on top. Or rather we lie there on a patch of black scree, smashed down by an icy gale hurling over the crest with demonic power. Though battered by winds, I am filled with a savage joy. Shey is ours. We have passed through the Himalaya with its sharp-edged peaks, and now the Asian highland, the Tibetan Plateau, lies ahead, wave after wave of rounded, rumpled hills, an immense landscape with every feature showing brilliantly clear. The descent from the pass into the snow caldron at our feet will be almost perpendicular at first, awkward but not very hazardous. I decide that only Jang-bu and I need continue to Shey. Lying curled with my back against the wind, I scribble a note to Peter with numb fingers, telling him that the route poses no problem and asking him to move all loads to the top of the pass. Phu-Tsering shivers as he tucks the note into his jacket. I check my altimeter: 17,800 feet. A cornice of snow blocks access to the slope, and we chop it away with a hoe brought from Ringmo for such a purpose. With Phu-Tsering and Jang-bu holding the rope, I lower myself over the lip, descending rapidly, cutting steps, until I reach a secure place, and Jang-bu can follow. Phu-Tsering waves good-bye and vanishes.

We kick steps into the crusted snow, bowed against the wind's fury. Where the slope levels the snow becomes powdery and I strap on my snowshoes to skim along, breaking trail for Jang-bu. After two hours we reach a small pond from which a valley extends northward, hemmed in by limestone cliffs. Alternately balancing on the slippery rocks of a streambed or floundering through deep snow, we slowly descend. Finally the valley widens and from a spur I see Shey Gompa far below at the junction of two streams, the monastery with its stupas very white against the winter-brown slope. But I am too tired to exult. We plod on and it is almost dusk when we pass some prayer walls, cross a bridge, and climb an embankment to the monastery. There are no people, no dogs, no signs of life; the houses are shuttered. The place is deserted, an ancient and dead world lost in the folds of the mountains. Then we see a lone white goat standing on a wall: someone must be here. Jang-bu shouts and shouts. A door opens slightly in an annex of the monastery, and a woman suspiciously peers out. Finally convinced that we are not bandits, she permits us to enter and stay the night. While we sip hot tea and eat boiled potatoes, the woman explains that only she and her two small children, as well as an old woman, remain at Shey. All others have gone to villages at lower altitudes one month earlier than usual because of the heavy snows. There being no porters, we now have interesting logistic problems. First we must move all our loads over the Kanga La to Shey. Peter plans to return to Kathmandu much earlier than I, in just three weeks. Who is to guide him back? Tukten and Gyaltsen could do so, if they can cross the Kanga La on their return from Jumla. I fall asleep thinking about these problems, the white goat snuggled against my sleeping bag for warmth.

The night has barely yielded its icy grip on the valley when I begin a search for bharal. To the south lies the canyon down which we traveled yesterday, as well as mountainsides deep in snow. However, the south-facing slopes, warmed by the sun, are still in autumn, with grasses dry and the leaves of low-growing *Lonicera* and *Caragana* shrubs brittle and brown. I see a bharal herd high above the monastery, mere blue-gray dots, and trudge upward, away from the biting cold toward the sun that now creeps down the slope. Casually approaching the bharal, I sit down about two hundred feet away; the animals, all males, continue to graze as if oblivious of me, perfect conditions for a study. I scan the snow-free slopes on the far side of the stream and within a few minutes discover three more herds. I also see several hermitages, some tiny, mere one-room huts used by people who wish to live in strict seclusion, others imposing, three to four stories high, constructed against sepia cliffs. As revealed by a Tibetan verse, hermitages require a certain location:

> *Gyab rii tag;*
> The mountain rock behind;
>
> *Dun rii tso.*
> The mountain lake in front.

Conforming to this tradition, these hermitages are ochre-colored eyries with a view, not of a lake, but at least of a river. According to our hostess, up to twenty-five monks, eleven of them women, reside at these hermitages in the summer. Far below me lies Shey. The monastery is ringed by eight stupas, two of them large, and with so many mounds of prayer stones that it seems as if some celestial construction project was never completed. To inscribe liturgical texts on these prayer stones, thousands of men labored thousands of hours over the centuries. Close to the monastery are four substantial homes and three huts, and farther up the slope, six more homes, two of them derelict, these signs of human existence tiny indeed in relation to the bleak sea of ridges and crags.

Shey lies at 14,700 feet, more than 3,000 feet lower than the Kanga La, and the following morning I wearily contemplate another ascent. Jang-bu and I travel rapidly upward, stopping at the small lake only to deposit some firewood and erect a tent. Six hours after leaving Shey we stand once more on the pass. Eight of our loads have been deposited there: Peter and the Sherpas have been working hard. Sliding and running, we descend the 1,300 feet to camp in twenty minutes. After briefing Peter, I shoulder a load of sugar and add it to our cache on top, the trip taking two hours. Then, very tired, I slip into my sleeping bag and Phu-Tsering brings me a cup of cocoa. Peter is annoyed with me, feeling that my note to him from the summit was impolitely curt, and that it implied failure on his part to keep the porters moving upward on the day I went off on my own. I explain in turn that it was I who had failed the expedition by being truant at a crucial time, but that, at any rate, the porters would never have gone beyond the pass. Peter has been remarkably even-tempered throughout our tribulations, and I suspect that high altitude coupled with extremely strenuous work has made both of us somewhat irritable, a common symptom when the body is deprived of sufficient oxygen. Having talked matters over, we relax and plan for the days ahead.

Another clear, cold morning. Peter and I each transport a heavy pack to the top while the Sherpas break camp and follow with the remaining loads. After Peter has kicked a small platform into the snow a hundred feet below the rim, I lower three loads by rope. One he shoulders and the others he permits to glissade on their own down the slope. As he retrieves these, Phu-Tsering, who has taken his place on the platform, releases a suitcase without looking. It bounces toward Peter, gathering momentum, and we all stand still, we on top watching its fateful course and Peter below not knowing how to elude its erratic descent. Stepping to one side, he falls flat into the crusted snow, and the suitcase leaps over the spot where he stood. Phu-Tsering laughs with relief. Having carried or rolled everything down the mountain, we gather the strewn loads into a mound. I carry a pack and drag a suitcase, moving steadily on my snowshoes to the lake. Peter and I decide to spend the night there; the Sherpas want to continue to Shey and we agree to meet tomorrow. I return up the snow basin for another load, but the snow is soft now, making the work here at 17,000 feet grueling; I stop often and pant from exertion. Returning to the tent in late afternoon, I start a fire and the reluctant flames finally heat enough water for a cup of soup, which, with a few crackers and sardines, constitutes our dinner.

The night temperature drops below 0° F., and we remain in bed until the sun touches our tents. Loaded heavily, we begin the final lap to Shey. On the way we meet Jang-bu and Phu-Tsering, ascending to retrieve more baggage; Dawa has remained behind, snow-blind again. We reach Shey at 1:15 P.M., so weary that we barely seem to move the final few feet up the bluff to the monastery. The Sherpas have taken possession of a hut, a smoke-blackened room, empty except for a conical clay fireplace but ideally suited to our needs. I pitch my tent on a flat spot in front of the hut, and Peter his in a nearby courtyard. Seeing a herd of bharal on the slope above the monastery, I grab my scope and climb toward them. Today is November 1, thirty-five days since we left Pokhara. A single purpose has sustained me, and now, finally, I can begin the research for which I have come so far.

Shey, November 2–December 5

The day after our arrival Peter and I walk westward along a trail up the Shey Valley. At this season it is the only route out of the valley, leading over the Saldang La to Saldang, Namdo, and other villages. About every half mile, on the crests of the ridges, are mounds of sacred prayer stones, *mani* mounds, which a Buddhist always passes on the left, so that, on returning over the same path, he or she will have circled it completely in deference to the wheel of life. The mounds consist of inscribed stones, dozens of them, each made by a man seeking credit in the next life. How differently we seek our destiny. The *mani* mounds, I discover, are also of interest for other more mundane reasons. Being conspicuous, they are used by wolves as signposts, as places where they leave evidence of their presence in the form of droppings. Not long after tucking a fecal sample into my pocket, I see far ahead, on the other side of a dry wash, two whitish animals. "Snow leopard!" I exclaim, verbalizing a hope though knowing as I speak that my identification is wrong; the movements of these animals are not those of cats. Instead my scope brings to life five wolves, large beasts with luxuriant coats, one almost white, another silver-gray, and three gray with tones of gold. The wolves have spotted us too. Three of them trot along a slope, and after perusing us briefly, angle to join the others. Soon all disappear in the hills, the moment of enchantment all too brief, no more than a minute elapsing between discovery and loss.

The following morning we climb high up a ridge behind the monastery and from there try to count bharal on the snow-free slopes across the valley. Scanning the hillsides in a grand sweep from north to south, from the wind-etched pinnacles bordering the impassable Shey canyon, past the hermitages, some crumpled with age, to the ramparts of Crystal Mountain, I tally four herds. One of these herds is small, only four females and two young. As we watch, the animals suddenly startle and bunch; running downslope toward them are two wolves, one of them white—the same distinctive animal we met yesterday—the other tawny. They bound side by side, the speed of their attack hampered by procumbent junipers and other shrubs over which they must leap. The bharal at first flee rather casually toward the nearest cliffs, but they sprint when the wolves get within 125 feet. Still the wolves gain. They are within about 60 feet of a lagging female when she angles sharply downhill to escape with the others onto a precipice where the predators dare not follow. Foiled, the wolves return uphill where they join two others who have not participated in the hunt. There are only four wolves: one of yesterday's members is not with the pack. The big white wolf leads the others to a small grassy glade where with tails wagging exuberantly they sniff and nuzzle each other and roll on their backs, reaffirming their friendship; then following their white leader, they trot from sight. All day Peter and I watch the slopes, but the wolves have gone; and all day, too, the six bharal remain on or near the safety of the cliff.

The incident reveals how important cliffs can be to bharal, for although they seldom venture onto them, preferring to feed and rest on nearby grass slopes, they retreat to precipices in times of danger. No matter how fine the mountain pastures, bharal do not use them unless cliffs provide a safe haven nearby. Thus the habitat requirements of bharal differ from their Asian relatives in that urials and argalis are not dependent on cliffs, whereas goats, including tahr, spend much of their lives on them. American bighorn and thinhorn sheep, as well as the Siberian snow sheep, all closely resemble bharal not only in choosing good grazing grounds near precipices but also in seeking refuge among them in times of danger.

Each morning, as soon as sun ignites the summits, I hurry into the hills to observe bharal. Icy winds slice through me while I stamp my feet to keep warm and scribble notes with fingers so numb they can barely hold the pencil. I want to miss nothing during these early morning hours when the animals are most active; I am determined to remake the bharal's image, to create a new reality. "He would seek to live in past, present, and future as one, one eternity of which he might be the intellectual master," wrote Loren Eiseley, and in a small way this applies to my endeavor here too.

After a few days the superficial aspects of bharal society at Shey become clear to me. About 175 to 200 animals winter around the monastery, the animals seeming almost sedentary, confined now to certain snow-free hillsides. As among sheep and goats, herds are fluid, members joining and parting from them at intervals. Average herd size is eighteen, with a range of from two to sixty-one. About a third of the males, especially adult ones, are still in bachelor herds, indicating that the main rut has not yet begun. I am surprised that the ratio of young to females is only 4 : 10 and that of yearlings to females 3 : 10; reproduction and survival of young is obviously poor. The comparable ratios from the bharal population at Lapche were 9 : 10 and 8 : 10. Why should the Lapche bharal be over twice as successful in raising young as are those at Shey? Predators are usually blamed when a wildlife population declines, and snow leopard and wolves do prey on bharal, but they do so in both areas (see Appendix, Table 2). Live-stock also provides both predators with food, as do marmots in summer when they are not hibernating.

With predators active at both Shey and Lapche, it is highly un-likely that they are the cause of such a drastic difference in the num-ber of bharal young. As I repeatedly observed, whether among wild goat in the deserts of Sind or among ibex in the Karakoram, the vigor of a population depends primarily on the condition of its range. When food is plentiful and nutritious the well-fed females give birth to large, vigorous young; when it is of low quality newborns tend to be weak and often die. Even a casual look shows that all is not well with the habitat at Shey. The slopes there are eroded, shrubs perching on pedestals of soil, clutching at the last fragments of fertility. Livestock trails crisscross the hillsides, and minced to a fine powder by many sharp hooves, the soil follows the wind. Much of the remaining grass, bharals' preferred food, is tucked beneath thorny shrubs where it is difficult to reach. Although livestock also uses the Lapche area, the habitat there is in better condition than at Shey and the difference is reflected in the increased survival of young.

The effects of nutrition pervade an animal's whole society. Popula-tions of low density on good habitat, as the bharal at Lapche, contain few old animals, whereas stagnant populations on overgrazed range live a long time. By counting horn rings I noted that only about 10 percent of the Lapche males lived longer than five years, in contrast to Shey where over half of them did so. The fact that animals living in a poor habitat survive longer than those in a good one may seem paradoxical. However, there is a logical explanation: before entering a physiologically demanding period, such as winter, animals generally store fat, but those that expend energy on matters other than mainte-nance may find their fat reserves depleted before nutritious food be-comes available again; with fat reserves exhausted, some die of malnu-trition, while others, weakened, become predisposed to disease and predation. The rut is an extremely demanding period, for males ex-pend excess energy in winter when they can least afford it. Valerius

Geist observed that bighorn sheep on good range begin to rut at an earlier age and fight more often and more vigorously than do rams on poor range. This raises the cost of living, it increases the probability that the animal will become undernourished. Early maturity also means that a ram reaches an advanced physiological age earlier; he literally seems to burn himself out. In contrast, males on poor range mature late and court lethargically—and live long. Females on poor habitat may also have a long life, but for a different reason. Although females, unlike males, dissipate little energy in social interactions, their body reserves are first drained by the fetus and then by lactation. Thus a female who fails to conceive or whose young die at birth retains her reserves and will better survive a stressful season.

Although such information is interesting, I am not engrossed by it. I find it more exciting to watch the intricacies of bharal society, the undercurrents of rivalry, the appropriation of certain roles, the fragile balance between aggression and submission. High above Shey, near the edge of the snow line, lives a bachelor herd of about a dozen males, and I often seek them out. Usually they ignore my approach, but if I come suddenly upon them, one may emit a startled call, *chit-chit* or a slurred *chirrt*, like an annoyed red squirrel. After this momentary alarm, they continue to forage and interact, constantly striving to maintain their rank. Bharal, like sheep and goats, carry their rank symbols with them in the form of conspicuous coat color, large body size, and massive horns. When meeting, two males casually evaluate each other's fighting potential, and the smaller then defers to the larger. Even if the smaller refuses to accept his subordinate position, a dominant male need not exhaust himself in asserting rank. Instead he can convey his status with such subtle gestures that at first I did not always recognize their importance. One male might halt by a second one, and standing broadside, casually show off his black and swollen neck and the sweep of his horns until the other just as casually averts his head in submission. Or two males may feed side by side until the subordinate animal moves forward. Should this happen, the other quickly noses ahead, it being the prerogative of the dominant to lead.

Bharal males also use more direct methods to express dominance, as when one male mounts another. A dominant individual can do this with impunity, but he considers it an affront if a subordinate attempts it, and therefore retaliates, sometimes by rearing bolt upright in a threatening manner. Occasionally, one male approaches another with neck lowered and muzzle stretched forward, the gesture perhaps followed by a gentle kick or more rarely by a sideways twist of the head; sheep often display their dominance in this manner whereas goats seldom do so. At times a bharal male may threateningly extend his crimson penis while standing in a hunched position broadside to an opponent, and may insert the penis into his mouth. As already mentioned, sheep do not use this gesture, but goats frequently mouth their penises and they may spray urine over their faces. After observing these and other displays, I realized that bharal behavior is in various forms intermediate between that of sheep and goats.

Some dominance problems can only be settled on the battlefield. The previous year at Lapche, I had on several occasions seen a male stand balanced on his hindlegs, and then, with head cocked sideways, crash his horns against those of his opponent. Here at Shey, with the rut near, males are even more energetic in their fights. Two males may dash some twenty feet apart, rear up, and on their hindlegs hop or run toward each other before bashing horns with a dull crack that reverberates among the hills. At Shey I confirm my earlier surmise that bharal fight more like goats than like sheep.

Occasionally, several males will mount, clash horns, and rub against each other seemingly at random, a melee without reference to dominance, without fear of retaliation. But after such an amiable interlude, every male once again returns to the confines of his rank. Sheep also have such free-for-alls, except that the rams stand in a huddle facing inward.

The males above Shey provide a marvelous evolutionary adventure, and during each visit I almost count on them for further insights into their behavior. Although in some ways I impatiently await the rut, an aspect of bharal life history about which nothing is known, I am also content just being near the animals. Toward noon they become less and less active and after pawing a bed, each animal reclines to chew cud, its eyes mere slits of satisfaction. The sun is often warm at this time of day, shade temperatures climbing above freezing, and the hills vibrate with heat waves. Beyond, to the north, are the enormous coppery cliffs of Shey canyon and the rounded dome of Purple Mountain; on the horizon a frieze of snow peaks guards the Tibetan border. Such vast wild spaces often produce fear; they seemingly threaten to crush and swallow a wanderer. But I know that mountains are not only wild, that we find in them what we seek, be it peace or violence, beauty or terror. Resting tranquilly near the bharal, I know also that animals are wild only because man has made them so. Wolf, snow leopard, and all other creatures could be as tame as these bharal if only we would permit them to be. However, before man can transcend the present, before he can view nature in this new dimension, he must first change himself.

As I roam these silent hills, the serene monastery as the center of my world, the cares of the past month slip away. The tranquility of Shey affects Peter, too. High on a slope, with a view of Crystal Mountain, he has prepared a place for meditation which he describes as:

> a broken outcrop like an altar set into the hillside, protected from all but the south wind by shards of granite and dense thorn. In the full sun it is warm, and its rock crannies give shelter to small stunted plants that cling to this desert mountainside—dead red-brown stalks of a wild buckwheat, some shrubby cinquefoil, pale edelweiss, and everlasting, and even a few poor wisps of *Cannabis*. I arrange a rude rock seat as a lookout on the world, set out binoculars in case wild creatures should happen into view, then cross my legs to regulate my breath, until I scarcely breathe at all.
>
> Now the mountains all around me take on life; Crystal Mountain moves. Soon there comes the murmur of the torrent, from far away below under the ice. . . . Even in windlessness, the sound of rivers comes and goes and falls and rises, like the wind itself. And instinct comes to open outward by letting all life in, just as a flower fills with

sun. To burst forth from this old husk and cast one's energy abroad, to fly . . .

In spite of our disparate reasons for being here, Peter on an inner search, I on a scientific quest, we are nevertheless travelers on similar paths. The aims of Buddhism and science are in some aspects alike, as a few comments by the Buddhist teacher Shunryu Suzuki show: "When you understand a frog through and through, you attain enlightenment; you are Buddha. . . . Without knowing the origin of things we cannot appreciate the results of our life's effort. . . . To study Buddhism is to study ourselves." But the meaning of these words far transcends scientific perception. Science still remains a dream, for it takes us no more than a few faltering steps toward understanding; graphs and charts create little more than an illusion of knowledge. There is no ultimate knowing. Beyond the facts, beyond science, is a domain of cloud, the universe of the mind, ever expanding as the universe itself.

Sometimes, while watching bharal, my eyes unconsciously leave the animals to climb along the skyline, and my mind struggles to escape its confines, traveling, searching, seeking, until on rare occasions a brief vision of shining clarity seems to define the world. Once I climbed high on a ridge where all was space and light and wind careened up the canyon over the weathered slopes. In fading shafts of sunlight the monotone of rock and snow had a metallic sheen, as from an inner glow. Looking down into the valley, I at first saw only the past, a fragment of a lifeless star. It was no more inviting than the earth as seen from outer space, hurtling through blackness, featureless, swathed in filaments of cloud. Then I detected the monastery, a fossilized remnant from another age. This ephemeral bulge on the earth's crust transformed the landscape. The view became liberating; it provided a glimpse of eternity. The compulsion to study bharal vanished. I knew my efforts were of little consequence, that this species, like all others, represents a mere passing phase of life in an ever-changing world. Man has pondered the transience of existence since he became man, yet such reflections recur in high and lonely places.

However, I let such thoughts slide away with the wind. Introspection may help me be less of a stranger to myself, but it accomplishes little. I have an inner obligation to remain a part of the present, to observe bharal, to discover something new; I am delighted with each new insight, even if utterly trivial in the grand scheme of things. The day I first saw rump-rubbing was cause for special elation: one bharal male walked up to a second male and for nearly a minute rubbed his face on the other's rump. I soon noted that it is usually a lower-ranking animal who rubs, apparently to convey his submission and to express friendliness. Another and even more subordinate male may join and rub the second-largest male, all three then standing amicably in a row, indulging in this curious gesture unique to bharal.

The district of Dolpo is an ethnic enclave of Tibetans, about 1,300 square miles in size, with a culture not yet disrupted by outside forces. In neighboring Tibet—of which Dolpo was part until the eighteenth century—the Chinese have almost extinguished the fires of religion, closing most monasteries since annexing the country in 1959, but here in Dolpo an ember of tradition still shines. Peter and I want to learn about this vanishing culture, to return if only for a moment to the Middle Ages. However, life at Shey has almost been suspended for the winter. Most people have gone to lower altitudes, the monastery is locked. We remain outsiders, wistfully looking; all we can do is wander among the culture's artifacts. We investigate the two large stupas. Ochre-colored clay frescoes depicting peacock, elephant, horse, and *garuda,* a mythical hawk, adorn the outside, symbolic creatures signifying the four directions; Buddhas and mandalas decorate the inside, and two rows of prayer wheels enable a supplicant to recite the sacred creed many times simultaneously by spinning them all. Suspended from one stupa is a tiny bell, a wind-bell which tinkles with the slightest breeze, producing a sound of such clear and delicate beauty that I sometimes detour past just to hear it. Surmounting the

monastery is an iron trident, around which is a cluster of shredded prayer flags sending its spiritual message in all ten directions. Piled beneath the prayer flags is an assortment of yak and bharal horns, and to my surprise, two bleached shou antlers with massive beams about 45 inches long. The shou or Sikkim stag, a subspecies of red deer, is believed to be extinct; at least no recent reports exist of shou from its home in the coniferous forests of Bhutan and in the Chumbi Valley and other parts of Tibet. These two antlers are nearly 400 miles west of the known range of the animal. How did they get here? Of the few people remaining at Shey none can provide me with information.

An old woman lives in one of the houses, but she fears us. Once when I drift close to her home to observe a robin accentor, a small brown bird with rusty chestband, flitting among the crumbling walls of her courtyard, she emerges from the shuttered darkness. Flapping her arms, she cries shrilly *"Kya? Kya?"* "What? What?" like a demented, dun-colored bird. Our hostess is more communicative. Her name is Tasi Chanjum but she prefers to be called Namu, or "hostess," for among Tibetans it is impolite to address a mere acquaintance by name. She is a woman of about forty, with sturdy pleasant features. She dresses in the coarse homespun and striped apron of married Tibetan women, and she wears a necklace of pink coral stones and large amber-colored beads. Two of her children are here, a thin boy of about seven and a chubby girl of two—"like a smiling potato given life," Peter says. Namu's husband, a lay priest who on request reads Buddhist scriptures at various households, is at present in Samling. No proper monks now live at Shey and some religious functions are performed by men like Namu's husband. The ancestors of such lay priests often built houses by monasteries because a family member was a monk, and, if so inclined, someone in each succeeding generation continues to participate in ceremonies.

When we query Namu about the Lama of Shey, she replies that he is in Saldang. Nevertheless, one day Peter and I head across the valley to look at Tsaking, his residence. We descend to the river and cross the small wooden bridge; a white-breasted dipper is there, as it often is. Beyond, the trail cuts up the slope, over a crest, and along the north-facing contour of a ridge, deep in snow. After traversing a fold of the hills, and another, the trail follows the base of a cliff. We first reach a cave with a small white stupa inside, and then a four-storied hermitage where for varying lengths of time, usually not exceeding three to four months, people seek seclusion to pursue their spiritual aims. But its many monastic cells stand empty now. Farther on, past a litter of rocks where in summer the *mani* stones are carved, is the lama's residence, a long structure built against the cliff face. On the patio, to our surprise, are two men. One, a youth of about twenty with close-cropped hair like mole skin, stitches boots; the other, somewhat older, sits cross-legged and rubs rancid butter into a goat hide. His face is coppery, and he wears a leather jacket and frayed pants of a color matching his face. With his high cheekbones and aquiline nose he looks like an American Indian, a Sioux or perhaps a Cheyenne. We smile at the two and they smile back, neither of us able to converse with the other. Passing some sliced, boiled potatoes drying in the sun, we continue past the hermitage to the crest beyond. There, by a stupa, we eat lunch. As a herd of bharal is grazing on a nearby slope, I remain to observe it while Peter ambles back toward the monastery. Dark snow clouds soon gather around the dome of Purple Mountain to the north, and then I also turn toward home, gathering juniper boughs for the evening's fire along the way.

Jang-bu discovers that Namu has misled us about the lama. To protect his privacy she had told us he is in Saldang, when, in fact, he is at his residence. Since his legs became crippled, possibly from polio or arthritis, about eight years ago, the lama has not left his home. One of the men we saw on our visit to the hermitage, the one I mentally referred to as "the Indian," is Karma Tupjuk, the Lama of Shey, the reincarnation of the founder-lama and the best authenticated of the five incarnate lamas in Dolpo. The young man, his helper, is named Takla. When David Snellgrove visited Shey in 1956 the lama had been in solitary meditation for three years and could not be disturbed, but now Peter and I hope for an interview. We send Jang-bu to arrange it. Peter and Jang-bu go together on the first visit, and some days later I join them, together with Tukten, on another.

Takla leads us into the dark interior of the lama's residence. We pass first through a storage room filled mainly with sacks of grain; a wolf hide hangs from a rafter. The lama owns fields in Saldang and these the villagers till and reap for him in exchange for half of the harvest. Climbing up a notched log, we reach a kitchen with many copper urns and pots around a clay hearth. Takla pokes a few twigs into the embers and sparks briefly light up the smoke-blackened room. The lama is in his study, a small, spare chamber with several books, a bench, and a row of butter lamps, all dimly lit by a shaft of sun piercing the window slit. Lacking a ceremonial *kata*, we present the lama with a packet of tea and ten rupees instead. He will talk with us later, he conveys through Jang-bu and Tukten, and we wait for him on the patio, in the sun. Takla serves us tea in porcelain cups, bitter, black Chinese tea salted and laced with butter, a heaped plate of *tsampa*, the roasted and ground barley that is the staple of Tibetans, and bits of sun-dried curd.

We eat and gaze at the mountains. The hermitage is on the quiet side of the hill, protected from the north wind. Below, the slope lies sere and rutted, its surface flecked with dark, low junipers like giant molds on the earth's crust. The opposite slope is alive, a dizzying, dancing, luminous white as heat waves flow viscously over the snow. The heights glimmer, the sky sways; and, above, Crystal Mountain, ice-veined, a mysticism of stone. Crystal Mountain is not an impressive peak. Hundreds, thousands of others in this land of rock are taller, sheerer, and have greater claims to beauty. At first Peter and I could not identify the mountain, the holiest in Dolpo, because we looked for a snow peak, white and sharp-edged like a crystal. But asking Namu, Jang-bu learned that Crystal Mountain is the gray-walled bulk guarding the entrance of the gorge leading to the Kanga La. The name of the mountain is derived not from its appearance, but from the veins of clear crystal lacing its flanks. As we sit on the patio, with the mountains moving before us in the sliding light, I can well imagine that this is a place for visions, that spirits and illusions dwell in these heights.

The holiness of Crystal Mountain is based on a legend. As related by Joel Ziskin in a *National Geographic* article, a thousand or so years ago the Buddhist ascetic, Drutob Senge Yeshe, visited Dolpo, where he found a people whose supreme god was a wild mountain spirit. Drutob meditated in a cave near Shey and attained enlightenment. He then tried to overcome the fierce mountain spirit, using a flying snow lion, a legendary companion of the snow leopard, as a mount, but the spirit resisted by unleashing hordes of snake beings. However, the snow lion reproduced itself 108 times, once for each book of the Buddhist scriptures, and with this reinforcement Drutob vanquished the spirit and transformed him into "a thundering mountain of purest crystal."

> I flew through the sky on a snow lion
> And there, among the clouds, I performed miracles.
> But not even the greatest of celestial feats
> Can equal once rounding on foot this Crystal Mountain.

Heeding Drutob's words, the people of Dolpo gather in July, before the barley harvest, to circle Crystal Mountain. On the day of the full moon the throng begins its trek. Now and then a celebrant scrapes rock dust from the sacred mountain and swallows it with water. The pilgrims cross a pass where prayer flags snap in the wind from a row of cairns, and bleached yak skulls mark the route. By a glacial lake, where the snow lions gamboled in victory, they join hands and dance in a circle to the music of a lute. This ten-mile circuit of the mountain ends in the cave where Drutob Senge Yeshe attained enlightenment and where a reliquary holds his ashes. There, in the depths of the mountains, final prayers are murmured.

After we have waited two hours, the lama appears, helped to a pillow on the patio by Takla. Amicably the lama answers our questions, about himself, about Shey, about wildlife. He has no aura of sagacity, no distant air of mystic vocation; he talks easily, as a farmer would of weather and crops. The large hermitage here, he says, was built about sixty years ago, before his time. He is fifty-two now and came to Shey as an eight-year-old boy from Manang, a village east of the Kali Gandaki. After the previous Lama of Shey died, emissaries from Dolpo searched far for a reincarnation of the founder-lama Ten-dzin Rä-pa, and by various signs the present lama showed that he was the chosen one. Even as a child he had known that one day he would be a *tulku*.

I ask him about the Sikkim stag antlers at the monastery. Yes, he remembers them well, for he brought them many years ago from the north, from the valley of the Tsang-po, but he never saw a live animal there. I query him about Tibetan argali, about whether this large sheep occurs here, for at the base of the flagpole in front of the monastery is a weathered skull. Ten years ago, even six years ago, the lama replies, he saw this sheep on the slopes of Purple Mountain, but they do not come anymore. I wonder why the animals disappeared since hunting is not intensive. Argalis cannot cope with deep snow. Have recent winters been severe? Last year and three years ago there was much snow, the lama relates, holding his hand about three feet above ground, so deep that much livestock died of starvation, and before that some other winters were bad too. I suspect that the argalis, living here at the edge of their range, died off during severe winters because deep snow deprived them of food and made them easy prey for wolves.

We talk on, of the snow leopard that wander the trails and the tiny hermitages that cling to the cliffs like limpets to a rock. Before we take our leave, Peter asks for and receives a prayer flag, printed on local wood blocks, for his meditation room at home. As we walk silently back to the monastery, lines from a poem by Robinson Jeffers might have been written for that moment:

> Soon, perhaps, whoever wants to live harmlessly
> Must find a cave in the mountains or build a cell
> Of the red desert rock under dry junipers
> And avoid men, live with more kindly wolves
> And luckier ravens, waiting for the end of the age.

When the sun of early November melts some of the snow off the high passes, travel becomes easier. The route north to Samling, across Purple Mountain, remains closed, but the one east to Saldang, a day's walk away, is open. One day four men come with yaks to transport sacks of *tsampa* and potatoes back to their winter homes in Saldang. One of them is Tundu, who in summer resides in a wing of the monastery. His face is long and his hair cropped short, and he wears a large turquoise in his right ear. We trade him some empty biscuit tins with tight-fitting lids, ideal storage containers, for potatoes. A few days later Ongdi, Namu's brother and the owner of the hut we have occupied, arrives. He possesses an immense smile, a torrent of words, and an insatiable appetite for possessions. His eyes roam constantly as he talks, and whatever they see he demands—lamp, bottles, jacket, suitcase, a pair of my boots. I trade him the last for *tsampa*. He shows us a *salegrami*, a smooth black stone with the dainty imprint of a plantlike sea creature, perhaps a brachiopod. Pilgrims along the Kali Gandaki, where such stones are common, consider them sacred, but Ongdi, ever avaricious, sells his to Peter, after considerable haggling, for a few rupees. Rent for the hut is next on the bargaining agenda. Ongdi wants a reasonable five rupees a day, but with our cash supply already depleted I am not certain we can afford this, and we agree to one rupee a day and a large can of tea.

On November 11, on returning to our hut late in the afternoon, I find Gyaltsen there, back from Jumla with supplies and mail. He has traveled alone over the Kanga La from Ringmo. Where is Tukten? Gyaltsen's story is confusing, but ill feeling between the two culminated at Ringmo, where, having drunk too much *rakshi,* they had a fight. Tukten is expected to arrive later today or tomorrow, and he does so at dusk.

I read my letters voraciously, the first ones from home in over a month and a half. However, Peter says, "I don't think I'll open my letters until I return to Kathmandu. They might contain bad news." His behavior puzzles me, but he does not explain and I do not pry, self-consciousness preventing us from sharing.

With the two Sherpas having returned, Peter can now depart for Jumla on November 18 as planned. He decides against crossing the Kanga La again, and instead plans on an alternate route via Samling and Namdo, a route with three passes, though none as high as the Kanga La. Tukten and Dawa will be his guides and porters. The helpful Tukten, with his quick mind and wide interests, should serve well as Peter's companion; the silent and phlegmatic Dawa has a powerful back for carrying loads. We are both relieved to settle the departure date. Peter has often been restless since his arrival at Shey. Although he finds contentment and spiritual solace at this Buddhist shrine, a part of him remains tense. Perhaps because of the recent death of his wife he is anxious to return to his children.

Almost daily Peter had broached the topic of how he might get out of Shey if Tukten and Gyaltsen did not return. I tried to deflect these discussions, for the Kanga La, though difficult, was open, and unless more snow fell the Sherpas would return. Besides, having just reached Shey the frequent talk of leaving disquieted me; for me the journey's purpose had only just begun. Partly to appease Peter, I sent Jang-bu

to Saldang to inquire about alternative routes to the south. Now, with
Gyaltsen and Tukten back and with plans settled, the future no
longer intrudes on the present.

Of the many mountain spirits at Shey, I seek to meet only one—
the snow leopard. Peter and I had found an old dropping but not
until the morning of November 12, the day after Tukten and
Gyaltsen returned, is there a fresh track in the dust of a trail. We
peruse the slopes carefully, knowing the cat is there, perhaps watching us with clear, unblinking eyes, but only a golden eagle quarters
the cliffs. Again that night the snow leopard patrols the slopes in
search of an unwary bharal. Near the hermitage trail is a shallow
cave, and at its entrance I pile rocks into a low wall behind which I
unroll my sleeping bag. Perhaps the snow leopard will pass my hiding place at dusk or dawn. I stretch a trip wire attached to a camera
flash across the trail to record any nocturnal visitor. My afternoon vigil
is futile, and finally, the night cold sends me to bed. The cave's ceiling
presses close, and in the dim light I can see in it scalloped shells,
fragments of bryophytes, and calcareous tubes, probably the former
retreats of marine worms. I lie among fossilized creatures of the ancient Tethys Sea, where long before man, waves pounded and life
pulsated in the abysmal depths. If I close my right eye, there is only
rock; I lie buried beneath the sediments of the ocean floor, and
perhaps my skull will become a *salegrami* stone. If I close the left
eye, my gaze is liberated, penetrating the emptiness beyond the first
evening stars.

The snow leopard crossed the slope just above my cave sometime
during the night and joined the trail 150 feet beyond the trip wire.
All that day and the next I look for its shadow among clefts and behind junipers. But spirits are made of dreams and their appearance
cannot be willed. Before dawn, on November 15, the snow leopard
passes above the monastery, and that same night a lone wolf trots
by our tents, going the other way, leaving only tracks to reveal their
furtive presence. After four days the snow leopard vanishes from

Shey, without having caught a bharal. Scavenger birds would have told me of a kill.

Snow leopard came to Shey just once more during my stay. Two animals, traveling together, passed through in late November. It seems surprising that no snow leopard settled at Shey to take advantage of all the bharal. However, I calculate that these 200 bharal could barely support one snow leopard on a long-term basis and still maintain their population level. Bharal also die from disease, accidents, wolves, and away from the protection of Shey, from human predation. When all causes of death are combined, the Shey bharal do not produce enough of an annual surplus to maintain even one large predator. Each snow leopard must travel widely to subsist.

To my knowledge only one bharal, a female, died during our visit. Her spark of life departed so suddenly and mysteriously that she collapsed in midstride on a trail near the monastery. Ravens and lammergeier discovered her. Seeing the birds, everyone at Shey came; Namu and her relative Sani, Tundu's wife, the old woman, and several visitors. Carrying knives and baskets, they ran to join the birds. But ahead of them all was Jang-bu. He reached the carcass first and thereby could claim a hindleg for our household. Scavenging is done here according to custom. For example, bharal dying on the hermitage side of the valley belong to the lama and those on the monastery side to the villagers. Jang-bu relates these events to me when I return home from bharal-watching that afternoon. I then visit the site of the female's death, descend to the river where she was butchered to collect a sample of stomach content, and visit Tundu's wife to examine the head. We have roasted bharal for dinner, tender, like good venison, our first meal with meat since we butchered a goat at Ringmo a month before.

November 18, the day of Peter's departure, arrives bringing a general exodus from Shey. Two of the Sherpas are leaving with Peter, Jang-bu and Gyaltsen are going to Saldang for a few days to trade a suitcase and other items of food, and I am accompanying everyone to the top of the Saldang La; only Phu-Tsering remains at the hut. We head east, between rounded hills, following the fresh tracks of a wolf pack. We are still on the animals' trail as barren scree replaces the last stunted plants. Plodding upward toward a cut on the skyline, we find on arriving that we are not at the anticipated pass, that we must penetrate farther into the mountains. But after ascending a narrow valley and a slope beyond, a new landscape explodes before us. We halt at the summit cairn to which each grateful traveler adds a stone to thank the gods for safe passage. My altimeter reads 16,900 feet. Toward the south is the jagged ice scarp of the Kanjiroba Range, sterile in its icy glory. "My eyes see that it is beautiful, my heart is touched by dread," wrote Peter of a similar view. However, to the north and northeast the brown maze of hills stretches on and on, into Mustang* and Tibet, beneath a sky that becomes deeper and deeper blue as it recedes. Peter and I shake hands, a silent affirmation of gratitude for what each has done for the other. It has been a good trip, a marvelous trip, and we wish each other luck in the days ahead. The trail sweeps downward across the face of a hill. I watch Peter's tiny caravan retreat and as I raise my arm in farewell the figures dissolve into the immensity of the land. We shall meet again, some centuries hence, in New York.

It seems quiet and lonely in the hut tonight. Phu-Tsering has borrowed a horse-headed lute from Namu, and he plunks a simple tune over and over.

Whether looking for bharal, choosing a trail, or relishing a hot cup of tea, I seldom think beyond the moment. My days follow a satisfying routine. The Sherpas sleep crowded in one corner of the hut like a cluster of hibernating marmots. When at dawn I hear twigs snap, someone, probably Gyaltsen, is building a fire, and it is time for me to get up. Tugging my shirt into the sleeping bag, I give it a few minutes to warm. Then, sitting up, I hurriedly pull the shirt

---

* Michel Peissel's book *Mustang, the Forbidden Kingdom* gives an excellent description of this remote corner of Nepal.

on as well as my down jacket. Unzipping the bag, I struggle into my pants, a complicated task in the confines of a low tent, and afterward my boots. As a butterfly emerges from its cocoon, I squirm out into the cold thin air. I glance at the sky. Another clear day. I check the thermometer at the side of the hut: 5° F. Shivering involuntarily, I duck into the smoke-filled room. Phu-Tsering has tea ready, and I sip it while he prepares oatmeal porridge or *tsampa* or a mixture of the two. He is a pragmatic cook. Once, for several days, I noted that whether he served tea or coffee it always tasted the same.

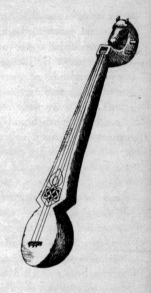

"Half and half, sah," Phu-Tsering explained. "Sherpas want coffee and Sahib wants tea."

When sun touches the summit of the peak on the other side of the valley, it is almost seven o'clock, time for me to leave. I travel the hermitage trail, looking for any one of several bharal herds which frequent these hillsides. Spotting several animals, I amble toward them. The lee of a small bluff gives me protection from the wind, and there, 300 feet from the bharal, I erect my tripod with scope. The sun's first feeble rays bring warmth and life to the slopes as the focus of my world narrows again to bharal. An adult male flays a juniper with sweeps of his horns, and I note his age and describe his behavior. A young male, two and a half years old, approaches a female with his muzzle and neck stretched forward, his tongue flicking, and then sniffs her anal area, to which she responds by trotting aside. Again I write down what happens. By recording each interaction, I can not only compare bharal behavior in detail with that of sheep and goats, but also detect changes in the rut. For example, until November 19 mainly young males showed interest in females, checking to see if by chance one might be in heat. Then, on November 20, the rut entered a new phase, tensions increasing palpably as adult males suddenly began to display to females. However, the bharal have done little today. It is almost noon; a lammergeier tilts along the cliffs; far away the Sherpas talk while collecting firewood. I become restless. Above, at the head of the small valley, is a saddle which I have not yet explored. Among shrubs I find tufts of bharal hair and then some bone splinters. Looking around I spot the skull of a male, and nearby, on a slab of rock, is an old wolf dropping, revealing how the bharal died. Searching further I find the contents of the bharal's stomach and place pieces of the shredded and dry plant material in a plastic bag. I will check it later to determine what the animal had eaten for its last meal. A skull, a dropping, stomach contents—it has been a good specimen day.

When I reach our hut at 2:30 P.M. Phu-Tsering is contentedly sitting in the sun pulling out his sparse whiskers with a pair of tweezers. He has seen me coming and is warming some leftover potatoes for my lunch. These he serves to me with rancid butter, a present from the lama. Butter is preserved for as long as a year by sewing it tightly into sheepskin. One day Takla brought us something that looked like a chunky ten-pound animal with mange: it was a skin bag of butter, well aged. The lama did not hesitate to ask for presents in return. From Phu-Tsering he requested a pair of pants, from Gyaltsen some socks, and from Jang-bu a pair of boots.

Since Jang-bu had only one pair and needed these for the journey to Jumla, I forbade him to part with it, noting that the lama cannot walk anyway. After eating, I do various small tasks, pressing bharal food plants for later identification, labeling exposed rolls of film, measuring horns. Shadows now rush down the slope, and the night cold arrives as suddenly as the sun drops behind the mountains. It is only 3:30 P.M., yet for us the evening begins.

As we sit cross-legged around the fire, Tundu's wife arrives to ask for a little sugar; tomorrow she may bring us *tsampa* or a handful of dried cheese. I transcribe the day's field notes into a permanent notebook while Phu-Tsering cooks dinner. Tonight I finish writing in only an hour, but on days when bharal have been active it may require three. We then eat a potato and turnip stew, a welcome change from our usual rice and *dal*. I compliment Jang-bu for obtaining turnips in Saldang on one of his recent trading expeditions. Jang-bu becomes bored with life at Shey, having little to do other than collect firewood, and greatly enjoys his forays to other villages. As we finish eating, Namu and Sani enter and join us by the fire. Sani is round and cheerful; when she smiles her eyes disappear behind her plump cheeks. She laughs and chatters and when the crowded bodies and fire make her hot, she leans back to open her *chuba,* letting cool air flow over her bare chest. Phu-Tsering adds more wood to the flames. After the two ladies leave, we talk in desultory fashion, the Sherpas asking questions about the United States, mainly what this or that item costs, and how much different jobs pay. Once, during such a quiet moment, Takla stumbled into the hut wanting to sleep with us. The lama, he said, had been angry and waved a stick at him because his *bogri*, a thick buckwheat bread, had not been well prepared. The Sherpas made him wash our dishes before permitting him to share their bed.

It is 7:30 P.M. I vacillate between drawing a little more warmth from the fire and going to bed. Deciding on the latter, I wish the Sherpas good night. Crystal Mountain looms above the stars and a sliver of moon casts a glacial glow on the snow. I light a candle, and tucked into my sleeping bag, write about the day's events and thoughts in my journal. My comments are brief, for my ballpoint pen freezes unless I warm it over the candle every minute or two.

For weeks now the herd of twelve bharal males has been on the slopes above the monastery. On November 25, at 8:40 in the morning, the animals descend into the valley, cross the icy stream, and determinedly head toward several females. I watch their progress with interest, realizing that the rut is entering a new phase. On joining, the bachelor herd breaks up as each male searches for a female in heat. But no females in this herd are ready to mate, and the males settle down with them to graze and rest. I note that only a few adult bharal males rove from herd to herd during the rut, in contrast to urial rams who always seem restlessly on the move. Male goats tend to remain with the herd. In this aspect of their behavior, like that of so many others, bharal are intermediate between sheep and goats.

Finally, on November 29, I observe males courting seriously, keeping close to certain females and chasing competitors away. They court impatiently, their actions lacking finesse this early in the rut. An incident from my field notes describes their behavior. The males are listed according to size, class V being the largest.

> A class V male and a female circle back and forth through a herd, running, trotting, and walking. Both are tired: they pant with tongues hanging out. Twice he mounts during his pursuit, but each time falls off as she continues to move. She leads him to a cliff, along a ledge, and into a rocky niche where he mounts her again. Restlessly she rushes off, cutting through and around the herd, the male still behind her, and then returns to the same ledge. The male mounts. A class II ventures near. The female bounds off pursued by the young male—but not the adult one. He tries to mount while running at high speed, but then further attempts are ruled out by a class IV male who hurries over to block him, yet ignores the female as she drifts away.

This female was obviously not in full heat or the adult male would not have permitted a young one access to her. However, the incident was typical in several ways. The female made no effort to escape the male; in fact, she seemed to entice not only him but any others in the vicinity by circling in or near the herd, sometimes gathering an entourage of suitors. As I mentioned earlier, should the largest male lose interest the one next in rank is ready to take over. Bharal retreat to cliffs mainly in times of danger. But females also seek lofty ledges during the rut, probably to reduce competition among males: there is seldom room for more than one to maneuver in such precarious retreats.

Sometimes at the height of passion the rank order among males breaks down temporarily before the dominant individual can once more create order out of chaos:

> Ten males are together when a female suddenly appears among them. As all converge on her she flees to a nearby cliff. Running along a ledge she reaches a platform. She stops there facing the wall while 6 males pile on her and on each other until she disappears beneath them. After much hooking and lunging only 3 males remain —two class V and one class IV. While the largest attacks a competitor, the female slips past him and escapes. She is pursued immediately by all males. A fleet class III mounts her on the run but a class IV butts him in the rump. Having lagged behind, the largest class V now arrives and displaces the rest as he follows the female to the same rocky platform. He first mounts her, then lunges at any suitor that ventures along the ledge. Suddenly the female departs, closely trailed by the males.

Although the rut is exciting to watch, I realize that the behavior of bharal is much like that of both sheep and goats, that courtship patterns have remained conservative in evolution. There are differences between species, especially in the frequencies of displays, with, for instance, urial twisting their heads sideways more often than do bharal, but these are minor vagaries. I want to observe the rut until the end, but know that this is not feasible. Our food is almost gone, except for a small hoard to be used only on the return journey. Daily, it seems, Phu-Tsering announces the demise of another item.

"Salt all gone, sah." I give him a frayed towel and ask him to trade it with Tundu's wife for coarse Tibetan salt.

"Soap all gone, sah." How can we be out of soap? Judging by appearances, we have not been contaminated by soap for weeks. A glutinous black soot from the juniper fires penetrates every crease and every pore of our skin; strange gray fuzz, like that found beneath an unswept bed, clogs our hair. We have discovered, as have Tibetans long ago, that the luxury of warmth far outweighs that of cleanliness. Namu gives us a little soda ash with which to scrub our dishes and pots.

A more urgent reason for leaving is the weather. The crisp November skies have given way to December storms. Dark cloud shadows hurry along the mountain flanks pushed by furious and bitter winds from which there is no escape. Wherever I hide, they find and pierce me like lasers. After only an hour of bharal-watching my hands and feet become senseless appendages. I stumble back to the hut, to the fire and a cup of tea, and then once more present myself to the elements. Any day the scudding clouds may bring snow and close the high passes, trapping us without adequate provisions until spring. I set our departure date for December 6.

The last few days are a time for summing up—filming neglected sequences, consolidating facts and impressions. Though much remains to be learned about bharal, I have gained valuable insights into the animal's natural history, and I have at least a reasonable answer as to whether the species is a sheep or goat.

Adult bharal males readily associate with females throughout the year, and in this respect resemble goats more than sheep. Only a few males roam during the rut, the animals being intermediate between sheep and goats. Males threaten each other directly by such means as lunging and clashing and, to a lesser extent, indirectly by

displaying themselves broadside and otherwise. Sheep use more indirect aggression and goats limit themselves almost wholly to the
direct forms. In spite of their stumpy horns, female bharal fight quite
often, behaving more like female goats than placid ewes. In general,
bharal society seems primarily goatlike with the addition of some
sheeplike traits. I surmise that the ancestors of bharal evolved on
cliffs, and that they later occupied less precipitous terrain where new
selection pressures modified their society in the direction character-
ized by sheep.

Turning to specific behavior patterns, one has to decide whether
similar traits have developed independently in two species, showing
convergent evolution, or whether they share a common origin. For
example, both bharal and sheep rub each other as a friendly gesture.
The part they rub is divergent—the former rub rumps, the latter
heads—and the evolution seems convergent. The fact that bharal and
sheep display the huddle may be convergent too, both habitat and
society having favored some means by which males can interact informally. There is a major difference in the way goats and sheep
clash: goats rear bolt upright and lunge down onto the horns of an
opponent; bharal often fight like that too, even though they do not
now spend much time on cliffs where this mode of fighting seems
safer than the long rush practiced by sheep. However, occasionally
they also run at each other like sheep, showing that selection for a
specific fighting style has been less rigid away from cliffs. Bharal
mouth their penises like goats, but they do not soak themselves with
urine. They also use their extended penises as display organs in
dominance, an elaboration not practiced by goats. A behavioral cline
exists, running from sheep that merely unsheath their penises, and
that rarely, to bharal that unsheath and mouth them, to goats that
unsheath and mouth them and also urinate on themselves. In this
respect bharal behave as if they are at an evolutionary stage prior to
that reached by goats.

What then can be deduced from these and other patterns about
bharal evolution? At Shey my thoughts dwelled on this topic, and

back home I tried to express them concisely in my book *Mountain Monarchs:*

> In general, the behavioral evidence confirms the morphological evidence that bharal are basically goats. Many of the sheep-like traits of bharal can be ascribed to convergent evolution, the result of the species having settled in a habitat which is usually occupied by sheep. But bharal do more than just show that a presumed change in habitat may modify behavior. Although bharal have clearly adapted to a mountain life, they remain rather generalized. Their horns are short, unembellished bashing instruments not quite like those of sheep or of goats. Their glands are either tenuously present or entirely absent. In their use of the penis the bharal also show an evolutionary hesitation to specialize beyond displaying it as a status symbol. The species has straddled an evolutionary fence, and if it had to make a choice of whether to become an *Ovis* or a *Capra* it could become either one with only minor alterations. Like the aoudad, the bharal probably split early from the ancestral goat stock. If I had to design a hypothetical precursor from which the sleep and goat line diverged, it would in many ways resemble a bharal in appearance and behavior.

It is December 5, my last day at Shey, and I take a vacation. Every so often I discard my cameras, tripod, scope, and other equipment, as well as my routine, and wander the hills unencumbered. At such times I must train myself to see again, to respond to creatures other than bharal. This day I spot a Tibetan hare beneath a shrub, brown and gray, drawn into itself with ears flattened against its woolly skull, its life devoted to remaining cryptic. Where the trail ends beyond the last small hermitage and across a rocky rib there are twisted birches, the only stand north of the Kanga La. It is a fine place for watching birds. Once a flock of great rosefinches, brown-mottled and streaked with a flush of red, swayed before the wind on the naked boughs like autumn leaves refusing to fall. Storms of Hodgson's mountain finches hurl up the canyon. Each flock swerves as with one mind, and skims low over the slope to settle suddenly among the brittle shrubs. I marvel at the energy, at the intense, internal fires that fuel these wisps of feather and bone in an environment where man breathes so laboriously. Birds can tolerate higher altitudes than can mammals because their circulatory system, particularly the network of air sacs, is better able to extract oxygen from the air. Bar-headed geese have been recorded at 30,000 feet heading south over Mount Everest, their wingbeats strong where men gasp and die.

On this last day I am given a special gift. The wolves are back, the same pack that Peter and I met five weeks earlier. I have been walking slowly, looking at tracks in the dust of a trail. The footprints of a vole are there, hurrying across the path, the delicate lines resembling a mysterious Tibetan script. *Alticola stoliczkanus* probably left these signs. It is a fluffy gray and white vole with furry boots, resembling a lemming except that it has a tail. I continue over the trail, then stop again for no known reason. My eyes are drawn up the slope and there they meet the calm gaze of the great white wolf, only his head visible and his ruff. Until now it has been a subdued day, with little emotion. Long, translucent clouds trail like ceremonial *katas* over the summits and even the wind has lost its edge. But the wolf's presence adds a new spark of vitality; his head is a glowing wedge against the sky. Imperceptibly he signals my intrusion to the members of his pack, perhaps with a whine, perhaps by the rigidity of his body, for three more heads appear. Then the white wolf stands up. Such a creature! I cannot decide whether beauty or power prevail, but in a wolf there is surely no difference between the two. Abruptly the animals vanish. I climb to where they rested. The mountains are vacant, as if the wolves have entered them through some mysterious crack.

For weeks now the heavy padlocked door of the monastery has remained closed. Once we asked Namu to show it to us but she was evasive, saying that Tundu's wife keeps the key; when later we inquired of Tundu's wife, she informed us that her husband needed to be here too, and besides a visit cost one hundred rupees. I displayed no further interest in the matter. Today, however, after meeting the wolves, I speak to Tundu's wife again and she agrees to show the monastery's interior for five rupees.

Slanting light from the open door illuminates a large assembly hall. Almost covering one wall are frescoes of Buddha and his helpers, and also hanging on it is a cloth on which are painted various animals, among them a tiger, a flying owl, a goat, and a hairy naked woman with flapping arms and big feet being chased by a wolf. I pass out of the well of light, past a bouquet of ancient swords and muzzle loaders, into the gloomy interior. Sitting platforms made of sturdy planks line the walls and several large drums hang from the ceiling. Toward the back stands a tiered altar with rows of butter lamps, and, as a monstrous intrusion, a vase with faded plastic flowers. Stacked nearby are wooden printing blocks, and heaped carelessly in a corner are books, typical loose-leafed Tibetan religious texts, the pages of each pressed between wooden slats and tied in silk cloth. Along the back wall, deep in shadow and shrouded in dust, are alcoves with bronze Buddhas; I count eleven and there may be more. My steps sound hollow on the wooden floor as I make my solitary round under the watchful eyes of Tundu's wife at the door.

Seen in these wintry circumstances the monastery is dead, like a long-forgotten museum with relics of another age. But this room, as the rest of Shey, merely lies dormant; in a few months, when the villagers bring their livestock to the summer pastures and till their fields, butter lamps will burn again and drums speak, as during the spring festival, celebrated in June at the time of the full moon. David Snellgrove witnessed this event during a visit here in 1956. Pilgrims come for the festival from far away, from Samling and Phijor and other villages, leading yaks and ponies. They replace their clothes of drab homespun with finery, pants and gowns of blue and gaily patterned shawls. Both men and women wear wide woolen trousers tied below the knee, a white shirt of silk or cotton, made of imported material, and over this a gown, long-sleeved for men and sleeveless for women. The monastery soon overflows with visitors. Several men mold *tormas,* or sacrificial cakes, which together with butter lamps are arranged as offerings on the altar. In the afternoon about a dozen celebrants begin to read a liturgy, "The Lama's Perfecter of Thought, Remover of All Impediments," the impediments being hostile spirits who obstruct the quest for enlightenment. This liturgy is intoned 108 times, the task requiring the rest of that day and all of the next. A monastic dance follows these monotonous incantations. Sitting cross-legged around the walls of the assembly hall in the flickering lights of burning butter lamps, the onlookers raptly watch three dancers, representing three divinities, whirl around and around, rejoicing in the offerings on the altar. Describing the next phase in the festivities, Snellgrove wrote:

> There now followed another ceremony in order to dispose of the eight classes of harmful divinities. For this thread-crosses were used representing space in general and the sphere of activity of these divinities in particular; they are enticed inside as it were, by the heaps of offerings that are piled around. The wood and thread structure, in which they are now caught like birds in a cage, is then carried outside the monastery and destroyed.

Offerings are consecrated on the third day of the festival. While lay priests read liturgy, the others dance in rings outside in the courtyard. Then, on the final day, comes the ceremony for which all have been waiting, the rite of life-consecration.

> O Lord Protector Boundless Life!
> Bestow thy consecration on these worthy sons,
> That life and knowledge may be widely manifest.

The officiants wave a wand, festooned with colored streamers, over several sacrificial items, a vase filled with water, a skull-cap with spirit, and a bowl with pellets of *tsampa.*

Oh you whose supernal life has wandered, strayed or disappeared!
The pure essence of the four elements of earth and water, fire and
air, the happiness and splendour of living things who dwell in the
threefold expanse of the threefold world, the whole essence derived
from the compassionate grace of the ocean of buddhas of past,
present and future, all this is compounded in the form of light rays
of various colours. It seeps through the pores of your bodies and
vanishes into the centre of the heart . . . the pure force of wisdom
itself; thus the well-being of your supernal life will be restored and
you will gain the perfection of deathlessness.

Men, women, and children then come forward to sample the life
pellets of *tsampa* and other consecrated items. All bestow long life
and health and progress toward enlightenment. After a final bless-
ing the festival is over. The villagers scatter to continue their normal
existence, and the monastery once again becomes sepulchral.

Shey to Jumla, December 6–15

As Phu-Tsering packs the last load, tucking in our breakfast dishes,
Gyaltsen and I carry the other three loads out of the hut where
Namu's husband waits. He has agreed to carry a load as far as
Namdo, a day's walk to the east, and Namu is coming too. Takla has
appeared to say good-bye and to scavenge anything we may discard.
Phu-Tsering borrows a small leather pouch from him; chanting, he
sprinkles incense from the pouch into the fire's embers and, outside,
flings a fistful of rice into the air, propitiating the deities on our
journey. Having finished these animistic ministrations, the five of us
leave Shey. For me a joyous scientific adventure is over but not completed. Any biologist experiences the anxiety of Tantalus: the more
one studies, the more one learns; and the more one learns, the more
unattainable truth becomes. There is always the painful realization of

somehow missing a wondrous opportunity, of not being clear-sighted enough to comprehend what nature unfolds. I neither stop nor look back until after three hours I reach the summit cairn of Saldang La. It is sterile with silence. Ahead the white and russet mountains roll endlessly into Tibet. Nothing relieves the severity of this vast, lucid space until below me a lammergeiier sails into view and glides stiff-winged down the valley toward Shey. I watch it disappear among the wind-beaten summits, carrying with it my vision of a lost horizon. To reach such a remote part of the world as Shey and to dwell there, one must make a quiet pact of friendship with the forces of nature and live as dictated by mountains and forests—but the cost is loneliness and isolation. I have now a powerful desire to go home again, needing the solace of my family, its warmth and love, and as my little caravan surmounts the crest, I hurry from the summit with a feeling of furious haste.

Our path sweeps along the hills and descends an ice-filled ravine before dividing at the rim of a limestone gorge, one trail leading down to Namgung Gompa and ours continuing eastward. We halt for lunch. Phu-Tsering passes me the boiled shoulder blade of a goat and a handful of doughy *tsampa* mixed with tea. The ochre-and-white stupas around the monastery shine with a final flare before retreating into an early dusk; but somewhat higher, in the recess of its coppery cliff, a hermitage continues to glow in the last wintry rays. Following the edge of the Namgung Valley, we soon reach its confluence with the Soliendo River, a major travel route north and south. Namu leaves us here to go to Saldang, whose houses are visible downstream. She departs abruptly, conveying by neither words nor gestures that we are parting, that our lives have touched across the depths of our cultures. We head south past numerous stupas and an almost continuous wall of prayer stones, some slabs as much as three feet high and crowded with tiny inscriptions. On reaching the small Namdo monastery, I note with interest that, as at Shey, a Sikkim stag antler adorns the roof. Jang-bu meets us. He has found accommodation for us with an old lady who lives in an annex of the monastery. The

room is low-ceilinged and so
crowded with a large wooden chest,
old goatskins, baskets, and other
items that only a small space remains for us around an iron pot in
which yak chips are smoldering. As
our hostess mixes a drink of but-
tered salt tea in her two-and-a-half-
foot wooden churn, Jang-bu relates
that he has had much trouble finding the three porters we need for
our trip south. Many people here,
both farmers and nomadic yak
herders, move for the winter to
Dunai, Tarakot, and other places at
low altitudes because Dolpo has a
severe fuel and food shortage, there
seldom being enough potatoes,
buckwheat, and barley until the
next crop is ripe. In order to survive for several months in the lowlands, many Dolpo men first trek
across the frontier into Tibet and
there collect soda ash, used as a
cleansing agent, along the shores of
shallow lakes, and they also obtain
salt. With loaded yaks they move
into southern Nepal and trade
these goods for food until in April
or May they head back to Dolpo to
plant their crops.

Our hostess is obviously delighted to have an audience and she

talks incessantly while holding a handful of sheep's wool and spinning thread on a small twirling distaff. Since she has absorbed everything of import in this valley, she is a valuable informant. Some fifteen years ago, she relates, a foreigner who transcribed religious texts also stayed with her. This must have been David Snellgrove, whose book *Himalayan Pilgrimage* so well describes the many shrines in Dolpo. Ten days ago six wolves killed a goat nearby and ate part of it before the herdboy drove them off. However, each spring the villagers now look for dens and kill the pups, and soon, she hopes, there will be no more wolves. Nine days ago near Namgung Gompa, one or perhaps two snow leopard killed two bharal and local people took all the meat. One snow leopard was shot near Namdo last year. As Jang-bu translates events for me, I realize that only a very large wildlife reserve can protect predators, that the wolves and snow leopard of her anecdotes are probably the same ones that hunt around the Crystal Mountain.

The three porters are anxious to leave in the morning because, they say, we must make our way through a canyon before 11:00 A.M., before the meltwaters from the snows raise the stream high enough, even at this season, to make passage difficult. Moving along the gravelly riverbed, we cross and recross the stream on brittle ice bridges. The hillsides are terribly overgrazed by livestock and deeply eroded, deterioration hastened by the fact that the animals are now largely cut off from their traditional winter pastures in Tibet; villagers also pull *Lonicera* and other bushes out by the roots to serve as fuel. The canyon cliffs are up to 3,000 feet high on the eastern side, and we hurry through the depths, facing a bitter wind under a frozen sky. Finally the walls give way to wide rolling hills. It is 10:30 A.M. And punctually at 11 A.M. a rush of gray water floods the dry channels and sweeps over the ice. At noon Phu-Tsering collects yak droppings for a fire and makes tea. The valley soon divides, the junction marked by a stone cairn on which are piled the skulls of about ten Tibetan argali and a few bharal. One of our guides tells us that he shot an argali near here last summer. A pack of three or four wolves has preceded us up the valley by only a few hours, and I am pleased to note from the tracks that one is a pup. It is only 2:00 P.M. when the porters stop, saying that it is too late in the day to cross the first of the two passes ahead. I feel uneasy, and to find an outlet for my tension, climb a high hill to look for argali. All I see is a low dark wall of cloud roiling toward us in the distance, and soon after I return to camp it begins to snow.

An awful night. The wind eddies fitfully around the tent, piling snow against it, and in the other tent the Sherpas and porters argue, undoubtedly about tomorrow's plans. The morning is but a thin solution of the night as, still in cloud and swirling snow, I join the others. The porters refuse to go on because even if we get across the passes more snow may prevent them from returning home until spring. With all landmarks obliterated, we have no means of finding the route by ourselves. But one man, a traveler who has attached himself to our group, agrees to take us as far as the first pass, the Raka La, without a load, in exchange for any items we may have to discard. Knowing that we must condense seven loads into four, his profits will be considerable. We repack our loads: out goes all food except a three-day supply of tea, *tsampa*, sugar and rice; out go an old tent, buckets, most pots and pans, and other kitchen equipment; and out go even such unessential scientific specimens as rock samples, fossils, and bharal droppings (which I wanted to analyze for parasite eggs). I hand over all my extra clothing to the thinly clad Sherpas. Gyaltsen is in knickers and tennis shoes, like a schoolboy on a picnic. I tell him to put on his boots, but he replies that he has no boots, that the money I gave him to buy a pair in Kathmandu was spent on other things. To cross passes nearly 18,000 feet high in midwinter in tennis shoes is a good way to freeze toes, I note dourly, and hand him my last clean pair of wool socks.

When at half past nine the clouds thin a little, we shoulder our packs and begin the ascent. The first part is steep and the slope slippery with a layer of fresh snow on ice, and we fall often and heavily, robbed of all agility by our seventy-pound loads. After only a few hundred feet our guide stops, vaguely waves one arm at the clouds, saying the pass is somewhere ahead, and flees down the mountainside. We trudge on, wholly lost in this featureless and form-less expanse. As the clouds engulf us again, it snows harder and the force of the wind increases. And then, just as we despair of finding the route, we hear above us the ringing of bells and the whistling and calling of men, *oo-oo-oo*. Out of the clouds, out of the gray nothingness, evolves a caravan of fifty or more yaks. In a single undulating line the heavily laden animals plow downhill, shaggy dark creatures, their coats encrusted with driven snow; the men are just as wild-looking in sheepskin *chubas* and long wind-tangled hair as they urge the beasts on with waving sticks and hollow cries as if dispersing a gathering of mountain spirits. Soon all vanish in the mists as if they have never been, and after a few minutes their tracks too have drifted over. But at intervals we now find frozen yak drop-pings, and using these as trail markers we toil toward the pass. Clouds scud along the slope and winds scream, whipping snow horizontally in gusts so savage that we must stand with our backs toward them until their force is spent. With visibility only a few feet, we remain close, seeking security from each other in this raging wilderness. Shouting above the howls of the blizzard, I suggest that we try to make a bivouac. Just then we hear bells again, coming toward us from below, and soon a ghostly caravan of six yaks driven by two men and two teenage boys emerges from the snow. The leader agrees to carry one of our loads on his yak. Our packs lightened by about fifteen pounds each and with yaks to break trail, we ascend with renewed vigor to the pass. A cairn surmounted by a gnarled pole marks the summit. One of the men takes from his snow-encrusted *chuba* a prayer flag and ties it to the pole as a votive offering; as I pass it, whipping in the gale, I also give my quiet thanks to the mountain gods.

We drop into a high broad valley, and farther on follow a canyon flanked by cliffs shadowy in cloud. At dusk we camp beneath a rock overhang. The Dolpo men unload their yaks and turn them free to find whatever meager forage exists beneath the snow. A bit of *tsampa* mixed with sugar and water is our dinner. Before falling into a weary sleep I note with satisfaction that the snow has ceased to fall and a wan moon shines through the thinning clouds. However, the weather remains unsettled the next morning and the Dolpo men inform us that they will be ready to go on after it has warmed up; but at 9:00 A.M. they are still beneath their blankets. No, they say, they will not continue today after all. We ask for a guide through this maze of peaks until the route to the next pass becomes obvious. After much vacillation and haggling one of the men, a young one in his twenties, agrees to come with us for an exorbitant price, to be paid in advance. After an hour of travel our guide walks so slowly that, suspicions aroused, I watch him carefully. While we drink at a rivulet, he walks ahead and falls purposefully, afterward moaning and rubbing his leg as if injured. Jang-bu hurries up to help him, but when I tell him of the deceit, his concern changes to fury. Jang-bu demands our money back, and when he finds out that it has been left in camp, his frustrations with the unreliability of Dolpo men erupts. He kicks the fellow in the legs with his heavy boots until I point out that if he does not stop the imaginary injury may well become real. Thereupon Jang-bu punches him in the head with his fists until he lies sobbing in the snow. Jang-bu orders him to pick up a load and carry it to the pass. His wind-chapped cheeks wet with tears, the man replies that the path to the pass is deep in snow, very difficult, but that the route down the Deokomukh Khola to Phoksumdo Lake is easy. I look at the canyon of the Deokomukh just ahead and know the descent is far from easy and that we will be away from a traveled route in case of mishap. But then I remember Gyaltsen in tennis shoes. With the weather clearing and temperatures dropping, Gyaltsen is hardly dressed for a high pass; tough and uncomplaining, he might not tell me if his toes are freezing. We discuss the pros and cons of each route. All three Sherpas vote for the Deokomukh and I concur with misgivings. Well, if the route is so easy the Dolpo man surely does not mind showing us the way and carrying a pack for a few hours. Prodding him to his feet, we begin the descent with myself in the lead and the three Sherpas in the rear to prevent the escape of our reluctant porter.

The canyon narrows almost immediately and in it a turbulent stream, covered with ice bridges, ricochets from wall to wall and leaps over precipices. Snow covers every boulder, and near the water's edge, everything is glazed with ice, making all footing treacherous. To cross the stream we must use the ice bridges. "You first, sah," urges Phu-Tsering. "You biggest." The logic of his suggestion is overwhelming: if the ice supports me, then the Sherpas can march across safely. Inching ahead, ready to leap back with the first hollow cracking, I barely breathe during each tense crossing. Most bridges ring solidly beneath my boots but a few rotten ones collapse with the first tentative tap of my foot. There are also questionable ones that groan and grumble yet seem strong, and sometimes they hold and sometimes not, only a desperate leap saving me from an icy immersion. During one crossing, the Dolpo porter suddenly drops his load and scrambles back up the canyon. No one tries to stop him; we have no more use for him. Soon after, the gorge narrows to the width of the stream, and there is a twenty-foot waterfall, a magic fall whose tumbling waters have been turned to clear shining glass. Water continues to flow between its ice-covered surface and the rock. I descend cautiously over the ice bulges, partly supporting my weight on a rope tied to a boulder. The others first lower the packs to me, and then descend too, hoping that the fragile shell of ice does not break. Farther on, a rocky slab slants from the stream. While traversing it, my boot slips and I fall into the water, soaking myself from the chest down. My clothes begin to freeze almost immediately, but we can now see the first birches and pines ahead, and I hurry on, trying to keep warm until we can find a good campsite and build a fire. Although a trail is now visible for the first time, I soon wish for rotten ice bridges and slippery boulders. To circumvent an impassable part of the gorge, the path climbs up the canyon wall, and, for a short distance, crosses the cliff face on a narrow snow-covered ledge, sloping outward. With bare fingers digging into frozen cracks of the wall and heels hanging over the abyss, I shuffle sideways, scraping with my toes little platforms on which the Sherpas can tread. But after this perilous path the canyon widens and in a copse of pine and birch, I build a fire. Soon my pants steam and as the warmth flows into me the strains of the past two days have already become memories. The worst part of the gorge is behind us; Phoksumdo Lake is near. A tawny wood owl hoots at dusk as I wait for the Sherpas.

The next morning we finally emerge from the dark canyon into bright sun. On a small plain covered with brush and grass, a snow leopard suddenly bounds away, across a stream, through a thicket, and into broken cliffs. For five weeks I sought a meeting with this species at Shey and was not once granted even a glimpse; now, on our last full day in the cat's mountain home, with my physical and mental energy sapped by altitude and hardship, I have this fleeting encounter. I drop my pack and search for its tracks on patches of snow, not following it into the cliffs, but retracing its path to discover what it had been doing before our arrival. I note immediately that not one but two medium-sized snow leopard have been here, one having vanished unseen. After coming down a hillside near Phoksumdo Lake, the two animals traveled up the valley along the banks of a rivulet, one usually behind the other. One made an occasional detour to investigate a boulder or the trunk of a downed tree, and depressions in the snow show where they reclined for brief rests. A leisurely morning until disrupted by our arrival.

There apparently being no path to Ringmo down the east shore of Phoksumdo Lake, we must loop around the north end. A livestock trail ascends the steep slope for 2,300 feet before following its contours. A snow leopard has traveled here too, a male judging by his large pugmarks. In the manner typical of his race, he marked his route with scrapes and feces, placing these on or near promontories. Full of delight, as if on a treasure hunt, I hurry along the trail collecting feces, old and fresh, and taking notes. Three snow leopard visited Shey and now I have evidence for three around Phoksumdo Lake, making at least six in about two hundred square miles. The naturalist Rodney Jackson was in Namlang Khola, just west of Dolpo, between December, 1976, and February, 1977, and there he estimated three to five snow leopard in 160 to 200 square miles. But local hunters killed two of the cats during his short visit. His report to the Nepal government describes the intensive hunting in that area:

> The hunting of musk deer, blue sheep and snow leopard by Dolphu villagers is rampant. Sale of musk at 1,000 to 1,200 rupees a tola represent the primary source of hard cash for many of the families in Dolphu. Some 30 hunters, operating from about seven base camps, spent November, December and part of January hunting the Namlang Valley and Kanjiroba Himal. Hundreds of poisoned bamboo spears were placed in the birch/juniper zones for musk deer, and along trails leading to water for blue sheep. Other spears were placed along rocky passes for the snow leopard, while stone deadfalls were used to kill rodents, martens and other mustellids.

We arrive at the western arm of the lake in midafternoon, too late to continue to Ringmo. I erect my tent on the same spot as on October 25, and with this act I mentally complete my journey. Near my tent swims a solitary tufted pochard, oblivious to bitter winds and icy shadows as it dives again and again. I watch the duck with calm detachment, one being casually interested in another. My wildlife survey is finished, my study done. And I have seen a snow leopard.

In the morning my boots are frozen so hard that I cannot pull them on. While Gyaltsen thaws them by the fire and Phu-Tsering cooks up the last of our food—a mixture of rice, *tsampa*, and tea—we discuss plans for reaching Jumla. There are only two heavily booked flights between Jumla and Kathmandu each week. I had asked Peter to reserve seats for us on December 17. It is now December 11, too late to reach Jumla loaded with heavy packs or with slow-moving porters who normally require ten days for the trip. It being doubtful that-all of us would find empty seats on the next flight, we decide to split up: Phu-Tsering and I will hurry to Jumla to catch the December 17 flight, while the others will travel slowly with two porters, reaching town in time for the December 21 flight.

This having been decided, we once again traverse the slender cliff trail above the lake to Ringmo. I note several musk deer tracks among the birches, and on a meadow above, a herd of bharal. Just before entering the village we meet three Hindu hunters from the lowlands.

Ringmo is almost abandoned, the people having moved to their winter villages at Murwa and Palam. However, Jang-bu finds one resident who is willing not only to sell us food but also to cook it. Our first course consists of buckwheat bread, heavy and warm, washed down with *chang,* and the second of boiled potatoes and omelet. Replete for the first time in days, I am almost willing to forgive the Ringmo people their earlier transgressions as porters.

It is time to part. Leaving Jang-bu and Gyaltsen to spend the night in Ringmo, Phu-Tsering and I turn toward the lowlands. We descend to Murwa and continue down the Suli Valley until at dusk we find a lean-to in which to sleep. Nearby is a Dolpo family, their yak saddle-bags stacked in a semicircle around the campfire as protection from the wind. We buy buckwheat from them. The evening is warm; for the first time in weeks my hands are not freezing as, resting in my sleeping bag, I write the day's notes.

All day we descend the Suli, passing the sullen village of Rohagaon at noon, and by evening reaching the mouth of the valley. Turning westward, our path follows a grass slope high above the Bheri River. At 8:00 P.M., long after dark, we lie down to sleep by the side of the trail, too tired to prepare a meal. We continue at dawn and within two hours reach the large village of Tibrikot. The Bheri swings south here, but we continue west, across denuded hills until these give way to stands of oak, and higher up, to mountain meadows and conifer forests. With the last light we reach 12,700-foot Balangra Pass. Our descent is slow, the weak beam of my flashlight barely illuminating the trail. Phu-Tsering follows so closely that he collides with me whenever I stop, and he chants continuously to keep dark spirits at bay. Another continent camp: no fire, no dinner. But lying on a litter of leaves I can see the starry sky through oak boughs.

An hour after dawn we reach a village. No one cares to sell us food and we continue to the next settlement where a woman not only provides us with eighteen eggs, but for a rupee extra also agrees to boil them. After eating eight eggs each for breakfast and saving one apiece for lunch, we march on, through villages and fields, up once more through mountain forests to the top of another pass as high as the one on the previous day, then down, down, hurrying to lose altitude, to escape the cold, as darkness overtakes us. For much of the next day we plod steadily along a narrow, gloomy valley, its slopes still densely forested since few people have cared to settle in its depth. By late afternoon we reach the village of Gajakot. A transistor radio blares. Jumla, we are told, is only a two-hour walk away. I am wholly relaxed as we eat goat stew by a cheerful fire in a small hut.

Already within me Shey remains only a strange combination of memory, dream, and desire. I know that all things in nature are transient, that species vanish and mountains dissolve, yet I hope that nothing will change at Shey, that from reincarnation to reincarnation the lama will still occupy his ochre-colored eyrie, that the medieval silence will continue to be broken by the clashing horns of fighting bharal, and that Drutob Senge Yeshe will fly forever on his magic snow lion around the sacred Crystal Mountain.

Appendix

TABLE 1

Subfamily Caprinae

	Genus	Species	Common name
Tribe *Rupicaprini*	Nemorhaedus	*goral*	Goral
	Capricornis	*sumatraensis*	Serow
		crispus	Japanese serow
	Oreamnos	*americanus*	Rocky Mountain goat
	Rupicapra	*rupicapra*	Chamois
Tribe *Ovibovini*	Ovibos	*moschatus*	Musk-ox
	Budorcas	*taxicolor*	Takin
Tribe *Caprini*	Ammotragus	*lervia*	Aoudad or Barbary sheep
	Pseudois	*nayaur*	*Bharal or blue sheep
	Hemitragus	*jemlahicus*	*Himalayan tahr
		hylocrius	*Nilgiri tahr
		jayakeri	Arabian tahr
	Capra	*aegagrus*	*Wild goat
		ibex	*Ibex
		falconeri	*Markhor
		pyrenaica	Spanish goat
		cylindricornis	East Caucasian Tur
		hircus	Domestic goat
	Ovis	*canadensis*	Bighorn sheep
		dalli	Thinhorn sheep
		nivicola	Snow sheep
		ammon	Argali
		orientalis	*Urial
		aries	Domestic sheep

* Species that I studied in South Asia.
  Some taxonomists also include the *chiru* and *saiga*, representing the Tribe *Saigini*, into the subfamily *Caprinae*, but most consider the two species to be antelopes of the subfamily *Antilopinae*.

TABLE 2

*Food Habits of Wolf and Snow Leopard at Shey and Lapche**

Food	Wolf†	Snow leopard	
	Shey	Shey	Lapche
Bharal	38%	50%	73%
Livestock	29	13	9
Marmot	32	31	9
Hare	3	—	—
Unidentified hair	—	6	9
Grass and forb	—	38	18

* The figures are expressed in frequency of occurrence of remains in the droppings.

† I found no droppings at Lapche, but villagers told me that packs visit occasionally.

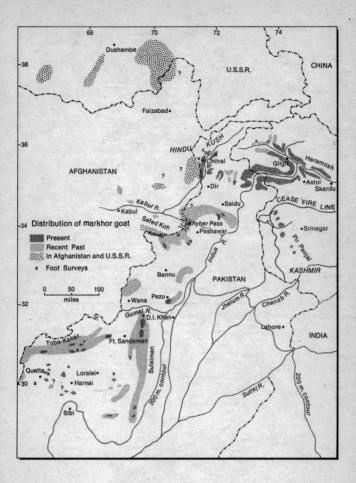

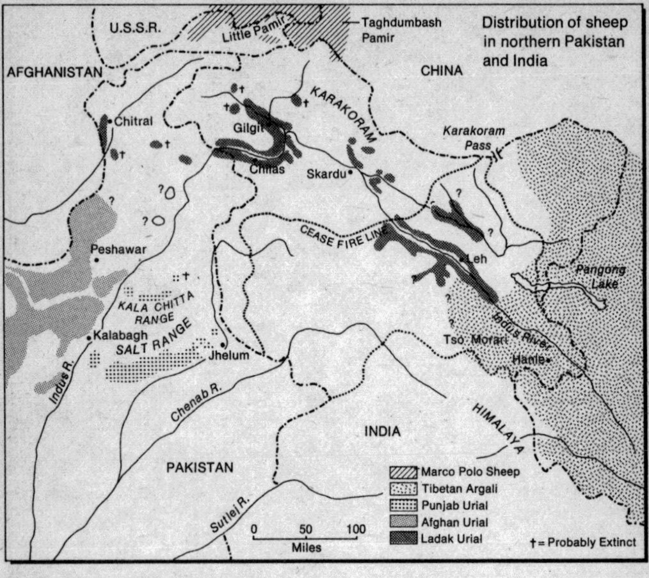
Distribution of sheep in northern Pakistan and India
U.S.S.R.
Little Pamir
Taghdumbash Pamir
AFGHANISTAN
CHINA
KARAKORAM
Chitral
Gilgit
Chilas
Skardu
Karakoram Pass
CEASE FIRE LINE
Leh
Pangong Lake
Peshawar
KALA CHITTA RANGE
SALT RANGE
Kalabagh
Jhelum
Indus R.
Indus River
Tso Morari
Hanle
Chenab R.
HIMALAYA
INDIA
PAKISTAN
Sutlej R.
0 50 100
Miles
Marco Polo Sheep
Tibetan Argali
Punjab Urial
Afghan Urial
Ladak Urial
† = Probably Extinct

Index

Abode of Snow (Mason), 103
Aferd Khan, 95, 99
Afghan urial, 136
Afghanistan, 3, 9, 13, 18, 19, 29, 42, 52, 60, 61, 65, 78, 82, 89, 91, 131
Afridi, Captain, 59, 66
Afzal, Muhammad, 106
Afzal, Subidar, 39, 40, 43, 45, 46
Afzal-ul-Mulk, 29
Aga Khan, 86
Alaska, 63, 104
Ali, Hussain, 107
Ali, Imtiaz, 79
Ali Bhutto, Zulfikar, 99
Ali Khan, Safdar, 83
Ali Shah, Wazir, 30
Alif Khan, 132
Alpine ibex, 42
Altai Mountains, 13
Amanullah, Major, 75, 85, 131, 132, 133
Aman-ul-Mulk, 28
Amir-ul-Mulk, 29
Anamalai Hills, 165, 167
Anamudi Peak, 166, 167
Annapurna massif, 204, 209
Aoudad, 150, 262
Appleton, H., 134
Apricots, value of, 55
Arabian Peninsula, 42

Arabian tahr, 151
Argali, 4, 78, 79, 238, 249, 269; *see also* Marco Polo sheep
Arkari River, 39, 45
Asad Khan, 139
Asad-ur-Rehman, Prince, 26, 28
Ashkole village, 106, 107, 108, 113
Ass, Tibetan wild (kiang), 98
Ayub Khan, 85

Babur (Moghul emperor), 28
Bachhal (guide), 123, 124
Baikal, Lake, 13
Balangra Pass, 276
Baltistan, 105
Baltoro Glacier, 74, 100, 107, 108, 109, 110, 111
Baluchis, 136, 137
Baluchistan, 18, 129, 130, 131, 133, 137
Bangitappal (India), 155, 157, 164, 165
Baroghill Pass, 52, 59, 60
Bashgali language, 14, 15
Bat, *Plecotus*, 58
Bear: black, 6, 12, 64, 71; brown, 52, 56, 61, 64, 65, 94, 98, 108
Beebe, William, 3
Beg, Ghulam Muhammad, 83, 85, 86, 87, 88, 89, 90, 95

Beg, Sher Ullah, 105
Beg, Zahid, Mirza, 11, 12, 15, 25, 134, 144
Besham Quila, 79
Besti Valley, 45, 47, 48
Bezoar stones, 122
Bhadauri Deorali Pass, 207
Bharal (blue sheep), 4, 5, 21, 98, 150, 176, 177, 196, 197, 199, 200, 201, 202, 204, 218, 219, 220, 221, 228, 233, 235–44 passim, 253, 256, 258, 259, 260–62; dominance among, 240–41, 259, 261; herd size of, 238; and ratio of young to females, 238; rutting behavior of, 256, 258–60
Bheri River, 221, 222, 223, 224, 276
Bhote Kosi River, 174, 175, 177, 184, 188, 201
Bhutan, 3, 151, 245
Biafo Glacier, 74, 107
Bimbahadur (porter), 212, 217, 218, 220, 221, 222
Birds: high-altitude, 4, 11, 262–63; in Kang Chu region, 182–83, 188; in Mudumalai Sanctuary, 159
Birds of Nepal (Flemings), 188
Blower, John, 176, 204
Blue sheep: see Bharal
Blyth, Edward, 107
Boar, wild, 163
Bokhan (guide), 157
Bombay Natural History Society, 154
B'on religion, 227
Bonatti, Walter, 111
Braldo River, 106, 112
Braldo Valley, 106, 108, 114
Broad Peak, 102, 111
Bruce, Charles, 28, 29, 35
Buddhism, 180, 190, 198, 209, 213, 227, 243, 248
Buffalo, 153, 160, 170, 176
Buhl, Herman, 111
Bulgaria, 130
Burhan-ud-Din, Prince, 30, 31, 32, 37, 38, 45

Burton, Richard, 6
Burushaski language, 14, 88

Capparis, 81, 120, 127
Caprinae, 4, 5, 117, 150, 279; see also Goats; Sheep
Cartier, Robert, 213
Cat, Temmincks, 187
Cattle of India, 159, 160, 161, 162
Caucasus Mountains, 42
Caughley, Graeme, 202
Central Asia, 3, 10, 13, 68, 82, 194
Chalt (India), 85, 86
Chamois, 152, 153
Cheetah, 119, 208
Chiantar Glacier, 61, 62, 67
Chilas tribe, 80
Chiltan Anari village, 134
Chiltan goat, 133, 134, 135, 137
Chiltan Range, 134, 137
China, 3, 52, 53, 68, 82, 83, 84, 85, 91, 192, 212
Chipko Andolan movement, 207
Chital deer, 153, 162, 163, 170
Chitawan National Park (Nepal), 170
Chitral region (Pakistan), 9, 10, 12, 14–19 passim, 21, 22, 25, 28–39 passim, 42, 45, 49–53 passim, 57, 64, 131
Chitral Scouts, 39, 59
Chitral town, 26–27, 37, 52
Chumbi Valley, 245
Churen Himal Peak, 215
Climbers, mountain, 104–105
Cockerill, George, 93
Conservation, 100, 147, 153, 159
Conway, William G., v
Cranes, 112
Cretaceous period, 117
Crystal Monastery: see Shey Gompa
Crystal Mountain, 204, 237, 242, 248, 257, 269, 277

Dachigam Sanctuary (Kashmir), 12
Dadarili Pass, 72

Dalai Lama, 214
Dang, Hari, 21, 33
Darkot Glacier, 59, 68
Darkot Pass, 68
Darwin, Charles, 129
Davidar, Reggie, 154–55, 157, 159, 167, 173
Davidson, Colonel J., 15
Dawa, Ang (Sherpa), 203, 217, 220, 222, 227, 230, 235, 251
Deer: chital, 153, 162, 163, 170; musk, 71, 191, 192, 275, 276; red, 7, 245; sambar, 153, 163, 164, 165, 170; swamp, 170; see also Stag
Deer and the Tiger, The (Schaller), 169
Deokomukh canyon, 272
Desert wildlife, body fluids conserved by, 124
Desio, Ardito, 104
Dhaulagiri massif, 204, 208, 212, 215, 219
Dhole, 159, 160, 162, 163
Dhorpatan (Nepal), 204, 212, 213, 214
Dilband-Moro massif, 136
Dipper, brown, 40
Dir (Pakistan), 14, 19, 34, 35, 36, 52
Dolpo (Nepal), 204, 213, 214n., 244, 247, 248, 268, 269, 275
Dorah Pass, 42, 65
Drutob Senge Yeshe, 248, 249, 277
Dunai (Nepal), 222, 224, 225, 268
Durga Puja (festival), 207–208, 210, 211

Ecology, 100, 176, 182, 206
Egypt, 42
Einstein, Albert, 147
Eiseley, Loren, 238
Emerson, Ralph Waldo, 104
Eocene epoch, 117
Eravikulam Plateau, 165, 166, 172, 173

Ethiopia, 39
Eurasia, 117, 118
Everest, Mount, 178, 189, 263

Face of the Tiger, The (McDougal), 170
Finch: Hodgson's mountain, 262; rosy, 65, 262
Forests of Nepal (Stainton), 204
Fossils, 130, 252
Fox, red, 19, 94, 108, 218, 220–21

Garmush Glacier, 63
Gasherbrum IV Peak, 111
Gates, Elgin, 85
Gaur, 153, 165, 167
Gauri Sankar Peak, 178
Gazelle, 119, 121, 138, 145
Geese, bar-headed, 263
Geist, Valerius, 128, 142, 144, 152, 187, 239–40
Genghis Khan, 26, 28
Ghabung Valley, 205
Ghadebar Gar Range, 137
Ghujerab Valley, 98
Ghusting River, 216
Gilgit (Pakistan), 29, 56, 67, 76, 77, 79, 82, 83, 84, 85, 96, 105
Gilgit River, 68, 70, 71, 82
Gilgit Scouts, 89, 90, 96
Gilkey, Art, 103
Gishk massif, 136, 137
Goat-antelopes, 150, 151, 152, 153, 186, 187
Goats (Capra), 4, 5, 11, 12, 17, 65, 117, 118, 119, 135, 137, 141, 142, 147, 153, 196, 238, 241, 261; American mountain, 152; Miocene ancestors of, 151; and sheep, differences between, 147–148, 261; trophies of, 44–45; see also Caprinae; Chiltan goat; Wild goat
Godwin-Austen Glacier, 111
Goethe, Johann Wolfgang von, 66
Golen Gol Valley, 21, 40, 43, 44
Gondwanaland, 117
Goral, 151, 152, 187

Gorilla, 157
Gouldsbury, J. C., 165
Great Himalaya Range, 3, 5, 178
Greece, 130
Gul Khan, 53
Gulab Singh, 76
Gulbas Khan, 45, 46, 47
Gulumbukt Valley, 47
Gupis, 68, 70, 71; Raja of, 70, 71
Gurkhas, 84, 175
Gyaltsen (Sherpa), 203, 220, 221, 227, 233, 251, 252, 253, 254, 256, 266, 270, 272, 275, 276
Gyanendra, Prince, 225

Halal, Ashok Kumar, 225
Hamilton, D., 153, 165, 166
Hamster (*Cricetulus migratorius*), 60
Handcock, Henry, 172
Haramosh Peak, 102
Hare, 13, 121, 262
Harpuchang Valley, 90, 91
Harrer, Heinrich, 104
Harris, Marvin, 160
Hashish, 57
Hassan, Mirza, 37, 38, 39, 43, 44
Hedgehog, long-eared, 122
Hedin, Sven, 6
High Range, 165, 172, 173
High Range Game Preservation Association, 165, 173
Highwavy Hills, 167
Himalaya Range, Great, 3, 5, 178
Himalayan Pilgrimage (Snellgrove), 204, 269
Himalayan tahr, 151, 176, 184–86, 187, 202; courtship displays by, 185–86
Hindu Kush Mountains, 3, 9, 10, 13, 25, 32, 43, 51, 59
Hindu Raj Mountains, 51, 61, 66, 67, 68
Hindu religion, 160, 208, 223–24
Hindubagh (Pakistan), 132
Hispar Glacier, 74
Hodgson, Brian, 176, 196
Hoopoe, 65, 66

Horseflies, 64
House, Brad, 35, 36
Houston, Charles, 103
Hrdy, Sarah, 224
Hunza, 14, 77, 78, 79, 82–88 *passim*, 97–101 *passim*
Hunza River, 83, 87
Hunza Valley, 83, 85, 86, 96
Hussain, Ijlal, 82
Hussain, Manzoor, 101, 102
Hyderabad (Pakistan), 118
Hyena, striped, 121

Ibex, 5, 31, 38, 39, 42–48 *passim*, 56, 61, 62, 69, 71, 85, 89, 90, 92, 101, 107, 109, 110, 112, 118, 129, 239
In the Throne Room of the Mountain Gods (Rowell), 102n., 105
India, 3, 5, 21, 27, 76, 77, 83, 117, 151, 153, 154, 159–63 *passim*, 169, 171, 172, 175, 176, 177, 212, 214
Indochina, 12
Indo-Gangetic Plain, 117
Indus Highway, 77
Indus Plain, 18, 35, 73, 118, 129, 138
Indus River, 3, 18, 19, 60, 74, 80, 82, 105, 106, 107, 130, 138
Iqbal, Muhammad, 76
Iran, 12, 129, 130
Ishkuman River, 65, 74
Ishkuman Valley, 64, 71
Islam, 160
Islamabad (Pakistan), 79

Jabba village, 139
Jackal, 144
Jackson, Rodney, 275
Jamal Khan, Muhammad, 84–85
Jang Bhanjyang Pass, 221
Jang-bu (Sherpa), 203, 208, 210, 212—23 *passim*, 227, 229, 230, 231, 232, 234, 235, 247, 248, 251, 253, 256, 257, 267, 268, 269, 272, 276

Japan, musk imported by, 192
Jeeps, traveling in, 36–37, 71
Jeffers, Robinson, 250
Jhelum River, 138
Journal of Bombay Natural History Society, 154
Jumla (Nepal), 227, 233, 251, 257, 266, 275, 276, 277
Junipers, 40–41

Kabul (Afghanistan), 28
Kafirs, 39
Kaghan Valley, 102
Kala Chitta Range, 137
Kalabagh Wildlife Reserve (Pakistan), 138, 144, 145, 146, 149
Kali Gandaki River, 207, 209, 210, 249, 250
Kami porters, 213, 214, 215, 216
Kancha (Sherpa), 178, 189, 191, 193, 195, 197, 201
Kang Chu River, 175, 177, 178, 179, 182, 184, 186, 188, 201, 203
Kanga La (Snow Pass), 226–27, 231, 232, 233, 234, 248, 251, 262
Kanha National Park (India), 153, 163, 164, 167, 168, 171
Kanjiroba Range, 254
Kao Hsien-Chih, 68
Karachi (Pakistan), 118, 119, 125
Karakoram (Maraini), 102
Karakoram Highway, 77, 78, 85, 98
Karakoram Mountains, 3, 74, 75, 76, 83, 100, 102, 137, 239
Karakoram Pass, 83
Karakoram 2 (K2) Peak, 74, 100–104 *passim*, 106, 111, 112, 114
Karambar Lake, 64, 65
Karambar Pass, 51, 53, 60, 63, 64, 65
Karchat Hills, 116–21 *passim*, 124, 125, 127, 128, 129, 146, 149
Kashmir, 6, 7, 12, 18, 21, 64, 70, 76, 77, 83, 131, 151
Kashmir stag, 7
Kathmandu (Nepal), 177, 192, 198, 201, 203, 207, 209, 212, 232, 251, 270, 275

Kazmi, Hussain Mehdi, 135
Keane, Richard, vi
Keats, John, 111
Kermani, W. A., 120
Keys, William, 153
Khampas, 214 and *n.*
Khan Muhammad, 134, 135
Khowari language, 14
Khunjerab National Park, 99–100, 106
Khunjerab Pass, 85, 93
Khunjerab Valley, 85, 88
Khushwaqt family, 28
Khyber Pass, 130, 131
Kiang (Tibetan wild ass), 98
Kilik Pass, 88, 89, 90, 91
Kinloch, Alexander, 64
Kipling, Rudyard, 78
Kirthar Mountains, 4, 117, 118, 129
Kitchener, Lord, 59
Knight, E., 84
Koh-i-Maran massif, 136, 137
Koh-i-Siah massif, 136
Kohistani language, 14
Kourban Ali Khan, 88, 89, 99
Kuban ibex, 42
Kublai Khan, 61, 79
Kunar River, 9, 27, 39
Kusang (Lapche monk), 193, 194, 198

Ladak (India), 77
Ladak urial, 44, 71, 85, 101, 107, 113, 137
Lahore (Pakistan), 11, 52, 65, 84, 145
Lambagar village, 178, 179, 183, 197, 201
Lammergeier, 24, 253, 256, 267
Lamnang village, 175, 179, 182, 183, 191, 197, 201
Land Rover, 86, 88, 93, 96
Langurs, 158, 163, 223–24
Langurs of Abu, The (Hrdy), 224
Lapche monastery, 191, 193–94, 197, 198, 201, 238, 239

Lapche village, 179, 180, 198
Laurie, Andrew, 120, 123, 125, 126
Leeches, 172
Leopard, snow: see Snow leopard
Lowari Pass, 34, 36, 52
Lydekker, Richard, 134

Macaques, 154, 187–88, 191
Machhapuchhare Peak, 204, 209
Mackeson, Frederick, 76
Magic and Mystery in Tibet (David-Neel), 213
Malakand (Pakistan), 34, 131
Malik Muzaffar Khan, 138, 139
Mammals of Pakistan, The (Roberts), 60
Mangars, 222
Mani mounds, 236
Maraini, Fosco, 102
Marco Polo, 61, 78
Marco Polo sheep, 4, 28, 52, 61, 78, 82–83, 85, 89, 91, 92, 93, 94, 98, 99; measurements of horns of, 94–95; see also Argali
Mardan (Pakistan), 35
Markhor, 3, 4, 5, 10, 11, 14–19 passim, 22, 31, 34, 38, 44, 45, 49, 71, 85, 98, 118, 129, 131–37 passim; Astor, 18–19; food of, 16–17; herd size of, 17; Kashmir, 19, 131; straight-horned, 18, 133
Marmot, 4, 47, 65, 75, 90, 95
Martz, Steve, 102
Masherbrum Peak, 75, 102, 111
Mason, Kenneth, 103
Mastuj village, 56, 70
Matiltan (Pakistan), 73
Matthiessen, Peter, 203, 205–22 passim, 225, 226, 227, 229, 230, 231, 232, 234, 235, 236, 242, 243, 244, 246–54 passim
Mayangdi Valley, 209
McDougal, Charles, 170
Merin (Pakistan), 17, 22, 23
Mianwali (Pakistan), 145

Mingma (cook), 178, 189, 191, 198, 201
Mintaka Pass, 82
Miocene epoch, 117, 151
Misgar (Kashmir), 88, 89, 96
Modi River, 207, 209
Mohidin (cook), 123
Mongolia, 89
Mongoose, 122
Monkeys, langur, 158, 163, 223–24
Montgomerie, T. G., 101
Mountain Monarchs (Schaller), 3, 147, 262
Mountain Sheep (Geist), 142
Mountain Travel (expedition outfitter), 177
Mountfort, Guy, 146
Mouse, Cairo spiny, 123
Mudumalai Sanctuary (India), 159, 162, 163
Muduwars, 166
Mukerti Peak, 155, 157
Mulberries, 55
Mundi Glacier, 111
Munnar Club, 165
Murdar Range, 137
Musk deer, 71, 191, 192, 275, 276
Mustang (Nepal), 213, 254
Mustang, the Forbidden Kingdom (Peissel), 254n.
Muta-ul-Mulk, Prince, 37, 38
Muztagh Pass, 111
Mysticism, Christian and Buddhist (Suzuki), 180

Nagars, 83, 84
Namdo monastery, 267–68
Namdo village, 236, 251, 266, 269
Namgung Gompa, 267, 269
Namu ("hostess"), 245–46, 247, 248, 250, 253, 254, 257, 260, 263, 266, 267
Nanga Parbat Peak, 81, 101, 102, 111
National Geographic magazine, 248
National Geographic Society, v, vi
Nazim Khan, 84, 85
Nehru, Jawaharlal, 160

Nepal, 3, 5, 21, 100, 170, 174–78 passim, 188, 192, 196, 198, 204–209 passim, 212, 214 and n., 219, 268, 275
Neve, A., 80
New York Zoological Society, v, vi
New Zealand, 186, 202
Newby, Eric, 14
Nilgiri Hills, 153, 154, 155, 157, 159, 165, 172, 173
Nilgiri tahr, 5, 151, 153–59 passim, 167, 184, 186 and n.; young of, 156–57
Nilgiri Wildlife Association, 154
Nizam-ul-Mulk, 28–29
Nowshera (Pakistan), 34
Nubian ibex, 42

Oman, 151
Ongdi, 250, 251
Ootacamund (India), 153, 154, 171
Oxus River, 60, 68

Paiyu campsite, 107, 108, 110, 113, 114
Pakistan, 3, 4, 5, 9, 18, 20, 41, 49, 64, 73, 76, 77, 78, 91, 94, 98, 105, 107, 113, 114, 117, 123, 130, 137, 138, 209
Pakistan-China Friendship Bridge, 87
Pallas, Peter, 14
Palni Hills, 165, 167
Pamir Mountains, 3, 13, 43, 51, 52, 59, 61, 66, 68, 78, 79, 94
Panah, Said, 53, 57, 60, 64, 70
Panah, Sher, 14, 15, 21, 25, 40, 43, 49, 53, 57, 60, 67, 70
Parachinar (Pakistan), 131
Partridge, chukor, 13, 49
Pashm (ibex wool), 63
Pa-Tenzing (Lapche monk), 193
Pathans, 29, 76, 82, 131, 137
Patterson, Leif, 114
Peissel, Michel, 254n.
Pervez Khan, 52, 56, 57, 60, 62, 63, 65, 66, 67, 69, 72, 73, 79, 82, 85, 86, 89, 90, 95, 96, 101, 105

Peshawar (Pakistan), 10, 29, 34, 35, 36, 37, 65
Petroglyphs, 48
Phoksumdo Lake, 226, 272, 274, 275
Phu-Tsering (Sherpa), 174, 178, 179, 188–89, 191, 198, 199, 201, 202, 203, 207, 208, 209, 215, 217, 219, 220, 221, 230–35 passim, 254, 255, 256, 257, 260, 266, 267, 269, 273, 275, 276
Pigeons, snow, 65, 225
Pistacia, 16, 19
Pleistocene epoch, 2, 49, 117, 151, 154
Pliocene epoch, 117, 148
Pokhara (Nepal), 203, 204, 205, 207, 209, 212, 235
Polo, 56–57
Porcupine, 121
Pound, Ezra, 69
Prayer wheel, 193, 194, 244
Pruchnik, Jean, vi
Pukhan (guide), 11, 12, 15, 22, 23, 25, 37
Punjab urial, 137, 138, 139–40
Purple Mountain, 242, 246, 249, 250
Putha Hiunchuli Peak, 215

Quetta (Baluchistan), 18, 130, 134
Qurban Shah, 90, 92

Radio telemetry, 37
Rafi, Meerza, 61, 65
Rain forests, 151
Rajapalayam Hills, 167
Raka La, 270
Rakaposhi Peak, 86, 87, 102
Rama Lake, 82
Ramayana, 224
Rana, Jung Bahadur, 176
Rangasany (guide), 166
Rä-pa, Ten-dzin, 249
Ravens, 228, 253
Rawalpindi (Pakistan), 10, 65, 96, 101
Records of Sport in Southern India (Hamilton), 153, 166

Redstarts, 65, 229
Rhinoceros, 176
Rice, Clifford, 186n.
Ringmo (Nepal), 223, 226, 227, 228, 229, 231, 251, 253, 274, 275, 276
Rizvi, S. M. H., 79, 99, 119, 120, 123, 135
Roberts, Tom, 60, 128, 129
Rogenali (Pakistan), 41
Rohagaon village, 225, 276
Rowell, Galen, 101, 102n., 105, 114
Rubruck, William von, 78, 79
Russia, 3, 6, 12, 18, 43, 52, 53, 91

Saif-ul-Maluke, H. H., 25–26
Saldang La, 236, 254, 267
Saldang village, 236, 246, 247, 250, 252, 253, 257, 267
Salt Range, 4, 117, 137, 138, 139
Saltoro River, 75
Salvadora, 123, 145
Samarkand (Russia), 28
Sambar deer, 153, 163, 164, 165, 170
Sani, 253, 257
Santayana, George, 177
Sayan Mountains, 13, 43
Schäfer, Ernst, 196
Schaller, Eric, 75, 81
Schaller, Hermann, 101
Schaller, Kay, vi
Schaller, Mark, 75, 81
Schaller, Robert, 101
Science, limitations of, 243
Seng Khola, bharal at, 219
Serengeti National Park (Tanzania), 19, 208
Serow, 151, 187
Shandur Pass, 70
Sheep (Ovis), 4, 5, 41, 65, 117, 118, 119, 137, 141, 142, 147, 153, 196, 238, 240, 241, 261; American mountain, 144, 238; and goats, differences between, 147–48, 261; Miocene ancestors of, 151; see also Caprinae
Shelley, Percy Bysshe, 56
Sher Afzal, 29

Sherpas, 178, 179, 188, 189; language of, 179; and wedding, 189, 190–91
Shey Gompa (Crystal Monastery), 204, 205, 220, 221, 222, 226, 229, 231–39 passim, 241, 242, 244, 245, 246, 251, 253, 257, 261, 262, 267, 277; Lama of, 246, 247, 249, 256, 257; spring festival at, 264–66
Shey Valley, 236, 242
Shigar River, 106
Shimshal Canyon, 88
Shogore (Pakistan), 37, 45
Shola, 155
Short Walk in the Hindu Kush, A (Newby), 14
Shou (Sikkim stag), 245, 249, 267
Shresta, Hem Bahadur, 197, 198, 201, 202
Shuinj Valley, 71
Shuja-ul-Mulk, 29
Shyok River, 74, 75
Siachen Glacier, 74
Siberian snow sheep, 238
Sierra Club Bulletin, 114
Sikkim, 175
Sikkim stag (shou), 245, 249, 267
Silk Route, 82, 88
Sind (Pakistan), 115, 119, 239
Sindhis, 137
Singh, Hari, 76
Sinkiang Province (China), 6, 53, 77, 78, 82, 85, 88, 89, 98
Skardu (Kashmir), 74, 101, 102, 105, 106, 107
Skink, 47
Snellgrove, David, 204, 228, 247, 264, 265, 269
Snow leopard, 2–3, 4, 8–9, 10, 13–14, 19–24 passim, 31, 32, 33, 34, 37, 38, 39, 40, 43, 45, 49, 50, 61, 71, 85, 91, 98, 107, 121, 187, 199, 200, 238, 242, 252, 253, 269, 274, 275; "calling cards" left by, 20; food habits of, at Shey and Lapche, 280; and prey, method of killing, 25

Snow pigeons, 65, 225

Soliendo River, 267
Sost village, 88, 93, 95
Southeast Asia, 151, 164
Sport on the Nilgiris and in Wynaad (Fletcher), 153
Squirrel, flying, 225
Srinagar (Kashmir), 76
Stag: Kashmir, 7; Sikkim (shou), 245, 249, 267
Stainton, J. D. A., 204
Stalking in the Himalayas and Northern India (Stockley), 21
Stanley, Henry, 6
Stein, Aurel, 29, 59
Stockley, C. H., 21, 43, 119, 131
Stupa, 227–28, 244
Sulaiman Mountains, 117, 129, 131
Suli Valley, 276
Sunquist, Melvin, 37, 40, 43, 49
Surghund massif, 132
Surguja, Maharaja of, 171
Sutlej River, 43
Suzuki, Daisetsu, 180, 181, 243
Swamp deer, 170
Swat (Pakistan), 14, 19, 34, 67, 72, 73, 130

Tahr (*Hemitragus*), 4, 5, 21, 150–59 *passim*, 165, 166, 167, 172, 173, 177, 182, 188, 201, 238; total world population of, 167; *see also* Himalayan tahr; Nilgiri tahr
Takhatu massif, 130
Takla, 247, 249, 256, 257, 266
Tamang porters, 222, 227
Tantric Mysticism of Tibet, The (Blofeld), 213
Tanzania, Serengeti National Park of, 19, 208
Tarakot (Nepal), 213, 214, 218, 220, 221, 222, 223, 268
Tennyson, Alfred, 180, 181
Tethys Sea, 117, 252
Thano Bula Khan village, 118–19
Thirty Years in Kashmir (Neve), 80
Thoreau, Henry David, 100
Thrush, Nilgiri laughing, 155

Thygarajan, Chief Forest Officer, 163
Tibet, 3, 5, 6, 13, 68, 76, 117, 174, 175, 177, 178, 179, 195, 196, 197, 199, 204, 209, 212, 214, 227, 231, 244, 245, 254, 267, 268, 269
Tibrikot village, 276
Tien Shan Mountains, 13, 43, 79
Tiger, 153, 167, 168–72, 176
Timur, 28
Tingri Himal Peak, 195
Tirich Mir Peak, 25, 47, 53
Tobar-Kakar Mountains, 131, 132
Todas, 153, 155
Tribhuvan, King, 176
Tukten (Sherpa), 212, 219, 221, 227, 233, 247, 251, 252
Tundu, 250
Tupjuk, Karma, 247
Turkey, 130
Turki language, 88, 89
Tushi markhor reserve, 31, 37, 38, 45
Twenty Years in the Himalaya (Bruce), 28

Uganda, 176
Umra Khan, 29
United Nations, 36, 77, 176
Upadya, Ragonath, 201
Urdu language, 14, 88, 132
Urdukas campsite, 110, 111, 112
Urial, 4, 5, 39, 44, 45, 71, 85, 101, 107, 108, 113, 119, 136–47 *passim*, 149, 238; and dominance among rams, 143; rutting behavior of, 139–41, 259; young of, 145–46
Ushu Valley, 72
Usman Khan, 145, 146

Vagavurrai Tea Estate, 165
Vale of Kashmir, 7, 18, 77
Vanishing Jungle, The (Mountfort), 146
Venkedachallam (guide), 155, 156
Viper, saw-scaled, 124
Virgil, 33
Vole, 60, 220, 263
Vultures, griffon, 22, 24, 75

Wakhan Corridor, 66, 78
Wakhis, 60, 61, 62, 88; language of, 88
Walia ibex, 42
Warble flies, 144
Ward, A., 21
Weasel, Himalayan, 111
Wegge, Per, 219
Welaswamy (guide), 166
West Bengal (India), 160
Where Three Empires Meet (Knight), 84
Whittaker, Jim, 101, 104n.
Wiessner, Fritz, 103
Wild goat, 5, 118–22 passim, 124, 125, 127, 128, 129, 130, 133–37 passim, 147, 149, 239; distribution of, 130; food of, 120, 123; gestation period of, 127; horns of, 121; rutting behavior of, 125–27, 129; young of, survival rate of, 127–28, 129
Wilson, E. O., 224
Wilson, Paul, 219

Wolves, 4, 19, 43, 49, 65, 71, 90, 107, 236, 237, 238, 242, 263, 269; food habits of, at Shey and Lapche, 280
World Wildlife Fund, 75, 86, 171
Wu-ti, Emperor, 82

Yaks, 6, 60, 61–62, 63, 92, 195, 199, 271
Yarkand (China), 83
Yarkhun River, 39–40, 51, 53, 56, 58, 59, 60, 61, 63
Yarkhun Valley, 52, 67
Yasin River, 68
Yasin Valley, 56, 68, 70, 71
Yasin village, 68
Younghusband, Francis, 111

Zaire, 157
Zarghun massif, 130
Zebra, 208
Zhuil village, 61, 65, 67
Zindikharam Valley, 67
Ziskin, Joel, 248

ABOUT THE AUTHOR

GEORGE B. SCHALLER is Director of Conservation for the New York Zoological Society. He has been doing field studies of wildlife since 1952, and his many books about his researches include *The Year of the Gorilla, The Serengeti Lion* (a National Book Award winner), and *Mountain Monarchs.* He is now doing research on jaguar and other wildlife in Brazil.